MW01251903

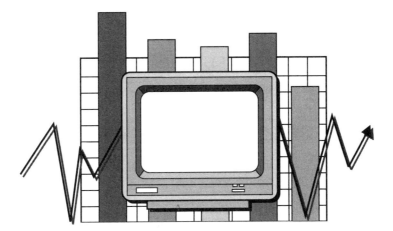

Welcome To...

Memory Management

Phillip Robinson

MIS: PRESS

A Subsidiary of
Henry Holt and Co., Inc.

Copyright 1994 © MIS:Press
a subsidiary of Henry Holt and Company, Inc.
115 West 18th Street
New York, New York 10011

First Edition—1994

ISBN 1-55828-343-9

Printed in the United States of America.

10 9 8 7 6 5 4 3 2

Library of Congress Cataloging-in-Publication Data
    Robinson, Phillip R.
    Welcome to — memory management / Phillip Robinson. — 1st ed.
        p.   cm.
    Includes index.
    ISBN 1-55828-343-9 : $19.95
    1. Memory management (Computer science)   I. Title.
    QA76.9.M45R67   1994
    005.4'3—dc20
                                       94-17282
                                         CIP

For details contact: Special Sales Director
                   MIS:Press
                   a subsidiary of Henry Holt and Company, Inc.
                   115 West 18th Street
                   New York, New York 10011

Publisher, *Steve Berkowitz*
Development Editor, *Laura Lewin*
Production Editor, *Patricia Wallenburg*
Assistant Production Editor, *Cari Littman*
Copy Editor, *Sara Black*
Technical Editor, *Mark Brownstein*

TABLE OF CONTENTS

MEMORY MANAGEMENT

Chapter 2

Chapter 3

Chapter 4

Chapter 5

Chapter 6

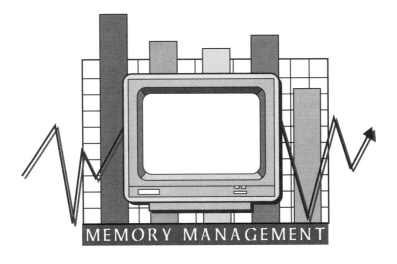

MEMORY MANAGEMENT

Introduction

Memory management is not a glamorous part of comput-ing. It doesn't dazzle like multimedia presentations or make money like spreadsheet calculations. But memory management is vital to all computing, especially advanced tasks such as multimedia and number crunching. Computers need mem-ory for everything they do and never have enough memory, so managing memory efficiently is absolutely necessary for getting the most from any system.

That's doubly true for PCs and compatibles. The Disk Operating System (DOS) that is the foundation for almost all PCs was designed way back in the early 1980s when 64K of memory was a lot. Arbitrary limits required most programs to operate in less than 640K of memory. Now programs want twenty times that much memory, and computer owners want to run many programs at once. Even if you put enough memory chips into your computer, DOS restricts programs from using most of them. The newer Windows software that makes the latest PCs easier to use than mere DOS doesn't eliminate all those limits—it just stretches them a bit. After all, Windows still needs DOS, so it must live by DOS rules. The result is too many programs chasing too little memory. If you don't manage memory carefully, your programs won't run well or won't even run at all.

You'll see error messages informing you that the computer is out of memory. You'll see your programs slow to a crawl or perhaps not even start. Sometimes they'll *crash* (stop working) because of insufficient memory. Or when you install a new peripheral—such as a sound card or mouse—or connect to some other system—such as through a network—your PC will inexplicably crash. This unexpected work stoppage happens when two programs or peripherals compete for the same limited memory.

Worse than having these problems is trying to cure them. Memory problems are famous for being irregular, for being complex, for being heartbreakers. They'll crash your computer and then hide when you go looking for causes. They'll make you remove every piece of hardware and software in your computer, replacing them one at a time as you ferret out the source of the problem. Memory troubles will sprout from obscure interactions of a half-dozen hardware and software components, all thinking they have a right to the same tiny sliver of memory. And sometimes they'll sap your computer's strength without ever giving you a clear indication that anything is wrong.

Ten years ago you needed to be a sophisticated programmer to manage memory. Five years ago you had to buy and understand a sophisticated memory management utility program. Two years ago DOS gained a free memory management utility of its own. Today the latest version of DOS automates that memory management utility, so that you can more or less keep your memory ship-shape just by typing a few quick commands.

But to master memory, to get everything from it, to push your PC as far as it can go, you still need to understand memory and your memory management utility software. This book is for anyone interested in understanding memory, for anyone who wants to give the orders that make memory run smoothly and efficiently. You don't need to be a programmer or even a computer expert to use it. It starts at ground zero, explaining what memory is and how it works; then it shows you the ground rules of the DOS memory management utilities and of some of the most popular alternatives.

What You Will Learn from This Book

First, you'll learn what memory is and what it does. You'll read about memory disks and chips, memory addresses, capacities, and speeds. That's for computers in general. Then you'll see how memory operates within PC compatibles. You'll see the hardware structure of memory and how the processor chip is the root of memory use. You'll see the software rules that organize memory. Finally, you'll learn how DOS sees memory and explore the restrictions it imposes. (Later chapters peek at memory management in other systems, such as other operating system software on PCs—OS/2, Windows NT, and UNIX—and on other computers—the Apple Macintosh.)

Then, you'll learn about memory management techniques such as relocating programs (called *loading high*), mapping memory (called *expanded memory*), and extending memory limits (called *extended memory*). It also shows you how to examine memory, to see just how much memory is in your PC and what it is doing. If you decide your PC doesn't have enough memory—and the book helps there too—it tells you how to buy and install more.

Along the way you'll see ways to use memory, especially any extra memory you've added or conserved. More memory can make your computing faster and easier through multitasking (with programs such as Microsoft Windows) and RAM disks.

The next section of the book tells you how to change your memory use, to manage memory by choosing relocations, mappings, and extensions. It first considers memory management with the DOS memory utilities, then with and for Windows, and finally with memory management utilities such as **QEMM**, **386-MAX**, and **Netroom**. This survey concludes with another peek, in more detail, at memory use in other systems.

When you finish reading this book you'll understand memory enough to manage it, troubleshoot memory problems, and make your PC faster and easier to use. You'll probably end up helping your computer-owning friends with their memory management or marveling that they muddle by with too little or mismanaged memory.

Note: This book focuses on IBM PCs and compatibles because they make up most of all computers in the world and because they have a more critical need for memory management than other popular computers.

CHAPTER

1

MEMORY MANAGEMENT

Understand Memory

emory is part of every computer. You can't compute without it. This chapter tells you about:

▼ *Memory basics*—what memory is and why it's important

▼ *PC design*—how a PC ties together memory, processor chips, and operating system software

▼ *Types of memory*—the ins and outs of different memory structures in a PC, such as conventional, extended, and expanded

▼ *Uses of memory*—what software lives in what type of memory

▼ *Memory management techniques*—how to coddle, conserve, and whip memory into shape, including how to use upper memory and disk caches

The first part of this chapter explains how memory works and defines the terms used to understand memory in a PC. The second part tells you the basic methods of managing memory. This introduction should prepare you for putting to work the more specific chapters on managing memory with DOS, Windows, or other utilities.

The Importance of Memory

The minimum computer must have a processor, memory, output, and input. The actual devices that the computer maker uses to satisfy those theoretical needs can vary tremendously. The processor could be the size of a room or the size of a gnat. The memory could be static electricity in a circuit or indentations on a sheet of plastic. The output could be marks on paper or flashes of light. Input could be a keyboard or a microphone. Still, those four elements are all in a computer in some way. Let's look at them one at a time.

Input is your way of telling the computer what to work on and when. Without input, the computer is no more than a complex doorstop, not able to follow your orders or even know you're there. The keyboard is the traditional computer input device.

Output is the computer's way of telling you "I heard your input" or "here are my results" or just "I don't know what to do next." Without output, you cannot control a computer nor benefit from what it does. The display, the printer, and the speaker are classic output devices.

The *processor* is often called the brain, but it's really only part of the brain—the central calculator part that adds numbers, compares letters, draws pictures, sequences sounds, and so on. Today's processors are almost all electronic circuits formed on chips of silicon called *microprocessors*.

Traditionally, we think of the *memory* as being added on to the brain, but really it teams with the processor to be the brain. It holds information to work on, information that has already been worked on, and even the scratch-pad information notes the processor makes as it works. What is that information? It is the numbers, letters, pictures, and sounds the processor works on.

But the memory isn't only for manipulating such information. It also holds the instructions you give the computer, the recipes you give it for working on information. This vital point isn't obvious to novice computer users—memory holds both data (the information to work on) and programs (the software instructions that tell what work to do).

The processor needs to find the programs to learn what step to take first. Then, it needs to find the data to take that step on. Finally, it has to know where to put the results, the data that comes from applying the recipe to the original data. And it does this over and over. The computer processor needs to know where to find and put each thing—programs, incoming data, and outgoing results. That place is *memory*. Figure 1.1 illustrates the process. What's more, for any complex calculation, the processor also needs a place to put temporary results, just as you need a place to put the numbers that you carry when you add or multiply larger numbers. This procedure also requires memory.

As you can see, a computer can't function without memory. Unfortunately, memory is often an unseen force, the unsung hero. You might say that "behind every successful processor lies an efficient memory." Well, maybe you wouldn't, but the idea would be correct.

We see and hear output devices—display screens, printers, and speakers—and so are easily comfortable with what they are and what they do (even if we don't know the details of how they do it— the shooting of electrons at the phosphorus screen, the spitting of ink dots at the page, the sounds that play through a speaker).

We touch input devices—keyboards, mice, and microphones—and are so comfortable with them and their importance to computers.

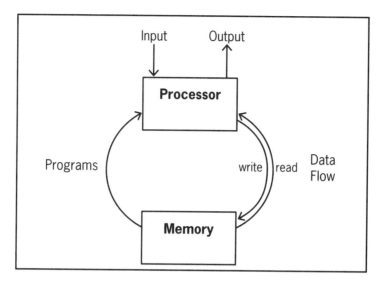

FIGURE 1.1

The flow of programs and data, between processor and memory, in a typical computer.

We read all the time about the "brains" of the computer, the processor electronics—often on a microprocessor chip—that compares, calculates, figures, and maybe even reasons. So, although it may seem magical, most people know there's a brain in that computer and are soon comparing official speeds of competing chips. Figure 1.2 shows a typical microprocessor, the star of computing today.

But we can't see memory, we can't touch it, and we don't hear so much about it. Too often it is simply overlooked. At best it becomes a measurement when buying a computer, a single number such as "My PC has 8 megs" or "get at least a 200 meg hard disk." After that, most of us forget about memory, hoping or just expecting that programs will find it when they need it.

The result too often is too little memory or poorly managed memory. If you don't have enough memory to hold programs and data, you won't compute. If you manage the memory you do have poorly, by inefficiently packing programs and data into some areas of memory while leaving other areas unused, your PC won't compute as fast or as easily as it could.

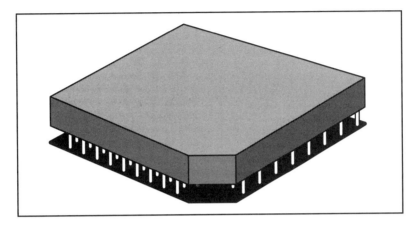

FIGURE 1.2
A typical microprocessor—the main brain chip inside a computer today.

Memory Basics

As you just read, memory holds programs and data as well as temporary processor notes. It must accept what the processor gives it, return what the processor asks back, and hold the information in between. The ideal computer would have endless amounts of memory that could hold information forever, accept new information instantly, and give back information just as instantly. And it would be free. But this is the real world, where nothing we make can be endless, forever, instant, or free—and certainly not computer memory. So computers must live within restrictions set by their memory, such as restrictions on capacity, volatility, speed, and cost.

Computer designers can choose from a variety of memory devices, each with its own combination of capacity, duration, speed, and cost. They must choose the right balance of those factors to get the appropriate computing ability for each situation. Nearly always this optimal configuration means building more than one memory device into every computer, to gain the advantages of each while lessening the weaknesses. The following sections explain those terms and the physical devices memory designers work with.

Capacity—Digital, Binary, Bits, Bytes, Kilobytes, and Megabytes

How much can memory hold? This capacity is always a finite amount, naturally, and as an ancient computer proverb grumbles: "A computer can never have enough memory." But how do you know how much you have, or might want? Just as you can't gauge a gas tank without knowing about gallons or liters, you can't measure memory without knowing about bits, bytes, kilobytes and megabytes.

Digital

Computers have been designed to work with many kinds of information, ranging from water pressures to punched holes in paper. But today, when we say computer, we always mean *digital electronic computer*. The *electronic* part explains itself: These computers operate on electricity. The *digital* part refers to the way the computers use that electricity.

Instead of the tricky task of calibrating just how much electricity is flowing this way or that, digital computers notice only electricity On or electricity Off. Each tiny electronic component in the computer can sense On or Off much more accurately than it could report "This flow is on 60%" or "That flow has decreased by half." Working only with whole values, such as On or Off, is called *digital*. (Working with percentages is called *analog*. A few computers, and many other electronic devices, such as the typical television set or radio, are still analog.)

Binary

Even simpler than digital is *binary digital*. *Binary* is a mathematician's term meaning base-two, or counting with only two values, typically called 0 and 1. That's easier for a computer to handle than counting in base-10, or decimal, where you have ten values, typically called 0, 1, 2, 3, 4, 5, 6, 7, 8, and 9. There aren't as many symbols to remember.

You count in binary using places, just as with decimal. For example, in decimal, after you count up to 9, the next number is 10. This means 1 ten and 0 ones. You can work that way up to 99, then you need another place, such as 100, which means 1 hundred, 0 tens, and 0 ones. Binary works the same way, but with fewer symbols and so a more frequent need for places. You start with 0, which means the same as in decimal: none. Then you have 1, which also means the same as in decimal: one. Then you are out of symbols, so you need a place to get higher values. In binary 10 means 1 two and 0 ones. That is, 10 binary equals 2 decimal. Then comes 11, which in binary means 1 two and 1 one, or the same as 3 decimal. Here's a demonstration of how more places let you continue up through values with just those two symbols:

Decimal	Binary
0	0
1	1
2	10
3	11
4	100
5	101
6	110
7	111
8	1000

You can continue this process forever, with binary equivalent ways to write any number, no matter how large. Because binary digital has fewer symbols, the binary way means more places and so longer values. These numbers are harder for humans to read and understand quickly, but they are better for computers to remain accurate with. Remember the ease of measuring electronic On or Off instead of percentages.

Bits

As you can see, the smallest information in today's computer is a single binary digit, a 1 or 0. Binary Digit is shortened to *bit*. The bit is the smallest piece of computer information.

Bytes

One bit can be one of two values: 0 or 1. Two bits together can be any of four values: 00, 01, 10, or 11. Three bits together can be any of 8 values; four bits, 16 values; and so on to eight bits being any one of 256 values.

To store text, you need to store letters, decimal numbers, and punctuation. In fact, to do a complete job of storing text, you need to store lowercase letters, uppercase (capital) letters, punctuation, special symbols, decimal numbers, and even some foreign language letters. There are at least 150 particular elements to storing text.

How can you get those elements into a computer? How can you represent those elements with bits? By teaming them into sets of 8, called *bytes*. Any byte can have 256 different values, from 00000000 to 11111111. If you tell the computer "this next stretch of bits is organized into bytes, and those bytes mean text," then the computer can process text information. The computer still just operates on binary numbers, but you can make the program understand that these represent text, using a table such as:

01000000 means A

01000001 means a

01000010 means B

01000011 means b

and so on, including punctuation, numerals, and so on, such as

10101011 means !

10100001 means @

00000111 means 7

 These bytes are just examples of a table you could make to represent text as binary values. They are not the actual values used in today's computers.

The code most computers use to represent text as bytes is called ASCII for American Standard Code for Information Interchange. A complete list of ASCII is shown in Figure 1.3.

0 to 15	☺ ☻ ♥ ♦ ♣ ♠ • ◘ ○ ◙ ♂ ♀ ♪ ♫ ☼
16 to 31	► ◄ ↕ ‼ ¶ § ▬ ↨ ↑ ↓ → ← ∟ ↔ ▲ ▼
32 to 47	! " # $ % & ' ( ) * + , - . /
48 to 63	0 1 2 3 4 5 6 7 8 9 : ; < = > ?
64 to 79	@ A B C D E F G H I J K L M N O
80 to 95	P Q R S T U U W X Y Z [\ ] ^ _
96 to 111	` a b c d e f g h i j k l m n o
112 to 127	p q r s t u v w x y z { ¦ } ~ ⌂
128 to 143	Ç ü é â ä à å ç ê ë è ï î ì Ä Å
144 to 159	É æ Æ ô ö ò û ù ÿ Ö Ü ¢ £ ¥ ₧ ƒ
160 to 175	á í ó ú ñ Ñ ª º ¿ ⌐ ¬ ½ ¼ ¡ « »
176 to 191	░ ▒ ▓ │ ┤ ╡ ╢ ╖ ╕ ╣ ║ ╗ ╝ ╜ ╛ ┐
192 to 207	└ ┴ ┬ ├ ─ ┼ ╞ ╟ ╚ ╔ ╩ ╦ ╠ ═ ╬ ╧
208 to 223	╨ ╤ ╥ ╙ ╘ ╒ ╓ ╫ ╪ ┘ ┌ █ ▄ ▌ ▐ ▀
224 to 239	α β Γ π Σ σ µ τ Φ Θ Ω δ ∞ φ ε ∩
240 to 255	≡ ± ≥ ≤ ⌠ ⌡ ÷ ≈ ° ∙ · √ ⁿ ² ∎

FIGURE 1.3
ASCII lets the computer work with text by representing every symbol as a byte of binary information.

Kilobytes and Megabytes

A byte holds a single letter, but that's not much. To get serious work done, your PC must work on words, pages, and even entire documents; consequently, you need lots of bytes. A typed page holds about 2000 characters. That takes up about 2000 bytes of memory. Because memory is binary, it doesn't work with nice, even decimal values such as 1000. Instead, it works in multiples of 2, such as:

2

4

8

16

32

64

128

256

512

1024

Because 1024 is the closest binary value to decimal 1000, computer scientists often use the metric *K* to stand for 1024. 1K of memory (1 kilobyte) is 1024 bytes of memory. So that typed page would fit in about 2K of memory.

Now because a document might have many pages, a single *K* or two of memory would rarely be enough. Also, you need memory room for the programs that process the text, as well as the operating system software that supports the text processor. That means you might want 10K, 100K, or even 1000K of memory. Again, working in binary means "1000" from decimal isn't the way the computer sees memory. Instead it works in 1024K at a time, also known as a 1M (read one megabyte) of memory. This measurement is a little more than 1 million bytes, more precisely 1,048,576 bytes or 1024 x 1024.

An even larger measurement is now useful, because computer memories keep getting larger and larger. The gigabyte or 1G is 1024M. Here's a comparison:

> 1 byte holds one letter
>
> 1K holds half-a-page of words
>
> 1M holds a book
>
> 1G holds dozens of encyclopedias

Programs can be as short as a few instruction lines, but useful, commercial programs are often much larger than that. They must take into consideration many possibilities and tell the processor what to do in each circumstance. They often include pictures of their own—to illustrate commands—and books full of explanations. For programs:

> 1 byte wouldn't begin to hold a program
>
> 1K might hold a small utility program
>
> 1M would comfortably hold a word processor
>
> 1G would hold hundreds of programs along with all sorts of reference and tutorial information

Volatility

No memory holds information forever. Even if you inscribe information on stone, the stone will wear away. Within electronic computers, some memory types are *volatile*, which means they lose their information as soon as you turn off their power supply. Other memory types are *nonvolatile*, which, as you might guess, means they hold on to their memory even when power is turned off.

Why would you ever use volatile memory, where information could be lost? Because it is often faster and less expensive than nonvolatile memory.

There's another facet to memory's duration: readability and writability. Storing information in memory is called *writing* to memory. Recalling information from memory is called *reading* memory.

Ideally any memory would let you write and read as many times as you might want. It doesn't work out that way. Some memory is not only nonvolatile, but permanent. This memory can have information stored to it only once. After that, the information can't be changed in that memory, like indelible ink on paper, you can't erase it. This is called *read-only* memory or ROM for short. Memory that you can change the information in many times is called *read/write* memory. Unfortunately, the acronym for that would be the unpronounceable RWM, so often the older and in this case not really appropriate term *RAM*—meaning Random Access Memory—is used instead.

Speed

The processor cannot store something in memory (write to memory) instantly. It takes a little time to tell the memory to get ready, for the memory to accept the information, and for the memory to tell the processor the writing is done. Nor can the processor get something from memory (read from memory) instantly. It takes time for the processor to ask memory for the information, for the memory to find it and serve it up. The time it takes to write or read from memory, and those times are often not the same, is the *speed* of the memory. Often it is measured in *access time*, the average time it takes to read one piece of information from the memory.

The faster the memory, the less the access time, and the faster your computer. But memory speed isn't the only factor that determines computer speed. For example, there's also processor speed. But memory speed is one of the most critical factors in computing speed, and today is often the weakest link in the chain. Slow memory often holds up a fast processor in today's typical computer.

Memories in today's computers measure their access time in fractions of a second. Some respond in *milliseconds*—thousandths of a second—*ms* for short. Some respond in *nanoseconds*—billionths of a second—*ns* for short. Why not use all fast memory? Because it costs more and is often volatile. It's necessary in most computers to have some slower, cheaper, nonvolatile memory and some faster, more expensive, volatile memory.

Cost

Faster memory, less volatile memory, larger memory: each improvement means higher cost. Designing a computer, even improving the performance of your own computer, always means balancing cost against performance. At some point a small increase in computing speed won't be worth the necessary price in dollars. But there are ways, as shown throughout this book, to ease the cost of memory. You can squeeze the most into what you have. You can use small amounts of faster memory to cache and thereby speed slower memory.

Real Memory Devices

All this theory is fine, but let's get to brass tacks: real hardware. The two most common real memory devices today are the chip and the disk. Chips are faster and more expensive; disks are slower and more capacious. Today's computers use both.

Disks

A floppy or hard disk holds information magnetically. It is a platter with a surface that can be magnetized in one direction or the opposite direction. Those directions are the 1s and 0s of binary information. As the disk spins inside a *disk drive*, an electromagnet presses against it and either reads (by sensing magnetic spots on the disk) or writes (by magnetizing the spots on the disk) information. The magnetic spots are organized into circular *tracks* on the disk. To read or write on the disk, the electromagnet must move to the appropriate track and wait for the desired spot to spin until it is directly under the electromagnet. Figure 1.4 shows a typical PC with its disk drives.

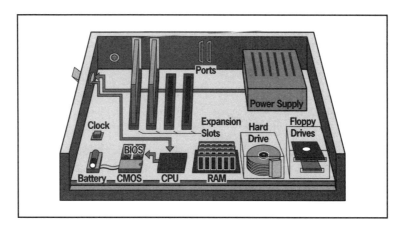

FIGURE 1.4
The disk drive in a typical PC-compatible computer.

The *floppy disk* is either 5.25" in diameter or 3.5" in diameter, as shown in Figure 1.5. Floppy disks hold from 360K to 1.5M of information. They are called floppy because the early ones were literally flexible. Floppy disks are typically used for delivering programs to computers, exchanging files from one computer to another, and backing up (making safe-keeping copies) of computer information and programs.

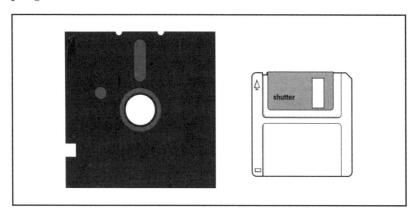

FIGURE 1.5
Floppy disks: 5.25" diameter and 3.5" diameter.

Hard disks, sometimes called fixed disks or hard disk drives, also have a magnetic surface. They also read and write information by sensing or magnetizing spots on that surface. Because they are protectively sealed into the computer and because their surface is much more precisely flat, hard disks can hold much more than floppy disks— from 10MB to 1000M (a full 10GB). That's ten to a hundred times as much as a floppy disk. Figure 1.6 shows a typical hard disk drive.

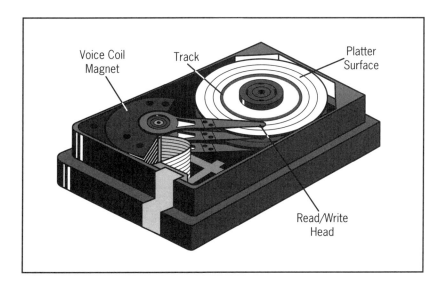

FIGURE 1.6
A hard disk (outside the computer where it would operate).

Hard disks also spin much faster than floppy disks, bringing magnetic spots under the reading/writing electromagnet much faster. They have an access time of 10 to 30 ms, one-tenth as long (and therefore ten times faster) than a floppy disk drive.

Hard disks are not removable, however. They stay sealed into the computer, so that they cannot be used to move information from one computer to another the way floppy disks are. A typical use of a hard disk is holding a computer's programs or holding a computer's data.

Hard disks are also much more expensive than floppy disks, in part because when you buy a hard disk you are buying the drive along with it, not just a replaceable floppy disk that can share use of a floppy disk drive along with dozens or hundreds of other floppy disks. A new floppy disk drive costs $50; a new floppy disk costs only $1. A new hard disk costs $200, although this holds 200 times as much as the floppy disk.

Both floppy and hard disks are nonvolatile. They retain their information even when the disks aren't spinning and the power is turned off.

Like floppy disks, *optical discs* are spinning platters and are removable. A superficial difference exists with a *c* appearing at the end of *optical disc* but a *k* taking the position at the end of *hard disk* and *floppy disk*. But floppy disks and optical discs are different in several other, more significant ways. They store information as tiny pits on the disk surface, which can be read by bouncing a tiny laser beam off the disc and seeing how much of it reflects. (That's the origin of the *optical* part of the name.) Because the laser can read a much smaller spot than the electromagnet in a hard or floppy disk can read, many more spots can be squeezed onto an optical disc. In other words, the optical disc has a much higher capacity. However, optical discs are much slower than hard discs, with access times of only 100 ms or more.

More importantly, most optical discs are ROMs. They cannot be written to by the home computer, instead they get their information when they are stamped out in a factory. That means they cannot be used to hold the constantly changing programs and data for the computer the way hard disks are. This information on the disc is nonvolatile it remains with or without power.

The most common type today is called the CD-ROM for Compact-Disc Read-Only Memory. *Compact* is part of the name because the discs are only 5.25" in diameter, compared to the older optical laser discs that were more than twice that diameter, and because the popular audio recording optical disc is called the Compact Disc.

The CD-ROM drive costs $200 to $500. The replaceable discs are inexpensive to produce, costing only a few dollars each. Consequently, they can be used to distribute software and information. CD-ROMs cannot replace hard disks: They aren't fast enough, and they can't read and write. CD-ROMs cannot replace floppy disks: They aren't widely available enough yet (not in enough computers) and they can't read and write.

A computer needs at least a floppy-disk drive, it runs faster when larger programs and documents load from a hard disk drive, and can accommodate much larger programs and reference materials with a CD-ROM drive. A complete computer system would have all three. But it would also absolutely need another form of memory: chips.

Chips

Chips are collections of electronic circuits made on the surface of a silicon crystal and then cut into pieces the size of this *O*, glued into plastic or ceramic holders the size of the title *Chips* of this section, and then plugged into a circuit board. Figure 1.7 shows a typical chip in its package.

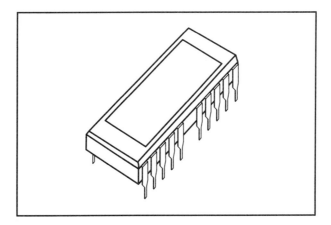

FIGURE 1.7
A chip.

Some chips are microprocessors, as described at the beginning of this chapter and in more detail later in this book. Some chips are memory chips. These chips have circuits that can hold and detect an electric charge and so can store 1s and 0s for binary information.

Every computer today uses memory chips, often lots of them. Memory chips are faster than disk memory, much faster. They have access times of 50 to 200 ns. That's almost a million times faster than disks because they depend only on electrical signals, which move at the speed of light, not the mechanical movement of spinning disks and moving electromagnets as in disk drives.

Memory Chips—RAMs vs ROMs, SRAMs vs DRAMs, DIPs vs SIMMs

There are many kinds of memory chips: ROM, RAM, DRAM, SRAM, and CMOS RAM.

ROM chips cannot be written to. We use them to hold permanently the fundamental programs the computer must always use, the programs that don't change (such as the BIOS or Basic Input Output System, which are explained later).

RAM chips can be written to and read from. Your computer needs large amounts of RAM because they hold the programs and data your processor works on. Disks can provide long-term storage for programs and data, but they are far too slow to serve programs and data up in the nanoseconds needed by the processor. Programs must be copied from disk to RAM to be run; data must be copied from disk to RAM to be worked on and then copied back to disk to save for later use.

Programs and data are stored for the long term on disk, but they must be copied into RAM chips whenever they are to run or be worked on. Your computer does this automatically when you start a program or open a document.

RAM chips come in three types: *DRAM* (Dynamic RAM), *SRAM* (Static RAM), and *CMOS RAM* (Complementary Metal-Oxide Silicon

RAM). DRAMs are less expensive than SRAMs, but they are slower. Because DRAMS are cheap, they make up almost all RAM in almost all computers. When someone asks "how much RAM is in your PC," they're asking about DRAM. SRAMs are faster but more expensive than DRAMs. Many computers use a small amount of SRAM to make the DRAM work faster. This is done with a *cache*, which is explained later in this chapter.

When you say that your PC has this or that many K or M of RAM, you're talking about DRAM.

RAM chips are measured in the bits they hold, not the bytes. A 1Mb RAM chip contains 1 million (actually 1024K) bits of memory. To turn the bits into the kilobytes and megabytes of a computer, where bytes are the minimum practical size, you need 8 chips (8 bits per byte).

In fact, the typical PC design uses a ninth bit with each byte for *parity*, a way of detecting any errors in the memory. So with parity, to get 1M in a computer you need nine 1Mb chips. Those chips in a gang are often referred to as a *bank* of memory.

RAM chips are now often teamed up on a tiny circuit board called a SIMM for Single Inline Memory Module. (The older packages were called DIPs—Dual Inline Packages.) A SIMM typically contains eight or nine memory chips, adding up to 1M or 4M of memory. Figure 1.8 shows examples.

Each year denser memory chips are developed, squeezing more bits onto the chips. Every couple of years this adds up to a quadrupling of memory in the typical chip, and prices keep falling so that those new chips cost no more than the lower capacity chips cost years before. In 1980 the typical memory chip held 16Kb. Buyers moved through the 64Kb and 256Kb generations in the 1980s, up to the 1Mb by 1993. Soon the typical DRAM chip will be the 4Mb.

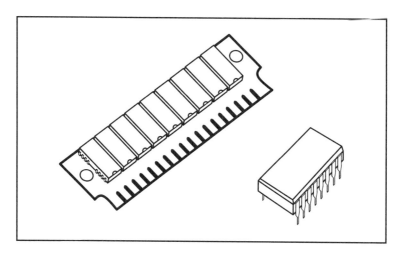

FIGURE 1.8
SIMM and DIP packaging for memory chips.

Chip Memory, Not Disk Memory

Disks are a form of memory and are slower and cheaper than chips. But when anyone speaks of memory management, they're referring to chip memory. Managing the space on your disk is a whole other subject.

Now you know:

▼ why memory is in computers (to hold programs and data)

▼ what the qualities of memory are (capacity, speed, volatility, cost)

▼ that chips and disks are the two key memory devices

▼ that chips come in DIP and SIMM packages

▼ that chips come in read-only or read-write versions

▼ that RAM chips come in faster, less capacious, more expensive SRAM or slower, more capacious, less expensive DRAMs

▼   that chip memory is the memory you care about for memory management

PC Design

Memory is vital to computing, as the previous section explained. But just how is memory included in a PC? How much is there? What devices are used? Which *chip forms*? This section answers all these questions.

DRAMs

PCs have disks, naturally. In fact, the newest PCs have a floppy disk drive (for installing new programs and backing up old), a hard drive (for holding programs you'll use), and a CD-ROM drive (for installing large programs, informational titles, and multimedia samples). But the memory you care about is the RAM memory. In fact, it is DRAM memory in all but a very few PCs. (SRAMs were used in a few, but you're unlikely to ever see one.) Nevertheless, everyone just calls them RAM.

Addresses

So your PC has RAM chips, say 1M of chips. They're hooked up to power and are ready to store information. But how does the processor write information to them and read information back from them? Consider how you send a letter to someone or receive a letter from someone else. You use an *address*.

The PC uses addresses, too. Each byte in memory is given its own numeric address, starting with zero (called the *bottom* of memory) and counting upwards (toward the *top* of memory). At that address there could be a byte of data, a byte of a program, or a random byte because nothing has been stored there yet. Just as each addressed house may have any of a variety of inhabitants, each address in memory may have any of a variety of values. And the inhabitant of the address is not the same as the address. In decimal this would look like:

0 a place that can hold one byte of information

1 a place that can hold one byte of information

2 a place that can hold one byte of information

and so on. Or, with some information stored there, it could be:

Address	Information
0	the letter *a*
1	the first spot of a picture
2	the first line of a program, perhaps the command **add**

and so on. Just remember that every byte in memory has its own address and that the value of that byte is unrelated to the address of that byte. Think of it as mailboxes (addresses) and mail (the information in those boxes).

Address Space

The total of all the addresses a computer can use—and this is limited by its processor and operating system as shown below—is called its *address space*. For PCs address space ranges from 1M to 4096M and is determined by the address bus.

Buses

How does the processor put that address out? It uses tiny wires or *lines* that carry electrical signals. One end of the line attaches to a *leg* of the microprocessor (one of the metal stubs coming out of it) and another end of the line attaches to a leg of the memory chip. In fact, the same line can attach to a series of memory chips, much as a single wire can connect to many light bulbs in a string. When a group of these lines run side by side, they're called a *bus*. (Just as a city transport bus carries many passengers from place to place, an electrical bus carries many signals from one place to another.)

In the PC there are three buses: data, address, and control. These buses are combined into one overall bus that runs from microprocessor to memory to input and output devices and so on. The *data bus* is a set of lines that carries the value from processor to memory or back from memory to processor. If you're getting a byte at a time, you have 8 data lines in the data bus. The *address bus* is a set of lines that carries the address the microprocessor wants to read from or write to in memory. 16 address lines can reach addresses from 0 to 64K. The *control bus* is a set of lines that carries signals telling memory what to do with the address and data it gets on the other two buses. Should it read? Should it write? Is the information headed for input or output devices instead of memory? The control bus lines answer these questions.

Hexadecimal

Now memory addresses could be counted in decimal, as above, but they rarely are. Because computers work in binary, as explained earlier in this chapter, addresses would more naturally look like:

0

1

10

11

100

and so on. This system of addresses soon grows cumbersome with large memories and, consequently, large addresses. Imagine an address near the top of final address in 64K of memory. In binary this could be:

Address	Value
1111101010000001	10100111

How would you like to rattle that address off in a hurry? Or copy it without making mistakes?

There's an easier way that sticks to the computer's binary heritage. It's called *hexadecimal*, counting in base-sixteen. Whereas binary has two digits (0 and 1) and decimal has ten (0, 1, 2, 3, 4, 5, 6, 7, 8, and 9), *hex* has 16, and here's what they equal:

Decimal	Binary	Hex
0	0	0
1	1	1
2	10	2
3	11	3
4	100	4
5	101	5
6	110	6
7	111	7
8	1000	8
9	1001	9
10	1010	A
11	1011	B
12	1100	C
13	1101	D
14	1110	E
15	1111	F
16	10000	10

The letters may look odd there, but hex-counters needed some symbol to, in a single space, stand for 10, 11, and so on, and for that they chose something familiar. *A* in hex means 10 of something; it has no relation to the text meaning of *A* other than looking similar.

Because hex uses base-sixteen, it doesn't need as many symbols for larger numbers as binary, or even as decimal. Because 2 is a root of 16, the fourth root (2 x 2 x 2 x 2 = 16), you can translate directly from binary to hex by converting each foursome of binary digits into a single hex digit.

> 1010 binary equals A hex
>
> 0000 binary equals 0 hex
>
> 10100000 binary equals A0 hex

In other words, the long address, near the 1M top of memory, would translate as:

> 1111101010000001 binary

or in other words, 1111 1010 1000 0001 binary equals FA81 hex.

Memory Maps

If you stack up the addresses of memory and place beside them the values at those addresses, you've created a *memory map*. This map shows how memory is being used. A memory map can be a simple diagram, as shown in Figure 1.9, or a detailed chart, as shown in Figure 1.10. As you can see, the addresses are in hexadecimal.

Segments and Offsets

Take a look at the memory map of Figure 1.11 and notice that the addresses are in hex. You may also notice that the addresses neatly divide each 1M of memory into 16 blocks of 64K each.

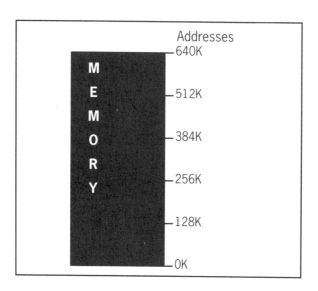

FIGURE 1.9
A simple memory map diagram.

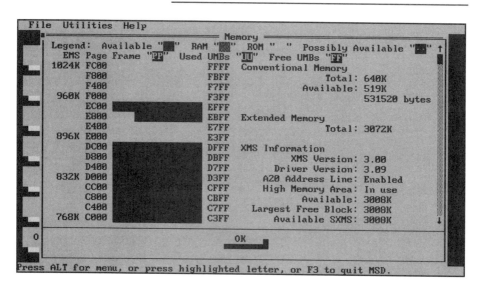

FIGURE 1.10
*A detailed memory map chart (from the MSD program
that comes with DOS).*

The PC has a peculiar way of addressing memory, grown from its early design. That design built each address in memory from a segment and an offset. The 4-bit segment address chose a 64K block from the 1M that an early PC could address. The 16-bit offset address chose a particular byte within that segment.

The segments neatly divide memory into the various PC uses, as you'll see throughout this chapter. The segments are named:

0 for addresses from 00000 to 0FFFF

1 for addresses from 10000 to 1FFFF

2 for addresses from 20000 to 2FFFF

and so on to

F for addresses from F0000 to FFFFF

Remapping

To make their addresses more flexible, some computers have the ability to *remap* memory. They start with the same basic addresses for memory but then reroute the information traveling the address bus, the new route depending on circumstances.

The PC can remap memory by keeping tables of address forwardings, so that when an address is sent out, for reading or writing memory, a table of the latest forwarding information is checked first to see if that address has been changed. If it has, the data are sent to, or read from, the new address, often without even telling the processor. The processor may not even know that it is dealing with memory that is not at the address it put on the bus.

The real-world analogy to remapping would be a forwarding service with a single office but many clients. That office would keep track of where the clients are; when mail came for them, the office would send it off to their current whereabouts, even though the original address on the envelope was always "the office."

By remapping memory, PCs can keep programs and data where they are most handy and even double-book the use of some memory so that as much use as possible is squeezed out of the limited address space. Memory mapping is the basis of many memory management techniques. It is possible only with the right *hardware* (memory management circuits) and *software* (memory manager utilities). Most of this book explains where you can find those and how to use them.

Processors and Their "Bits"

Processor chips are central to PCs, as you've seen above. Their abilities help determine the PC's abilities, especially:

▼ the processor's speed in calculation

▼ the processor's data bus size—how many bits it handles at once

▼ the processor's address bus size—how many bits it uses to address memory, and so how much memory the computer can use

▼ the processor's remapping ability—circuits it has to juggle addresses

The processor's *speed* is often measured in megahertz (MHz). (Processor speed is actually a combination of the way calculations work in the processor and how fast the processor carries them out—the *clock speed* measured in megahertz or millions of operating cycles per second.) The original IBM PC ran at about 5 MHz. The slowest 386 PC runs at about 16 MHz. Today's fast 486s and Pentiums run at 50 to 100 MHz.

The processor's *data bus size* is typically either 16 or 32 bits. A processor handling 32 bits at a time can get work done twice as fast as a 16-bit data-bus processor, even running at the same clock speed. (In the same way, a person carrying 100-pound sacks can load a truck twice as fast as a person carrying 50-pound sacks, if they lift and place at the same speed.)

The processor's *address bus size* can be 20 bits (in the original PC), 24 bits (in a 286 PC), or 32 bits (in a 386, 486, or Pentium).

> 20 bits can address 1M as in 8088 and 8086 PCs
>
> 24 bits can address 16M as in 80286 PCs
>
> 32 bits can address 4096M as in 386, 486, and Pentium PCs

Processors are often categorized by the size of the data buses. There are 8-bit, 16-bit, and 32-bit processors. Early PCs had the 8088 and 8086 processors, with 8-bit data buses and 16-bit address buses (plus that 4-bit segment mentioned earlier, for a 20-bit address). The 80286 processor in the IBM AT and compatibles has a 16-bit data bus with a 24-bit address bus. The 386 and 486 processors are fully 32-bit, with 32-bit data buses and 32-bit address buses.

Operating Systems and Processor Modes

The *operating system* is the fundamental software in the computer. It works with the processor to set basic abilities. Programs such as word processors, spreadsheets, and so on are really written to work with the operating system, not so much to work with the PC hardware itself.

The most popular operating system for PCs is called DOS. There are many versions, both because the operating system has changed over the years (and so had evolving version numbers such as 3, 4, 5, and 6) and because several competing companies (such as Microsoft, IBM, and Novell) sell DOS. See Chapter 4 for more details on these versions. DOS, which was written for the original PC with its 8-bit data bus and 20-bit addresses, was phenomenally popular. Lots of programs were written for that PC and that DOS.

Then along came the IBM AT with its 80286 processor chip. This chip could reach more memory with a 24-bit address bus to reach 16M instead of the mere 1M the original processor chips could read.

Programs could have been written to use the AT's new abilities. But DOS stayed the same, unable to work with the full 24-bit addresses. To use the new AT abilities and that wider address bus, computer owners would have to give up DOS and all the programs written for it. Most weren't willing to do so.

80286—Real Mode and Protected Mode

The 80286 designers guessed that people would still want to run their older programs, so they gave the 286 a special switch. This switch when turned one way lets the 286 run in Real mode where it pretends to be an 8086 chip, only much faster (it has higher clock speeds and moves more data in each operation). If you turn the switch the other way, the 286 is in Protected mode where it can use the larger address bus and still run faster than the 8086.

DOS is a Real mode operating system. If you run DOS on a 286, your computer will behave as though it has just a very fast 8086 processor. It can still run the programs written for DOS and 8086 computers such as the original IBM PC.

DOS cannot use Protected mode for basic programs. Some recent DOS utilities make some limited use of Protected mode—switching to it to get at more memory and then switching back to run programs that don't understand Protected mode. But DOS remains a Real mode operating system.

386, 486, Pentium—Real Mode, Protected Mode, Virtual-86 Mode

Then, the 386 processor came along. It had a 32-bit address bus and some memory management circuits for remapping memory addresses. It too was given a Real mode, so that it could run DOS and DOS-understanding programs. It was also given Protected mode, so that it could run programs written for the 286 computers (although there were very few). Finally, it was given a new mode, *Virtual-86 (V-86) mode.* This mode gives access to the full 32-bit address bus, and so to an address space of 4096M. Using the memory-remapping circuits, this mode is also able to give 1M of memory, anywhere in that 4096M, to any DOS program that wants it. That is, it creates a Virtual 8086 PC with that 1M of memory and part of the processor's time, fooling the DOS program into thinking it is running on a very fast 8086 PC. At the same time, the 386 can run many other DOS programs in their own little virtual worlds. And it protects them from one another in memory so they can't interrupt or bother one another, or even know about one another.

The 486 and Pentium chips follow this same design, with Real, Protected, and Virtual-86 modes.

DOS and Windows

DOS cannot use Protected mode on the 286, and it cannot get at Virtual-86 mode on the 386. It is limited to Real mode. But if you get the right operating system or software that can get a 386, 486, or Pentium started in V-86 mode, then that operating system should be able to run any number of DOS programs in their own memory areas.

Windows is the best-known other operating system for PCs. Early versions were really just additions to DOS, even though they could run in Real mode, in Standard mode (their name for Protected mode), and then in 386-Enhanced mode (their name for V-86 mode). In other words, Windows could switch the 286 processor into Protected mode or the 386 processor into Protected or V-86 mode when it started. The latest version, Windows 3.1, drops Real mode, offering only Standard and 386-Enhanced modes. By using these modes, Windows can work with at least 16M of memory (the address space for Protected mode), and it can run DOS programs. In 386-Enhanced mode it can run many DOS programs at once, side by side, using the V-86 mode. For more information, see Chapter 5 on managing memory in Windows.

OS/2 is another operating system. In its latest version, 2.1, it is able to run a 286 processor in Protected mode or a 386 processor in Protected or V-86 mode. The result is that it can run DOS programs side by side, as well as its own programs—with their natural reach to 16M or more memory. In fact, OS/2 can even run Windows programs, at least those written for Windows 3.0. (Competitive difficulties are leading Windows-maker Microsoft to make it harder for OS/2-maker IBM to make OS/2 compatible with the latest Windows.)

Windows NT and UNIX are other operating systems that use the most powerful and flexible modes—such as Virtual-86—of the latest processors.

Types of Memory

The *x86* (meaning 8086, 80286, 386, 486, or Pentium) processor in your PC compatible and the operating system (typically DOS) that runs on it determine how memory is organized and used.

DOS sets stricter rules than the processors. As explained above, DOS is a Real mode operating system that can address 1M of memory. If you change to Windows or OS/2 or some other operating system, your memory organization changes and so do your memory management techniques.

But if you stick with DOS, you're officially stuck with using just 1M of memory. I say *officially* because you can use some tricks and clever programs to get at more—sometimes and for some purposes. The tricks and clever programs do this by dividing memory into several *types*, based on how the processor can get at it for reading and writing. All of this memory is RAM chips, the types just determine how it is addressed.

Conventional Memory, Upper Memory

DOS can directly address 1M of memory. Unfortunately, it can't just use all of this memory as it pleases. The processor chip could, but DOS won't let it. When DOS was created, way back when the typical PC had barely 64K of memory chips, the original DOS program-mers put up a wall, *the 640K wall.*

Below the 640K address would be the area for DOS itself and for the programs that you would run. This memory, called *conventional memory*, would also hold any data for those programs. Above the 640K address would be the area for PC housekeeping chores. After all, the PC needs somewhere to put such software as:

▼ **BIOS ROM**—Basic Input Output System, the software that starts the PC and then hands power over to DOS

▼ **Peripheral BIOS ROMs**—The BIOS software for any extra peripherals you connect such as network adapter boards or new hard disks

▼ **Video Memory**—The RAM memory that holds the image to display on the screen

This 384K area, from the 640K address to the 1024K address at the top of DOS memory, is reserved for such system uses. It is called by lots of names including high DOS memory, upper memory, and reserved memory. Figure 1.11 is a memory map of conventional memory and upper memory. (Remember that, as you read back ear-lier in this chapter, the 0 address is called the bottom memory and the 1024K is the top.)

Now you know the fundamental facts of PC and DOS memory man-agement. There is only 1M of RAM that DOS can see, and it can use only 640K of this conventional memory for most programs. If you add RAM chips beyond the 1M, DOS won't see them. Even if you have 1M, DOS will use only 640K for programs, unless you learn to outwit it. Read on.

CMOS Memory

CMOS memory is not a different memory area, but rather it is memo-ry that uses a few RAM chips made with the CMOS (Complementary

Metal-Oxide Silicon) method. This memory has a small battery attached, to hold a small amount of vital, must-be-remembered-from-one-session-to-the-next DOS information, such as what type of disk drives are in the computer. Because CMOS memory uses very little power, it can keep its information when a tiny battery is connected to it. Most PCs now have a small amount of CMOS memory, which is actually addressed by the system within conventional memory. You won't know about it unless and until something changes in your computer—such as a newly added drive or memory board—that conflicts with the information in CMOS. Then, you'll see an error message suggesting that you use a Setup program to change the CMOS settings. Some utility programs also promise to save what's in CMOS to disk, in case you make changes to CMOS settings that don't work out or the tiny battery fails and you need to recover your CMOS settings.

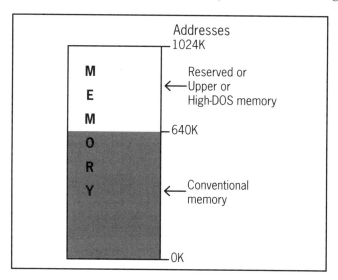

FIGURE 1.11
Conventional memory.

Cache Memory

Sometimes you'll hear or read of a memory *cache*, a small amount of fast memory that holds the most frequently used information from a larger, slower memory. If you direct the processor always to look first into the fast memory cache, and you have a program that keeps the latest important information there, your system will run at nearly the speed of the faster memory, despite being mainly stuffed full with data from the slower, cheaper memory.

Caches are critical to making fast, affordable computers. There are two common uses of cache: to speed RAM access and to speed disk access.

Speeding RAM access should be called *RAM caching*. This type of access typically uses a small amount of expensive SRAM memory, perhaps 32K to 256K, to hold the most recently, and most frequently read information from the larger, slower DRAM. The SRAM doesn't really have an address—it just stands in for whatever addresses the DRAM has. So you don't think of a cache as being in conventional or upper or any other memory. Figure 1.12 diagrams the operation. Most of today's PCs have a RAM cache because processors have become faster than the DRAM chips.

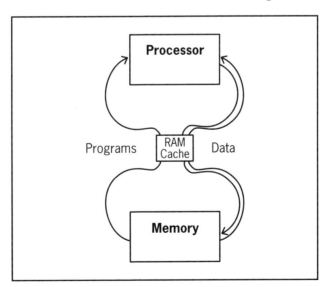

FIGURE 1.12
RAM caching.

Speeding disk access should be called *disk caching*. But because it is typically done by using some RAM memory to hold the most frequently accessed information from disk, it is sometimes referred to as making a disk cache in RAM or a RAM cache. It's confusing! Figure 1.13 shows how disk caching works. A disk cache in RAM could be in conventional memory or upper memory or even some other type of memory (such as expanded and extended memory, which are described below). It just depends where the *disk cache program*—the software that sets aside the memory and keeps it loaded with the most frequently used information—puts the cache. A disk cache could be anything from 32K of memory to 1M or more, even though a typical PC size is about 256K.

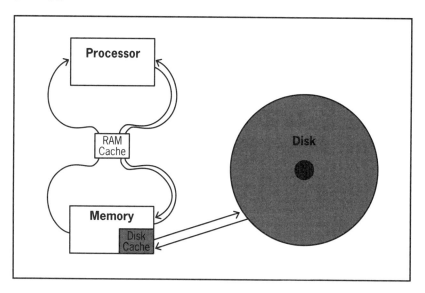

FIGURE 1.13
Disk caching.

Just remember that RAM caches add a little fast RAM to make all RAM look faster and don't use any conventional or other type of memory. Disk caches borrow a little RAM to make the disk look faster, and the borrowed RAM could be conventional, upper, expanded, or extended.

Some disk cache utilities include a *write cache* option. The cache not only holds the most frequently read information from the slower memory but also holds the latest written information, only writing it through to the slow memory in efficient batches. Write caching can speed operation even more but risks losing the written information if memory loses its power before the information makes its way to disk.

Extended Memory

Remember how Protected mode on the 286 chip and Virtual-86 mode on the 386 and 486 chips can get at more than 1M of memory? Those megabytes beyond the first 1M are called *extended memory*, as shown in Figure 1.14.

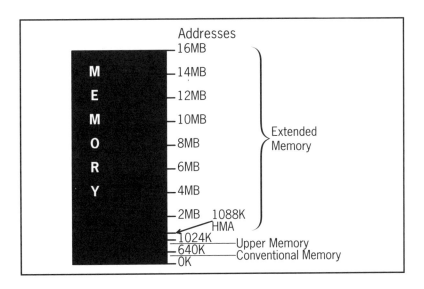

FIGURE 1.14
Extended memory map.

DOS programs can't get at this memory, because DOS is a Real mode operating system and those extra megabytes required Protected or

V-86 mode. However, by adding special software to DOS you can use extended memory, sometimes even for programs. The final section of this chapter, on memory management techniques, goes into more detail. The latest standard for working with extended memory is called XMS for Extended Memory Specification.

XMS means extended memory.

1M Installed Means 640K Conventional and 384K Extended

This point is very important. PCs that have 1M, or more installed memory almost always have 640K of that memory mapped as conventional memory and 384K more mapped as extended memory. See Figure 1.15 for a diagram.

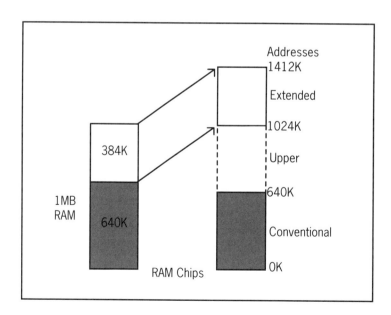

FIGURE 1.15
1M installed means 640K conventional and 384K extended.

Why is the 384K extended memory instead of upper memory? We are talking about where the memory chips, the RAM chips, are addressed. The addresses from 640K to 1024K, the 384K worth of addresses there, are reserved for ROMs and other such uses. They don't need RAM chips. The video RAM for the video adapter is on the adapter card itself; it is not part of regular memory. Many of the addresses may not even have ROMs, which take up only part of the reserved addresses. In that case, there is nothing at all in those unused addresses. Remember this point later when reading about memory management techniques.

Expanded Memory

Even before the 286 chip brought the possibility of Protected mode and its 16M and the 386 chip brought V-86 mode and its 4096M, PC users wanted more than 1M of memory. Spreadsheet users, particularly, wanted more memory for their huge sets of numbers. But DOS lets programs work only with addresses under 1M.

Programmers came up with a trick to get around that limit. They added megabytes more RAM chips to some PCs and some electronic circuits for remapping memory addresses (later included in the 386 and 486 chips) and called the result *expanded memory*. More specifically, they called it *LIM* (Lotus Intel Microsoft—for the three companies that started it) EMS (Expanded Memory Specification). LIM EMS version 3.2 specified how 8M of expanded memory could hold data for programs. LIM EMS version 4.0 (which borrowed from a short-lived, competing specification called EEMS expanded memory) is more flexible, specifying how not just data but programs as well can use as much as 32M of expanded memory.

How do programs get at those megabytes if they don't have addresses under 1M? They use remapping. Figure 1.16 shows how. Information is stored in 16K chunks called *pages* in those extra megabytes of expanded memory. Programs written to understand expanded memory ask for information by pages, giving each page a *handle* (a name). The remapping circuits keep track of the pages and their names. A 64K chunk of memory in upper memory addresses is set aside as the *page frame*, with room for four pages.

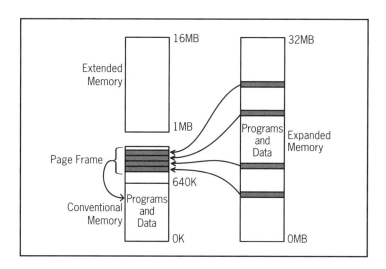

FIGURE 1.16
Expanded memory diagram.

When a program asks for an information page, that request is sent to the expanded memory hardware. This hardware looks up where that page is in the expanded memory megabytes. When it finds the page, the expanded memory hardware remaps the page frame address to it. Suddenly, the processors think that the 16K page in expanded memory is located in the page frame area in upper memory. In other words, that 16K page is within the 1M of addressable memory, so that DOS and DOS programs can get at it.

When a program needs information from another page, the expanded memory hardware can remap addresses again, taking the page frame address away from some unused page and giving it to the now needed page. The four 16K stretches of the page frame may each be mapped to information pages that are megabytes apart in the expanded memory.

Backfilled Memory

The expanded memory in LIM EMS 4.0 allows the page frame to be larger and to be in conventional memory. You can even remap pages all the way down to the 256K address. (Although to do this with expanded memory, you'll need an expanded memory board with enough memory chips and a main memory board—a motherboard—that let's you "disable" the chips that are already at those addresses.) If you can *backfill* conventional memory addresses with expanded memory, as shown in Figure 1.17, your PC will be better suited to *multitasking*—running more than one program at a time. After all, new programs can be brought into useful memory just by tiny remapping operations, rather than by wholesale copying to and from disk.

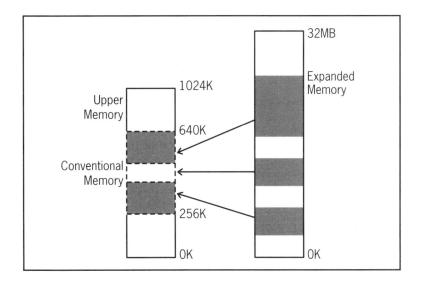

FIGURE 1.17
Backfilling conventional memory with expanded memory.

Expanded Memory Circuits: Boards, 386, or Chipsets

To use expanded memory you'll need remapping circuits, which come on the expanded memory boards, either in version 3.2 or in version 4.0. The expanded memory circuits are built into the 386, 486, and Pentium chips. They can remap memory even better than EMS boards can.

But some PCs built before the 386 generation have another kind of remapping ability. These PCs have a *chipset* (the collection of chips that connect to the microprocessor to help it deal with input, output, and memory) that contains some remapping abilities. In expanded memory program manuals these chipsets are referred to as Chips & Technologies NEAT, LEAP, or AT/386 chipsets. With them you can sometimes get some of the benefits of expanded memory management, as explained later in this chapter, as long as you also add an expanded memory manager program.

Virtual Memory

Virtual memory has nothing to do with chips. Instead, it refers to a utility program that pretends part of your disk is actually RAM chips. This program works by copying information from real RAM to disk and then copying other information, more immediately needed, to that same RAM. The effect is to multiply the effective RAM space. Figure 1.18 shows how this works.

The great advantage is that disk space is far more plentiful and less expensive than RAM space. The disadvantages are losing some disk space and, more importantly, losing RAM speed because the disk is so much slower. All that copying back and forth to disk eats up performance.

DOS doesn't use virtual memory. Some programs come with their own virtual memory schemes built in. Windows has virtual memory, as detailed in Chapter 5.

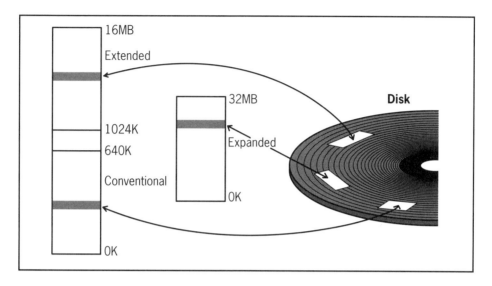

FIGURE 1.18
Virtual memory diagram.

What's in Memory

Memory holds programs and data, as mentioned earlier in this chapter. But not all programs and data have equal rights to each type of memory. Here's a rundown on what you'll find in memory and where you'll find it.

DOS

DOS is not a monolith. It is instead a collection of many parts that do many things. They fit into different areas of memory. Figure 1.19 lists a typical PC's use of conventional memory, including DOS and the other elements mentioned here.

The *kernel* is the heart of DOS. It fits into the lowest area of conventional memory, as you can see in Figure 1.20, where it is called **MSDOS.SYS** and **IO.SYS**. In addition, you can see the BIOS Data

Area and *interrupts*, which keep track of what the PC is doing whenever it has to change direction suddenly and handle a request for a disk or printing or program change and so on.

```
Modules using memory below 1 MB:

    Name          Total       =   Conventional   +   Upper Memory
    --------     ------------     ---------------     ---------------
    MSDOS          13677  (13K)      13677  (13K)          0    (0K)
    HIMEM           1168   (1K)       1168   (1K)          0    (0K)
    COMMAND         2912   (3K)       2912   (3K)          0    (0K)
    SNAP          105872 (103K)     105872 (103K)          0    (0K)
    Free          531616 (519K)     531616 (519K)          0    (0K)

Memory Summary:

    Type of Memory       Total      =      Used      +      Free
    --------------     -----------     -----------       -----------
    Conventional        655360 (640K)    123744 (121K)     531616  (519K)
    Upper                    0   (0K)         0   (0K)          0    (0K)
    Adapter RAM/ROM     393216 (384K)    393216 (384K)          0    (0K)
    Extended (XMS)     3145728 (3072K)    65536  (64K)    3080192 (3008K)
                       -----------      -----------       -----------
    Total memory       4194304 (4096K)   582496 (569K)    3611808 (3527K)

    Total under 1 MB    655360 (640K)    123744 (121K)     531616  (519K)

Press any key to continue . . .
```

FIGURE 1.19
List of DOS and other elements in conventional memory.

DOS also has a *command interpreter* called **COMMAND.COM**, a program that watches your keyboard and tells the rest of DOS what you're typing. This program takes up conventional memory, too, and in fact can be loaded accidentally before each of several programs in memory, taking up more space than is needed.

DOS drivers help DOS work with parts of the computer such as the printer and video display. These drivers stay in conventional memory, too.

DOS resources, such as its **FILES**, **BUFFERS**, **FCBS**, take up memory space. They specify how many files may be open at once, how many small memory areas to set aside to hold disk information, and so on. Chapter 4 gives details.

Device Drivers

When you add some new devices to your PC, such as a mouse or CD-ROM drive, DOS won't know how to work with them. It needs more software to understand them. This added software is called a *device driver*. Typically, you tell DOS to load it when starting the PC, as explained later in this chapter. Drivers take up more conventional memory, as shown in the example of Figure 1.20.

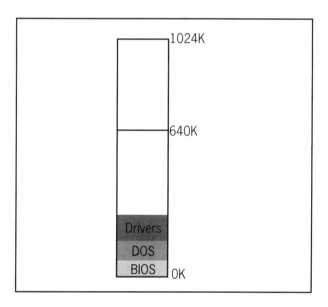

FIGURE 1.20
Drivers take up conventional memory.

Network Adapters

When you connect a PC to a network, DOS needs several new pieces of software to understand and work with the other computers and printers on the net. This software—called *network drivers* or other names—all fits into conventional memory.

Applications and Utility Programs

Programs take up memory when they *load*—that is, when they're copied from disk into RAM chips and start running. These programs are the *applications* you use for processing words, numbers, pictures, and so on, as well as the *utility programs*, which are smaller than applications and aimed at housekeeping chores on the PC such as organizing the hard disk or finding a file.

Programs are loaded in this way: You type a command to start a program, **COMMAND.COM** passes that command on to the rest of DOS, **COMMAND.COM** unloads from memory, the program is copied from disk into memory, and you see the program's menus or options. Figure 1.21 shows this procedure.

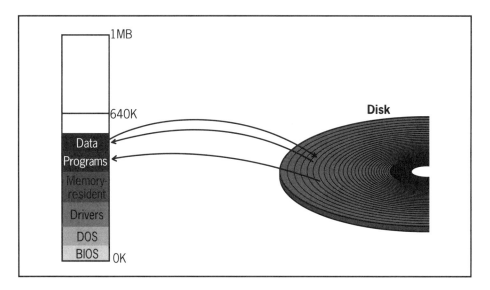

FIGURE 1.21
Loading a program into memory.

When you're done with a program—quitting, exiting, or terminating it—**COMMAND.COM** is copied back into RAM again, and the program is ignored. It isn't really erased, but DOS acts as if it isn't there and copies other things over it without regret. After all, there's still the original copy on disk, so you're not losing anything.

Data

When you have the program running, you may choose to open a file or start a new document. Starting a file will take some more conventional memory, even though very large documents are probably kept partially in memory and partially on disk.

Memory-Resident Programs (TSRs)

Some programs aren't ignored when they terminate. Some leave instructions not to be copied over by anything else. These programs remain in memory, ready to be used again without having to be copied back from disk to RAM. They're called *Terminate and Stay Resident* or TSRs. I call them *memory-residents* in this book to avoid extra acronyms. As you can see in Figure 1.22, memory-residents take up conventional memory, too.

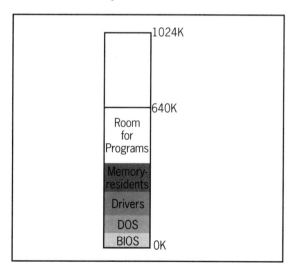

FIGURE **1.22**
Memory-residents take up conventional memory.

Memory-residents take up conventional memory. The first memory-residents were actually parts of DOS, such as the **PRINT.COM** utility. Later memory-residents were calculator utilities, calendars, and then even full-size programs such as spreadsheets and word processors. However, with the parade of programs, drivers, resources, adapters, and DOS elements wanting into conventional memory, this didn't last long. Soon the use of TSRs was fading, and memory management techniques were born that could get those still necessary out of the precious conventional memory. Check out the next section to see how this is done.

Disk Cache

A cache makes slow memory work faster by putting the most frequently needed information into a smaller element of faster memory. A disk cache makes the disk appear to read and write faster by putting its most recently used information into a small area of memory.

There are many disk cache programs, including DOS's own **SMARTDrive**. The **SMARTDrive** controlling software runs in conventional or upper memory (it can load high). But the memory holding cache information can be in extended or expanded memory too, which is a good idea if you have a cache as large as 256K or 512K. See Chapter 4 for details. Figure 1.23 shows how this works.

RAM Disk

Often confused with a disk cache, a RAM disk is a very different use of memory. It takes an area of memory and treats it just like a disk: storing files to it and reading files from it. A RAM disk is normally much larger than a disk cache, and although it doesn't make the main disk run any faster, it runs very fast itself (chips are much faster than disks).

DOS comes with a RAM disk utility called **RAMDrive**. The controlling **RAMDrive** software runs in conventional or upper memory, but the RAM disk itself can be in extended or expanded memory. That's vital given the 1M to 4M size of many RAM disks.

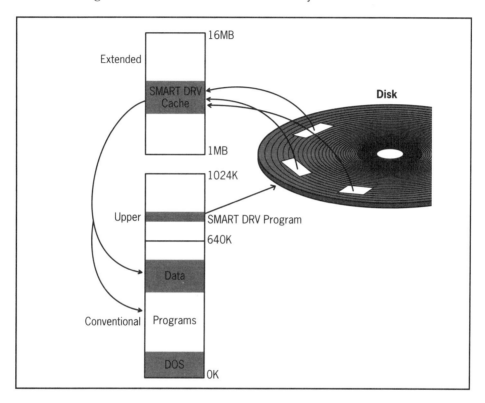

FIGURE 1.23
SMARTDrive diagram.

A RAM disk's speed is very useful if you can load entire applications into it—then they run much faster. But it can still be useful if only large enough to hold:

▼ a document as it is processed

▼ the temporary files many programs make as they work

▼ parts of a program, such as spell checkers, that reach to disk often

▼   batch files often executed under DOS

Figure 1.24 shows a typical RAM disk diagram. Chapter 4 has more detail on **RAMDrive**.

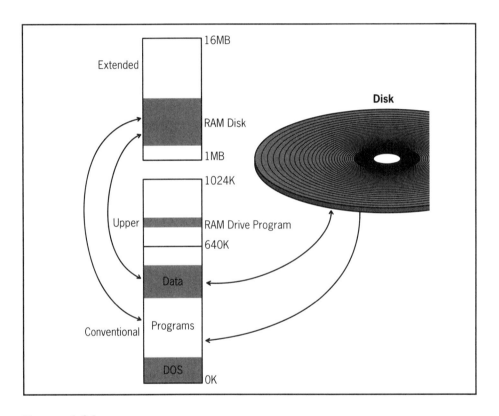

FIGURE 1.24
Diagram of a RAM disk.

Management Techniques

So far, this chapter has explained how a PC compatible running DOS (and that's almost all PCs) has many types of memory, including extended, which few programs can use; expanded, which few programs can use; upper, which is walled off from programs; and conventional memory. It must cram DOS itself, DOS resources, device drivers, memory-residents and more into conventional memory. This fact makes the 640K of conventional memory the most precious memory in the PC.

Memory management has two goals: to find ways to make extended, expanded, and upper memory usable and to find ways to conserve and do more with conventional memory. This section lists the most popular schemes to accomplish both goals. The rest of the book explains how particular utilities help implement those schemes. (Chapter 4 will interest most people first, because it tells how DOS's own utilities can help with memory management.)

Loading High

The most common way to manage memory uses extended or expanded RAM to free some conventional memory. It's called *loading high*. It needs five elements:

- ▼ software elements in conventional memory that can relocate
- ▼ some unused extended or expanded RAM
- ▼ some unused memory addresses
- ▼ remapping circuits
- ▼ memory management software

Here's how it works. All PCs have conventional memory, most have at least 640K of it. (That is, most PCs these days come with that much or have RAM chips added to equal at least 640K.) Too often what starts as 640K of useful conventional memory is whittled down—by loading DOS, drivers, memory-residents, and so on—to 600K, 580K, or even less. That memory may not be enough to load an important program, or maybe just not enough to load all the drivers and network connections you want.

Although some of the software in those conventional memory addresses may not work at any other addresses, most of the drivers and memory-residents available today are created to work from other addresses. (The programmers know about the importance of memory management and loading high.)

Most PCs now also have some extended or expanded memory. Old PCs may have an expanded memory board. Recent PCs come with 4MB or more RAM installed. The first MB is 640K conventional and 384K extended memory, RAM that won't be used by most programs.

In the upper memory area, most of the addresses aren't used by system functions. Figure 1.25 shows a typical memory map, where there is 200K or more of *unused addresses*, areas with no ROM and no RAM.

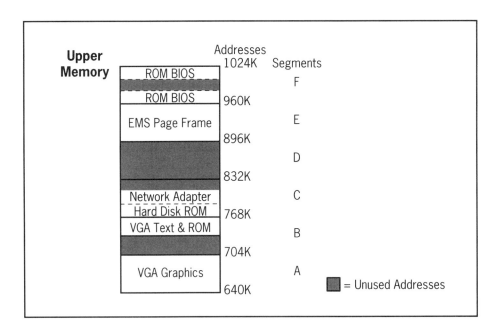

FIGURE 1.25
Unused addresses in upper memory.

With the help of a memory manager program, remapping circuits in expanded memory hardware, special chipsets, or a 386 or 486 chip can pretend that the unused extended or expanded memory is at those unused upper memory addresses. That puts the previously unused RAM into conventional memory where DOS can get at it. This is called creating *Upper Memory Blocks* or just making UMBs. Figure 1.26 shows what I mean.

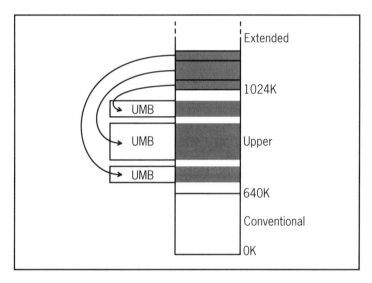

FIGURE 1.26
Creating UMBs from unused addresses and unused RAM.

Memory management software can then load as many drivers, memory-residents, and other software elements as possible into UMBs instead of into conventional memory. This relocation, by *loading high* means that less goes into conventional memory, leaving more conventional memory free. On some systems memory managers can get 620K or even more free. Figure 1.27 shows an example.

Loading Order

Because memory-residents and drivers are different sizes, fitting them into the variously sized UMBs is a challenge, similar to finding the optimum way to pack a truck full of various-sized boxes. Doing this packing and repacking manually can be tough. For example, if you load a small driver into a large UMB, you may not have enough room for a large UMB later. If instead you load the large UMB first, as shown in Figure 1.28, you may have room for the smaller UMB later, so that both are successfully loaded high. Many memory managers now come with optimizing utilities that test all the possible loading orders, sometimes running through millions in a few minutes, to find the best solution.

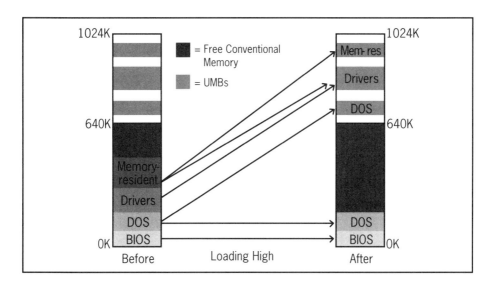

FIGURE 1.27
Loading drivers and memory-residents high frees conventional memory.

Initialization Size

Another complication of loading high is initialization size. As you can see in Figure 1.29, some memory-residents occupy more memory during loading than when they are set in memory. The difference can be large—such as initializing with 67K but residing in only 3K. If the loading high process sets aside 67K for such a memory-resident, 64K would soon be wasted. The most intelligent memory managers take initialization size into account when figuring the best loading order. Some even "borrow" temporarily from memory that isn't yet settled but eventually will be—such as the expanded memory page-frame—and then give that memory back to its final use after initialization.

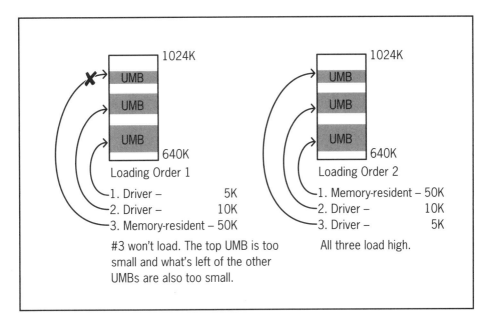

Loading Order 1

1. Driver –   5K
2. Driver –   10K
3. Memory-resident – 50K

#3 won't load. The top UMB is too small and what's left of the other UMBs are also too small.

Loading Order 2

1. Memory-resident – 50K
2. Driver –   10K
3. Driver –   5K

All three load high.

FIGURE 1.28
Loading order affects loading high efficiency.

Shadow RAM is a feature on some PCs, but you may need to disable it to load high. *Shadow RAM* maps some unused RAM into the addresses of upper memory ROMs and copies the ROM contents to that RAM. This procedure speeds system performance because the software runs faster from RAMs than it did from ROMs (the chips are faster at reading and writing information).

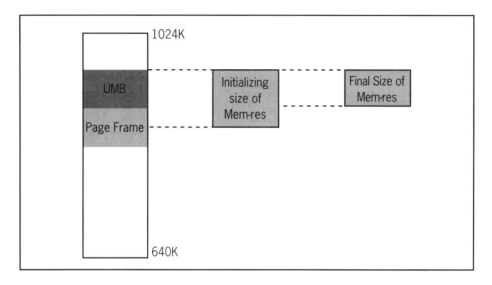

FIGURE 1.29
Initialization size may be much greater than resident size, complicating loading high.

 Some memory managers know which parts of system ROMs are no longer important—such as the old version of BASIC in the ROMs of some old IBM PCs. These memory managers can then *compress* those ROMs by copying only the important parts to RAM and mapping that RAM to the ROM addresses.

Double-Mapping

Some memory managers have begun to use the same upper memory addresses for both RAM and ROM use, which is not the same as remapping a RAM into a ROM's addresses or unused addresses. *Double-mapping* means keeping a table of what the addresses are in use for and switching the address maps when either a ROM instruction or a RAM data or program byte is called for. It can be dangerous, because if a mistake is made the computing will crash. But it can increase upper memory by hundreds of kilobytes. Figure 1.30 diagrams double-mapping in action.

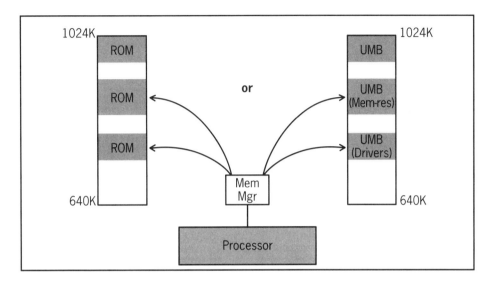

FIGURE 1.30
Double-mapping upper memory addresses.

HMA and Moving DOS

Not all of extended memory is completely off limits to DOS. In fact, because of an odd detail of addressing on the 286, 386, and 486 processors, PCs built on those chips have a special area called the *HMA* in extended memory that DOS can use sometimes, for some uses. The HMA or High Memory Area (not to be confused with high memory as in upper memory) appears in Figure 1.31.

Addresses for Real mode that are given at the top of memory, just below 1024K, are intended to wrap around to the bottom of memory again, back to zero K. But if the A20 address line which permits access to memory beyond 1024K is controlled properly, these addresses, still part of the 1M of DOS memory, will reach up 64K (minus 16 bytes that is) into extended memory. This area is the HMA, which is nearly 64K large.

The right memory management software can load something high into the HMA. That keeps it from using UMBs and so can make even more room in conventional memory. There's only one draw-back: The HMA can hold only one program at a time. If you put a small program there, you don't get much use from the HMA. But only some utilities—such as **DESQview**, which can put 63K of itself into the HMA, or even DOS 6, which can put more than 50K of itself into the HMA—make good use of the HMA.

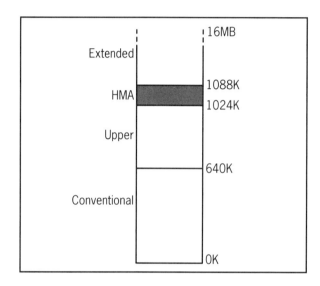

FIGURE 1.31
The HMA.

Novell's new DOS can load some software high right into extended memory, without using UMBs. This ability saves UMBs for other programs that won't load into extended memory.

Borrowing Video Memory

Just above the 640K barrier of conventional memory is an area of upper memory reserved for use by video adapters. Here you'll find addresses for the small video adapter ROMs and for the RAM memory that video adapters use to hold screen images. Figure 1.32 maps video memory use.

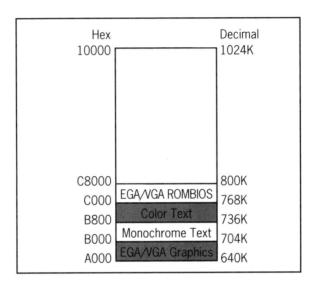

Hex		Decimal
10000		1024K
C8000		800K
C000	EGA/VGA ROMBIOS	768K
B800	Color Text	736K
B000	Monochrome Text	704K
A000	EGA/VGA Graphics	640K

FIGURE 1.32
Map of video memory use.

Often there is a lot of unused memory here. The less resolution and color in the display, the less memory is used here. The monochrome adapters use only 2K. Other adapters use more, but only when you reach SVGA is the memory almost all used. The unused memory could be turned into UMBs. But some memory managers can use it instead as conventional memory. Because it is contiguous with conventional memory, they can attach unused video memory to conventional memory. On EGA and VGA systems you could get as much as 736K or even more conventional memory. Figure 1.33 shows how this works.

Not every PC program can use this borrowed conventional memory.

You cannot switch back to the graphics modes that need the borrowed conventional memory until that memory is released by the memory manager that took it.

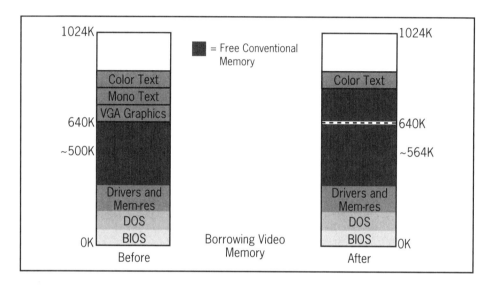

FIGURE 1.33

Borrowing unused video memory to add to conventional memory.

Protected Mode Programs and Virtual-86 Mode Programs

Some programs can prod DOS into using Protected mode or V-86 mode and so let DOS programs use extended memory, at least in some circumstances. For example, some extended mode utilities, such as the **VDISK** RAM disk, run themselves in conventional memory but use extended memory for their target memory.

DOS Extenders, programming that you can build into a program, are found in programs such as AutoCAD 386 and Paradox 386. They temporarily switch the PC into Protected mode to run the software and then switch it back to Real mode whenever DOS actions are necessary. The most famous DOS Extender program is Windows, which lets the PC start in Real mode for DOS and then moves into Protected mode or V-86 mode when Windows runs. Chapter 5 tells more about Windows.

CONFIG.SYS and AUTOEXEC.BAT

Throughout memory management you'll find two files mentioned over and over: **CONFIG.SYS** and **AUTOEXEC.BAT**. They're both part of DOS, files that DOS reads when it starts your PC to see how you want the PC set up.

CONFIG.SYS is the configuration file. It is the place to tell which drivers and DOS resources to load into memory. It is also the place most memory managers load themselves into memory to work. Chapter 4 explains this in more detail.

AUTOEXEC.BAT is the automatically executing batch file. You put into it commands and programs that you want to run automatically when you start your PC but after the configuration is set up. These programs may be memory-residents that load into memory and stay there. Many memory managers also put commands into **AUTOEXEC.BAT** to tell programs where they should be in memory.

Both files are *text-only*—they have pure text lines only but do not contain special formats or commands. To edit them, if you have MS-DOS 4, 5, or 6, you can use the pure text editor built into DOS. To start it, just type:

```
edit
```

and the name of the file you want to edit, such as:

```
edit config.sys
```

You'll see it appear, or if it doesn't exist yet, a blank screen will await, as shown in Figure 1.34. When you're done making or changing it, press **Alt+F** and then **X** to get back to DOS.

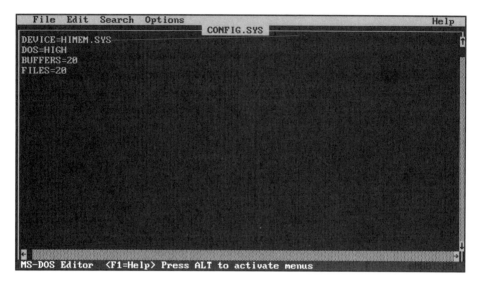

```
   File   Edit   Search   Options                                    Help
                              CONFIG.SYS
DEVICE=HIMEM.SYS
DOS=HIGH
BUFFERS=20
FILES=20




















MS-DOS Editor   <F1=Help> Press ALT to activate menus
```

FIGURE 1.34

*Use the DOS Editor to work on the CONFIG.SYS
and AUTOEXEC.BAT files.*

To see the results of any changes to **CONFIG.SYS** and
AUTOEXEC.BAT, you must restart your PC—press
Ctrl+Alt+Del or turn off the power and then turn it on
again.

CHAPTER

2

MEMORY MANAGEMENT

Measure Memory

You can't manage memory unless you know how much is there and what it is used for. You can buy some sophisticated utility programs to answer these questions, but DOS can provide some answers for free. Early versions of DOS can give only the roughest answers, but DOS 5 and 6 can answer in some detail. DOS comes with commands and utilities that let you determine how much memory is in your PC and what that memory is doing.

When you turn on your PC you'll see initial test displays of the total amount of memory in the PC. Then, you can use the **CHKDSK** command to see how much conventional memory is in the PC or the **DEBUG** utility program to view individual bytes of memory. If you have DOS 5 or 6, you have more options. The **MEM** command has four options—**FREE**, **CLASSIFY**, **DEBUG**, or **MODULE**—to tell you how much conventional, expanded, and extended memory your PC has and how it is used. The **MEM** program can even detail which *modules* (programs and drivers) are in memory and where.

The MSD (Microsoft Diagnostics) program that comes with DOS 6 is even more detailed, analyzing not just memory but all other software and hardware aspects of the computer. This program has many analysis categories and options that can tell you how your PC is configured—even letting you view the configuration files, such as **AUTOEXEC.BAT**, **CONFIG.SYS**, **WIN.INI**, and **SYSTEM.INI**.

In fact, almost any memory manager that you can buy and add to DOS comes with its own system analyzer utility. **QEMM**'s **Manifest** and **386MAX**'s **ASQ** are good examples.

When You Turn the PC On: Rough Answers

The first thing a PC does when you turn it on is test its own chips and connections. This is called a *Power-On Self Test* or POST. Part of that test is searching for memory chips and making sure they are working properly. Most PCs are set up so that you can see the results of this test on the screen. Look quickly! The test results don't stay long, flashing on screen for several seconds before they are replaced by the news that DOS is loading itself and its various drivers and programs from **CONFIG.SYS** and **AUTOEXEC.BAT**.

At best, the POST will tell you how many bytes of conventional, expanded, and extended memory you have. On a few PCs you'll also be told if BIOS shadow RAM or video shadow RAM is in effect. (See Chapter 1 for an explanation of shadow RAM.)

When the PC Is Running: Measuring Conventional Memory

The **CHKDSK** (pronounced *checkdisk*) command aims to analyze your disk, telling what parts of it are misarranged or damaged. As a byproduct, though, it tells how much conventional memory is in your PC. To see this for yourself, type:

```
chkdsk
```

As you can see in the example of Figure 2.1 (your own numbers will almost certainly be different), the end of the CHKDSK report tells you how much conventional memory the PC started with and how much of it is still free. Try this again after loading a TSR program or another driver, and you'll see the bytes free amount has changed.

```
C:\>chkdsk
Volume Serial Number is 3338-14EB
Errors found, F parameter not specified
Corrections will not be written to disk


    5 lost allocation units found in 5 chains.
      10240 bytes disk space would be freed

85714944 bytes total disk space
   79872 bytes in 2 hidden files
   51200 bytes in 15 directories
41213952 bytes in 904 user files
44359680 bytes available on disk

    2048 bytes in each allocation unit
   41853 total allocation units on disk
   21660 available allocation units on disk

  655360 total bytes memory
  485968 bytes free

C:\>
```

FIGURE 2.1

CHKDSK command can tell you how much conventional memory your PC started with and how much is still free.

If CHKDSK doesn't work, your PC isn't finding it in the current directory or through the PATH established for searching the disk. Just change to your DOS directory to use CHKDSK or other DOS utility.

Seeing or Changing
What's in Memory: DEBUG

One other command is available to all versions of DOS. It's called **DEBUG** and is actually an entire program, not just a command. This program lets you see and change what's at any address of memory. To use **DEBUG**, type:

```
debug
```

Enter or **Return** is required after all commands are typed. The result is not imposing—a simple hyphen telling you that **DEBUG** is waiting for a command. See the hyphen prompt at the top of Figure 2.2 for an example.

To see all the commands of **DEBUG**, from inside **DEBUG**, just type a question mark:

```
?
```

You'll see a list similar to that in Figure 2.2, with the names of commands, the single letter you use to get that command, and the options that can come after the command letter.

The version of **DEBUG** with early versions of DOS, such as DOS 2 and 3, cannot work with expanded and extended memory the way **DEBUG** of DOS 5 and 6 can. Early **DEBUGs** are limited to conventional memory. Also, **DEBUG** can make changes that are difficult to undo. Unless you're a PC expert, skip it and use MSD, which is described later.

```
-?
assemble       A [address]
compare        C range address
dump           D [range]
enter          E address [list]
fill           F range list
go             G [=address] [addresses]
hex            H value1 value2
input          I port
load           L [address] [drive] [firstsector] [number]
move           M range address
name           N [pathname] [arglist]
output         O port byte
proceed        P [=address] [number]
quit           Q
register       R [register]
search         S range list
trace          T [=address] [value]
unassemble     U [range]
write          W [address] [drive] [firstsector] [number]
allocate expanded memory        XA [#pages]
deallocate expanded memory      XD [handle]
map expanded memory pages       XM [Lpage] [Ppage] [handle]
display expanded memory status  XS
-
```

FIGURE 2.2
The DEBUG utility can tell you what's in memory, but it is hard to use. Press ? to see a list of DEBUG commands for viewing and changing what's in memory.

Learning all the ins and outs of **DEBUG** could take up half a book, and has done so in many manuals. Just try an example here with the **D** command, which stands for *DUMP*. It's a traditional computer command meaning give me a complete readout of what's in that area of memory, give me a *memory dump*.

At the **DEBUG** hyphen prompt, type:

d

(You don't need to use an uppercase *D*.) You'll see a dump with the address on left, the data (in hexadecimal values) in the middle, and the ASCII translations of that data on the right. Figure 2.3 is an example.

```
C:\>debug
-d
2F0E:0100  8A FF F3 0A 1B AE 47 1F-8B C3 48 12 B1 04 50 50   ......G...H...PP
2F0E:0110  8B C6 F7 D0 D3 48 DA 2B-D0 73 00 D8 34 00 FD 2E   .....H.+.s..4...
2F0E:0120  D3 E0 03 F0 8E DA 8B C7-B6 0D 16 C2 16 C0 16 F8   ................
2F0E:0130  8E C2 00 00 AC 8A D0 4E-AD 8B C8 46 8A C2 24 FE   .......N...F..$.
2F0E:0140  3C B0 75 05 00 55 AC F3-AA EB 06 3C B2 75 6D 6D   <.u..U.....<.umm
2F0E:0150  80 A2 13 A8 01 74 B1 BE-32 01 8D 8B 1E 90 40 8E   .....t..2.....@.
2F0E:0160  FC 33 D2 29 E3 13 8B C2-03 C3 15 00 69 0B F8 83   .3.)........i...
2F0E:0170  FF FF 74 11 26 01 1D 00-A0 E2 F3 81 FA 00 F0 74   ..t.&..........t
-
```

FIGURE 2.3

DEBUG dump command can tell you what's in memory.

You may also add an address to the dump command to see a pin-pointed part of memory. For instance, the example in Figure 2.4 shows what starts at 0000:0500 in one PC's memory, where the ASCII translation shows that this area of memory is tracking various system programs. To see this, type:

d 0000:0500

```
C:\>debug
-d 0000:0500
0000:0500  00 00 20 20 00 00 20 20-53 59 53 27 00 00 00 00   ..  ..  SYS'....
0000:0510  00 00 00 00 00 00 00 30-6A 1A 02 00 16 9E 00 00   .......0j.......
0000:0520  4D 53 DF 02 25 02 12 1B-FF 54 F6 01 08 00 00 00   MS..%....T......
0000:0530  00 00 00 00 00 00 00 00-6A 1A 16 00 FA 94 00 00   ........j.......
0000:0540  44 4F 53 20 20 20 20 20-20 20 20 10 00 00 00 00   DOS        .....
0000:0550  00 00 00 00 00 00 67 6C-CC 1A 4C 00 00 00 00 00   ......gl..L.....
0000:0560  57 49 4E 44 4F 57 53 20-20 20 20 10 00 00 00 00   WINDOWS    .....
0000:0570  00 00 00 00 00 00 83 6C-CC 1A B0 0B 00 00 00 00   .......l.......
-
```

FIGURE 2.4

DEBUG dump command for the 0000:0500 address.

When you're done with **DEBUG**, you can use the **Q** or **QUIT** command to get out of it and back to DOS. Type:

q

and you'll be back at the DOS prompt.

To find out what version of DOS you're using, and so which memory commands you can use, try the **VER** command. Type:

```
ver
```

You'll see a description of the brand and version of DOS as in this example line:

```
MS-DOS Version 6.00
```

MEM Command (in DOS 5 and 6) Gives Memory Details

DOS 5 was the first version of DOS to have memory management abilities. As is explained in Chapter 4, these include drivers to manage expanded and extended memory and utilities to relocate TSRs and drivers to high memory. DOS 6 added automatic configuration for these, in the MemMaker utility.

DOS 5 and 6 have a command called **MEM** that analyzes memory. This analysis can tell you lots more than the **POST**, **CHKDSK**, or **DEBUG** of previous DOS versions. And it's very easy to use. Just type:

```
mem
```

You'll see a display such as in Figure 2.5.

This is the basic MEM report. You see how much conventional, upper, adapter, and extended memory the PC started with and how much is still free—after loading the various drivers, programs, and parts of DOS. (The actual numbers in your report will certainly differ from these.) The basic report also tells you how much expanded memory there is and how much is free. Finally, you'll be told if DOS is using the HMA—that first 64K above the 1024K address, the first 64K of extended memory. If it is, that reduces how much DOS is in conventional memory (see Chapter 1 for details).

```
C:\>mem

Memory Type          Total  =  Used   +  Free
------------------   ------    ------    ------
Conventional          640K      121K      519K
Upper                   0K        0K        0K
Adapter RAM/ROM       384K      384K        0K
Extended (XMS)       3072K       64K     3008K
------------------   ------    ------    ------
Total memory         4096K      569K     3527K

Total under 1 MB      640K      121K      519K

Largest executable program size        519K   (531520 bytes)
Largest free upper memory block          0K        (0 bytes)
MS-DOS is resident in the high memory area.

C:\>
```

FIGURE 2.5

The MEM command (available in DOS 5 and 6) tells you how much memory is in your PC in far more detail than POST or CHKDSK.

You can get more details than are available in this basic report by using one of MEM's options. To see what these are, type:

```
mem /?
```

Figure 2.6 shows you this always-available description of MEM and its options.

A *switch* is another name for an option. To use a switch, you type the command, a space, a slash mark, and finally the option's name or abbreviation.

MEM's Free Memory Option

The **Free** option tells you more about how much memory is left free in conventional and upper memory even after DOS, drivers, memory-residents (TSRs), and other resources load into those kinds of memory.

To learn the details of free memory, type:

```
mem /f
```

You'll see a report like that of Figure 2.7.

```
C:\>mem /?
Displays the amount of used and free memory in your system.

MEM [/CLASSIFY | /DEBUG | /FREE | /MODULE modulename] [/PAGE]

   /CLASSIFY or /C  Classifies programs by memory usage. Lists the size of
                    programs, provides a summary of memory in use, and lists
                    largest memory block available.
   /DEBUG or /D     Displays status of all modules in memory, internal drivers,
                    and other information.
   /FREE or /F      Displays information about the amount of free memory left
                    in both conventional and upper memory.
   /MODULE or /M    Displays a detailed listing of a module's memory use.
                    This option must be followed by the name of a module,
                    optionally separated from /M by a colon.
   /PAGE or /P      Pauses after each screenful of information.

C:\>
```

FIGURE 2.6

MEM has several options, and you can learn about these with the DOS on-line help as shown here.

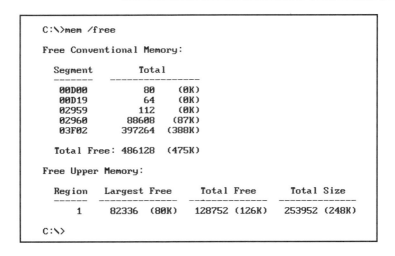

```
C:\>mem /free

Free Conventional Memory:

   Segment        Total
   -------    ----------------
    00D00            80   (0K)
    00D19            64   (0K)
    02959           112   (0K)
    02960         88608  (87K)
    03F02        397264 (388K)

   Total Free: 486128  (475K)

Free Upper Memory:

   Region   Largest Free     Total Free      Total Size
   ------  --------------   --------------   --------------
      1     82336  (80K)    128752 (126K)    253952 (248K)

C:\>
```

FIGURE 2.7

The MEM /FREE command can report in detail what memory is free.

As you can see, this report tells you where the free memory is in both conventional and upper areas and does more than the basic MEM report, which just tells you how much total memory is free. This report tells you the size of the pieces you can use, information you can then use to relocate software from conventional to upper memory (see Chapter 1 for details), or to calculate what you can run in conventional memory.

In fact, though, I don't think you'll often use the **Free** option. If you're interested in knowing more than just ballpark estimates from the basic MEM report, you'll want the grittier details from the **CLASSIFY** or **DEBUG** or **MODULE** options.

MEM's CLASSIFY Option

Use the **CLASSIFY** option by typing:

```
mem /c
```

You'll see a display similar to that in Figures 2.8 and 2.9.

If your memory use is complex, which it often will be, then the **CLASSIFY**, **DEBUG**, or **MODULE** options will report with more than a single screen of details. This means that the first things reported will scroll off the top of the screen before you can read them. There is a solution: use the **PAGE** option as shown in these examples:

```
mem /c/p
mem /d/p
mem /m/p
```

Abbreviate each option to a single letter and give each option its own slash, with a space after *mem* and none necessary between the options.

This **CLASSIFY** option tells what programs are in memory and describes exactly how much conventional and upper memory they occupy. Then it summarizes memory use—much like the basic MEM report. Let's look at the example of Figures 2.8 and 2.9. You can see that in conventional memory DOS uses about 4K of memory—4189 bytes to be precise—and **QEMM386** uses 800 bytes. **SMARTDRV**, **LOADHI**, and **COMMAND** also use a little conventional memory and no upper memory. The result is 632K free conventional memory on this example PC. That's very good—only 8K less than the full 640K of possible conventional memory (without stealing any video RAM). The summary shows this, on the continuation of the display, as shown in Figure 2.9. As the bottom line of Figure 2.8 says, press any key (try the **Spacebar** for instance) to see the next screen of the CLASSIFY report.

```
Modules using memory below 1 MB:

    Name          Total        =    Conventional    +    Upper Memory
    --------    ---------------     ----------------     ----------------
    MSDOS          47405   (46K)        47405   (46K)           0    (0K)
    386MAX          1072    (1K)         1072    (1K)           0    (0K)
    386LOAD           80    (0K)           80    (0K)           0    (0K)
    COMMAND         4992    (5K)         4992    (5K)           0    (0K)
    QCACHE          9840   (10K)         9840   (10K)           0    (0K)
    SNAP          105856  (103K)       105856  (103K)           0    (0K)
    MSDOS            160    (0K)            0    (0K)         160    (0K)
                   15792   (15K)            0    (0K)       15792   (15K)
    MSDOS          98352   (96K)            0    (0K)       98352   (96K)
    --------        3792    (4K)            0    (0K)        3792    (4K)
    MSDOS           6976    (7K)            0    (0K)        6976    (7K)
    --------         128    (0K)            0    (0K)         128    (0K)
    Free          614768  (600K)       486016  (475K)      128752  (126K)

Memory Summary:

    Type of Memory        Total       =       Used        +        Free
    ----------------    ---------------     ---------------     ---------------
    Conventional          655360  (640K)       169344  (165K)      486016  (475K)
Press any key to continue . . .
```

FIGURE 2.8

MEM's CLASSIFY option can tell you what programs are in memory and how much memory they use.

```
MSDOS        6976   (7K)          0   (0K)        6976   (7K)
--------       128   (0K)          0   (0K)         128   (0K)
Free       614768  (600K)     486016  (475K)     128752  (126K)

Memory Summary:

  Type of Memory         Total      =        Used       +        Free
  ----------------    -------------      -------------       -------------
  Conventional        655360  (640K)      169344  (165K)      486016  (475K)
Press any key to continue . . .
  Upper               253952  (248K)      125200  (122K)      128752  (126K)
  Adapter RAM/ROM     393216  (384K)      393216  (384K)           0    (0K)
  Extended (XMS)     2891776 (2824K)      630784  (616K)     2260992 (2208K)
  ----------------    -------------      -------------       -------------

  Total memory       4194304 (4096K)     1318544 (1288K)     2875760 (2808K)

  Total under 1 MB    909312  (888K)      294544  (288K)      614768  (600K)

  Total Expanded (EMS)                   2457600 (2400K)
  Free Expanded (EMS)                    1867776 (1824K)
  Largest executable program size         485856  (474K)
  Largest free upper memory block          82336   (80K)
  The high memory area is available.

C:\>
```

FIGURE 2.9

*MEM's CLASSIFY option can have more than a single screen of informa-
tion. If you use the /P option too, you can see each screen in turn.*

If you want yet more detail, not just a summary of the programs in
memory but a list of programs and drivers by their order in memory, try the **DEBUG** option.

MEM's DEBUG Option

Here's the maximum detail **MEM** can give. When you use the
DEBUG option, you get a full list of all the programs and drivers in
memory. Type:

```
mem /d/p
```

to see an example. (Be sure to use that **/P** option along with it. This
report is sure to take up several screens.) As you can see in Figure
2.10, you'll get a bottom to top list of the programs and drivers in
memory, showing memory segment, memory size of this area, name

of module using the area, and what type that module is (driver, program, and so on). Figures 2.11 and 2.12 show the rest of this report, down to its extended summaries of memory use.

Module is the name given to a piece of software that occupies an area of memory. This could be a driver, environment, program, vector, or other software, ranging from only a few bytes to megabytes in size.

```
Conventional Memory Detail:

    Segment            Total        Name          Type
    -------        -------------    ------------   --------
    00000              1039   (1K)                 Interrupt Vector
    00040               271   (0K)                 ROM Communication Area
    00050               527   (1K)                 DOS Communication Area
    00070              2656   (3K)   IO            System Data
                                     CON           System Device Driver
                                     AUX           System Device Driver
                                     PRN           System Device Driver
                                     CLOCK$        System Device Driver
                                     A: - C:       System Device Driver
                                     COM1          System Device Driver
                                     LPT1          System Device Driver
                                     LPT2          System Device Driver
                                     LPT3          System Device Driver
                                     COM2          System Device Driver
                                     COM3          System Device Driver
                                     COM4          System Device Driver
    00116             42816  (42K)   MSDOS         System Data
    00B8A              1264   (1K)   IO            System Data
                       1056   (1K)          EMMXXXX0  Installed Device=386MAX
    Press any key to continue . . .
```

FIGURE 2.10

MEM's DEBUG option report (listing all the programs and drivers in memory).

The DEBUG report can help when you want to know what's where in memory and perhaps notice multiple environments or awkwardly placed drivers that could be relocated. But that three-screen—or more—report might be too long for you. If you are interested in one specific module from that long list, then you need the last option for **MEM**, the **MODULE** option (which is not available in DOS 5).

```
                          64   (0K)     386LOAD$   Installed Device=386LOAD
                          80   (0K)                FILES=6
         00BD9          4720   (5K)     COMMAND    Program
         00D00            80   (0K)     MSDOS      -- Free --
         00D05           272   (0K)     COMMAND    Environment
         00D16            48   (0K)     QCACHE     Environment
         00D19            64   (0K)     MSDOS      -- Free --
         00D1D          9792  (10K)     QCACHE     Program
         00F81           112   (0K)     SNAP       Environment
         00F88        105744 (103K)     SNAP       Program
         02959           112   (0K)     MEM        Environment
         02960         88608  (87K)     MEM        Program
         03F02        397264 (388K)     MSDOS      -- Free --

     Upper Memory Detail:

      Segment  Region       Total       Name        Type
      -------  ------  ----------------  ----------  --------
       0C000     1          80   (0K)               Data
       0C005     1       15744  (15K)               Program
       0C3DD     1          80   (0K)               Data
       0C3E2     1          48   (0K)               Environment
       0C3E5     1       82336  (80K)   MSDOS       -- Free --
       0D7FF     1       69648  (68K)               Data
     Press any key to continue . . .
```

FIGURE 2.11

Second screen of MEM's DEBUG option.

```
       0E900     1       28656  (28K)   MSDOS       -- Free --
       0EFFF     1       20496  (20K)               Data
       0F500     1        3040   (3K)   --------    Data
       0F5BE     1          96   (0K)               Data
       0F5C4     1         864   (1K)               Data
       0F5FA     1          80   (0K)   MSDOS       -- Free --
       0F5FF     1        8208   (8K)               Data
       0F800     1         960   (1K)               Data
       0F83C     1         128   (0K)               Data
       0F844     1         752   (1K)   --------    Data
       0F873     1         288   (0K)               Data
       0F885     1        4288   (4K)               Data
       0F991     1         480   (0K)               Data
       0F9AF     1       17680  (17K)   MSDOS       -- Free --

     Memory Summary:

      Type of Memory       Total       =      Used       +      Free
      ---------------  ----------------   ----------------   ----------------
      Conventional      655360  (640K)     169344 (165K)      486016  (475K)
      Upper             253952  (248K)     125200 (122K)      128752  (126K)
      Adapter RAM/ROM   393216  (384K)     393216 (384K)           0    (0K)
      Extended (XMS)   2891776 (2824K)     630784 (616K)     2260992 (2208K)
      ---------------  ----------------   ----------------   ----------------
     Press any key to continue . . .
```

FIGURE 2.12

Third screen of MEM's DEBUG option.

MEM's MODULE Option

If you want to know about a module of software in memory, you can use **MEM**'s **MODULE** option. You need the module's name to use this option. You can find a list of all named modules in memory from the MEM /DEBUG listing already described. Then you can use that name like this (to use the SNAP memory-resident as an example, from Figure 2.13), type:

```
mem /m snap
```

You'll see a quick synopsis of that module's memory use: the memory size and address for the module, as shown in the example in Figure 2.13.

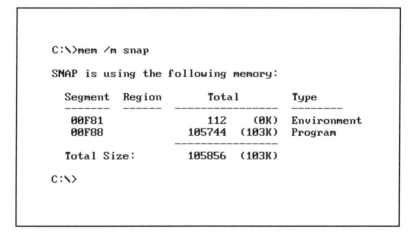

FIGURE 2.13
MEM's MODULE option (for details on a single program or driver in memory).

The information in this report can help you decide what to relocate from one place in memory to another or what programs to eliminate.

MSD Complete Reporting

DOS 6 comes with a program that can tell you all about what's in your PC. Microsoft Diagnostics analyzes your PC's processor, memory, disk drives, other peripherals, and so on, and tells you all about them.

To start MSD, locate its directory (probably the DOS directory, or put that directory in your path) and type:

```
msd
```

For a few seconds while MSD analyzes the PC, you'll see a title screen display. Then, you'll see the main choices screen, as shown in Figure 2.14.

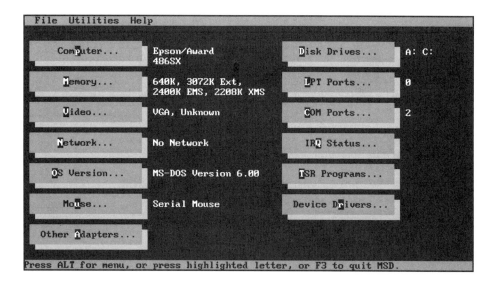

FIGURE 2.14
MSD main screen.

You can see summary information such as which processor, how much memory, what operating system, which video adapter is hooked up, and other information. But when you get into details, there's so much information on your PC that it must be divided into the following categories:

▼ *Computer* describes the processor, keyboard, bus, and BIOS.

▼ *Memory* maps in the first megabyte and summaries conventional, extended, and expanded memory use.

▼ *Video* tells what type of video adapter you have and what mode it is in.

▼ *Network* tells what kind of Network adapter is connected.

▼ *OS Version* tells what operating system is running, which version is being used, and what path it is set to, including the ENVIRONMENT for DOS.

▼ *Mouse* tells which mouse is connected and what driver it uses.

▼ *Other Adapters* tells about such extras as a game adapter.

▼ *Disk Drives* tells you about the floppy and hard disks, and also shows CD-ROM and other disk drives on the system— how large they are and how they're organized.

▼ *LPT Ports* tells how the parallel ports are set up.

▼ *COM Ports* tells how the serial ports are set up.

▼ *IRQ Status* tells about the interrupts stored in memory for handling all the peripherals.

▼ *TSR Programs* tells you what TSRs are loaded into memory and how much memory they're occupying and at what address.

▼ *Device Drivers* tells you what drivers are loaded into memory and what address they're at.

MSD tells you as much as it can, but sometimes it cannot divine from analysis of RAM and ROMs just who made a BIOS or other peripheral. Sometimes you'll see blanks in the various report screens.

From here you can:

▼ press the highlighted letter of any category to see details on it.

▼ press **Alt+F** or **Alt+U** or **Alt+H** to see menus of other choices.

▼ press **F3** to quit MSD and return to DOS.

▼ select a menu option with your mouse.

If you want to print any MSD analysis, press **Alt+F** and then **P**. Then move the cursor—with Arrow keys and **Tab**—to the report you want and make sure that there's an *X* in that parenthesis. You can print to a port—parallel or serial—or to a file on disk, and you could give that a name. You can also tell MSD to print a report using your mouse to choose the above items.

The most important categories for memory management, not surprisingly, are the Memory, OS Version, TSR Programs, Device Drivers, and Video. Network can also come into play.

MSD Memory Analysis

Once you're in MSD, press **M** to get the Memory analysis. You'll see a display similar to that in Figure 2.15. On the left you see a map of the first megabyte of memory, showing what areas are used by RAM, ROM, expanded memory Page Frame, and upper memory blocks, and which of those areas are free for use. On the right are summaries of the conventional, extended, and expanded memory available. When you're done with this information, you can press **ESC** or **Enter** to return to the main MSD screen.

```
 File  Utilities  Help
━━━━━━━━━━━━━━━━━━━━━━━━━━━━━ Memory ━━━━━━━━━━━━━━━━━━━━━━━━━━━━
  Legend:  Available "██"  RAM "██"  ROM "  "  Possibly Available "██"    ↑
    EMS Page Frame "PF"  Used UMBs "UU"  Free UMBs "FF"  Free XMS UMBs "XX" █
 1024K FC00 UUUUUUUU             FFFF  Conventional Memory
       F800 UUUUUUUUUUUUUUUU     FBFF             Total: 640K
       F400 UUU UUUUUUUUUU       F7FF         Available: 474K
  960K F000 UUUUUUUUUUUUUUUU     F3FF                     485872 bytes
       EC00 UUUUUUUUUUUUUUUU     EFFF
       E800 UUU UUUUUUUUUUU      EBFF  Extended Memory
       E400 UUUUUUUUUUUUUUUU     E7FF             Total: 3072K
  896K E000 UUUUUUUUUUUUUUUU     E3FF
       DC00 UUUUUUUUUUUUUUUU     DFFF  MS-DOS Upper Memory Blocks
       D800 UUUUUUUUUUUUUUUU     DBFF         Total UMBs: 247K
       D400 FFFFFFFFFFFFFFFU     D7FF    Total Free UMBs: 80K
  832K D000 FFFFFFFFFFFFFFFF     D3FF  Largest Free Block: 80K
       CC00 FFFFFFFFFFFFFFFF     CFFF
       C800 FFFFFFFFFFFFFFFF     CBFF  Expanded Memory (EMS)
       C400 FFFFFFFFFFFFFFFF     C7FF         LIM Version: 4.00
  768K C000 UUUUUUUUUUUUUUUF     C3FF  Page Frame Address: D800H    ↓

                         ━━━━━━ OK ━━━━━━
Memory: Displays visual memory map and various types of memory.
```

FIGURE 2.15
MSD memory analysis.

MSD can also show you a block display of memory use. At any point within MSD just press **Alt+U** and then **M** or make the selection with your mouse. You'll see the menu appear and then the block display shown in Figure 2.16.

On the left you'll see a list of modules in memory with the address each starts at and the amount of memory they occupy. You can press the Arrow keys to select any one of these modules, highlighting it on the screen. You can also pick an area in the Allocated memory column using your mouse. On the right you'll see a map of that section of memory, showing how it is taken. If you want to scroll through this map, press **Tab** to move to the section on the right. When you're done, press **Esc** to get back to the main MSD display.

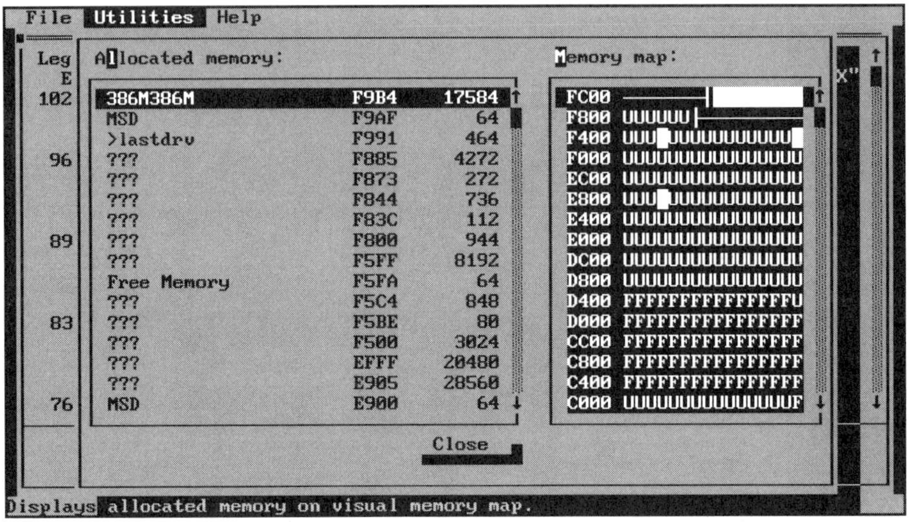

FIGURE 2.16

MSD's memory block display.

Or you could use MSD's Memory Browser (press **Alt+U** and then **B**), and you'll see a display similar to that in Figure 2.17. Here you can choose an area to browse and see a map on the right of that area. Near the bottom you'll see a Search String area. **Tab** to this area and then type any string you want to find in memory. Then, press **Enter** to see if that *string* (sequence of characters) is in memory and, if so, where.

OS Version

If you press **O** (for the highlighted letter of OS) from the main MSD screen, you'll see a description of the DOS version you're using, along with its path and environment settings. Figure 2.18 shows an example.

As you saw in Chapter 1, the version of DOS you use affects how much memory is used. The environment takes up some memory—although not much.

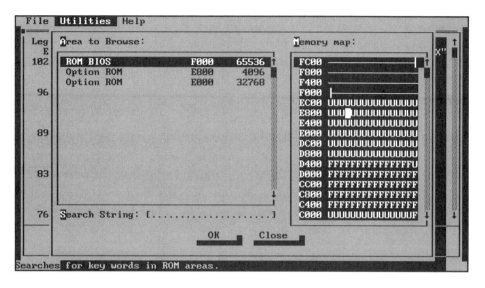

FIGURE 2.17
MSD's Memory Browser example.

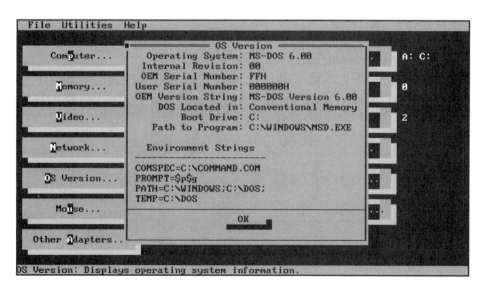

FIGURE 2.18
MSD Operating System analysis example.

MSD TSR Programs Analysis

As explained in Chapter 1, memory-resident programs load into memory and stay there even when they are not active. Many load from instructions in the **AUTOEXEC.BAT** file when you start your PC. These programs take up memory that normal programs, which dump out of memory when stopped, don't use. To manage memory you need to know what the memory-resident programs are, how much memory they occupy, and where they are in memory. Then, you can choose to eliminate them, minimize them, or relocate them to other, less vital memory areas. See Chapter 1 for details on that house cleaning.

To see MSD's analysis of TSRs in your PC, press **T** from the main MSD screen. You'll see a display similar to that of Figure 2.19. The TSRs names are on the left, the address they start at and the amount of memory (in bytes) they need is next, and any parameters that were on the command line that loaded that TSR are last.

MSD Device Drivers Analysis

Device drivers, as explained in Chapter 1, are pieces of software that help interface one hardware or software element to another. They load into memory from **CONFIG.SYS** when you start your PC and stay there, as explained in Chapter 1. MSD includes an analysis of these, showing what drivers are in your PC and where they are in memory. To manage memory you need to know what they are, how much memory they occupy, and where they are in memory. Then, you can choose to eliminate them or relocate them to other, less vital memory areas.

To see MSD's analysis of drivers in your PC, press **R** from the main MSD screen. You'll see a display similar to that in Figure 2.20. The names of the TSRs are on the left, the address they start at and the amount of memory (in bytes) they need is next, and any parameters that were on the command line that loaded that TSR are last. If there are more drivers than can appear on one screen, you can press **PgDn** or the **Down Arrow** key to scroll the display and view them in the list.

```
 File  Utilities  Help
                                TSR Programs
   Program Name        Address   Size   Command Line Parameters          ↑
   -----------         -------   ----   -----------------------
   System Data         0B8A      1248
     386MAX            0B8C      1056   EMMXXXX0
     386LOAD           0BCF        64   386LOAD$
       File Handles    0BD4        80
   COMMAND.COM         0BD9      4704
   Free Memory         0D00        64
   COMMAND.COM         0D05       256
   QCACHE.EXE          0D16        32   /S:768
   Free Memory         0D19        48
   QCACHE.EXE          0D1D      9776   /S:768
   SNAP.EXE            0F81        96
   SNAP.EXE            0F88    105728
   MSD.EXE             2959        96
   MSD.EXE             2960    316576
   MSD.EXE             76AB      8192
   MSD.EXE             78AC     10032                                     ↓

                             ┌─────────┐
                             │   OK    ██
                             └─────────┘

 TSR Programs: Displays allocated memory control blocks.
```

FIGURE 2.19
MSD's TSR analysis.

```
 File  Utilities  Help
                              Device Drivers
 Com ┃  Device     Filename  Units    Header      Attributes        ↑
     ┃  ------     --------  -----    ------      ----------
     ┃  NUL                           0116:0048  1.............1..
 Me  ┃  386LOAD$   386LOAD            0BCF:0000  1...............
     ┃  SMARTAAR                      F845:0000  11..1...........
     ┃  386MAX$$                      0B8C:0012  11..............
 Ui  ┃  EMMXXXX0   386MAX             0B8C:0000  11..............
     ┃  CON                           0070:0023  1.........1..11
     ┃  AUX                           0070:0035  1...............
     ┃  PRN                           0070:0047  1.1.....11......
 Net ┃  CLOCK$                        0070:0059  1...........1..
     ┃  Block Device           3      0070:006B  ....1...11....1.
     ┃  COM1                          0070:007B  1...............
 OS v┃  LPT1                          0070:008D  1.1.....11......
     ┃  LPT2                          0070:009F  1.1.....11......
     ┃  LPT3                          0070:00B8  1.1.....11......
 Mo  ┃  COM2                          0070:00CA  1...............
     ┃  COM3                          0070:00DC  1...............  ↓

 Other                        ┌─────────┐
                              │   OK    ██
                              └─────────┘

 Device Drivers: Displays installable device driver information.
```

FIGURE 2.20
MSD's device drivers analysis.

MSD Analysis of Video and Network

If you need to know what kind of video you're using, what network adapter occupies a spot in your PC's memory, or what other adapters might impact memory, you can use MSD to find out. Press **V** or **N** or **A**, and you'll see a report on each.

MSD Views AUTOEXEC.BAT

As explained in Chapter 1 and mentioned previously, part of memory is full of TSR programs that load when you start your PC. These load from instruction lines in the **AUTOEXEC.BAT** file on your disk. You need to know what's in this file to manage memory. You'll often want to change what's in it.

MSD lets you view the **AUTOEXEC.BAT** file, without your having to start a separate word processor or text editor. Just press **Alt+F** and then **1** to see the file, as shown in the example in Figure 2.21.

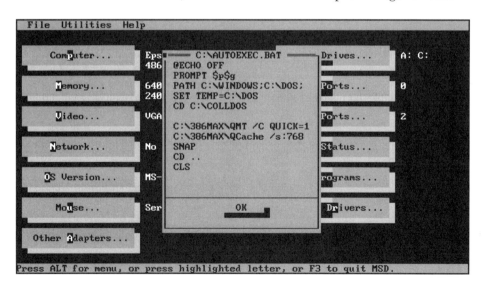

FIGURE 2.21
MSD can view the AUTOEXEC.BAT file.

MSD Views CONFIG.SYS

As explained in Chapter 1 and mentioned previously, part of memory is full of device driver software that loads when you start your PC. This software loads from instruction lines in the **CONFIG.SYS** file on your disk. You need to know what's in this file to manage memory. You'll often want to change what's in it.

MSD lets you view the **CONFIG.SYS** file, without your having to start a separate word processor or text editor. Just press **Alt+F** and then **2** to see the file.

MSD Views SYSTEM.INI and WIN.INI

Windows has two configuration files. As **AUTOEXEC.BAT** and **CONFIG.SYS** configure DOS itself, **SYSTEM.INI** and **WIN.INI** configure Windows. MSD lets you view these files without starting the Windows Notepad or other text editor. Figure 2.22 shows an example. To see these files, you just get into MSD, press **Alt+F**, and then press **3** or **4**. These files are almost always more than one page long, so you'll need to use your mouse or scrolling keys to see the entire file.

Inserting a Command into a Configuration File

When you manage memory, you need both to view and often to change the configuration files: **AUTOEXEC.BAT**, **CONFIG.SYS**, **WIN.INI**, and **SYSTEM.INI**. MSD offers some power to change these files. Press **Alt+U** and then **I** (for Insert command), and you'll see a display offering a number of common changes in a list, as shown in Figure 2.23. If you want to add one of these statements to a configuration file, you highlight it in the list (use the Arrow keys to move the highlighting to it), **Tab** to the **OK** button (you'll see the blinking cursor appear in it), and then press **Enter**.

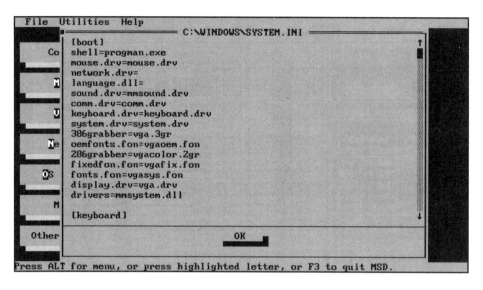

FIGURE 2.22
MSD can view the Windows configuration files, such as SYSTEM.INI.

Another window will appear and ask if this is truly the command you want, the section it should fit in (the Windows configuration files have sections devoted to different tasks), and the file you want it in. You can change each of your responses and then press **OK** or **Cancel**.

Yet another window will follow and ask if you want to just add that line and if you want to replace other similar lines. At the end you'll see a view of the configuration file.

Measuring with Other Memory Managers

Memory managers such as **QEMM** and **386MAX**—described later in this book—sometimes come with their own memory and system analyzer utilities. **QEMM**'s **Manifest** does a lot of what MSD does.

386MAX's **ASQ** is similar. But **386MAX** also comes with **RAMExam**, a memory-testing utility that not only tells you how much memory you have but also how well the memory chips are working. Other system testing that will exercise every part of your system, including the memory chips, are available too.

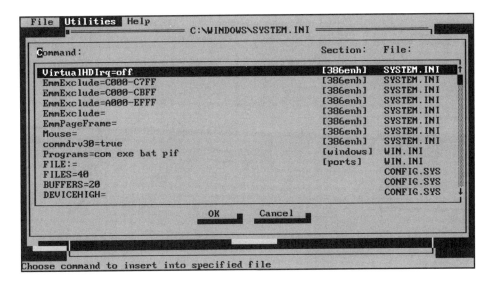

FIGURE 2.23
MSD lets you add commands to configuration files.

Now on to...

Now that you know what's in your PC, you're ready to add more memory (if needed) and then manage the memory, with DOS's own or other utility programs.

CHAPTER
3

MEMORY MANAGEMENT

Add Memory

Memory is chips. Most PCs have room to let you add more chips. Should you? As you know from Chapter 1, it isn't enough to have memory chips. You can't necessarily use all the chips that are in the PC, but it is important to have enough chips. Even the best memory management in the world can't make something out of nothing. This chapter is about putting more memory into your PC, so that there's more to manage and make the most of.

How Much is Enough?

If your PC doesn't have enough memory, you should add more. How much is enough? That depends on what you want to do with your PC and what kind of PC you have. Here are some guesstimates for you. Of course, you can always add even more for disk caches, RAM disks, and multitasking.

In the following table, *minimum* means simple word processing or spreadsheet calculating, and *optimum* means fancy word processing with fonts, drawing graphics, and calculating large spreadsheets.

Type of PC	Use of PC	Operating System	A Good Amount of Memory
8088, 8086 PC	Minimum	DOS	640K conventional
8088, 8086 PC	Optimum	DOS	640K conventional plus 2M EMS expanded
80286 PC	Minimum	DOS	1M (the first 640K is conventional; the 384K remaining is XMS extended)
80286 PC	Optimum	DOS	1M (the first 640K is conventional; the 384K remaining is XMS extended) 4M EMS expanded (backfill if can)
80386 PC	Minimum	DOS	2M (the first 640K is conventional; the rest is XMS extended)
80386 PC	Optimum	Windows	6M (on the motherboard or an extended memory board)

continued

Type of PC	Use of PC	Operating System	A Good Amount of Memory
80486 PC	Minimum	Windows	4M (on the motherboard or an extended memory board)
80486 PC	Optimum	Windows or OS/2	12M (on the motherboard or an extended memory board)
Pentium PC	Minimum	Windows or OS/2	8M (on the motherboard or an extended memory board)
Pentium PC	Optimum	Windows, OS/2, or Windows NT	16M (on the motherboard or an extended memory board)

So now you have some idea about how much memory you need. Do you know how much you have? If you're a pro, you can look inside the PC and see. If not, and even for pros, the easy way is to use some of the commands found in Chapter 2 to measure your memory. Then come back here to consider buying that memory.

Where Will You Add the Sockets, Slots, and Boards?

Before you buy more memory chips, you need to know where you're going to plug them in. There are four possible places:

▼ on the motherboard

▼ on a special high-speed memory board plugged into a special 32-bit slot

▼ on an EMS expanded memory board plugged into a slot

▼ on an XMS extended memory board plugged into a slot

You may have all of these sources ready and waiting, or you may have none. If you have none, then you'll need to add a memory board with open slots if you want to add memory chips.

Where should you choose to add memory first? On an 8088, 8086, or 80286 PC, you should first fill an expanded memory board (and then use the memory manager software to backfill conventional memory).

On a 386 PC, 486, or Pentium PC, you should fill the motherboard first and then fill any high-speed board (if your PC has one) followed by an extended memory board. When you know where you're going to add memory, you need to discover how many sockets are available there and what type of sockets (DIP or SIMM) they are. There are only two ways to do this: open the case yourself and look or have someone else open the case and look.

You could choose to first fill all available sockets on the motherboard on the 8088, 8086, or 80286 and then fill an expanded memory board. Backfilling, though, is more flexible, at the cost of disabling 256K to 384K of memory and losing it, as explained in Chapter 1.

Not even the memory measurement programs mentioned in Chapter 2 can tell you just where the sockets are or what type they are. What you're looking for are DIP sockets for DIP chips as explained in Chapter 1 and SIMM sockets for SIMMs, which is also explained in Chapter 1. See Figures 3.1 through 3.4 for examples.

Have your PC's manual handy, too. You'll probably want its help in identifying any particular order for installing chips.

Count the DIP sockets that are open and refer to your manual (or read the tops of the chips filling neighboring sockets) to determine the capacity of the chip that fits here. You'll need to add DIP chips in groups of 2, 4, 8, or 9—depending on your particular computer.

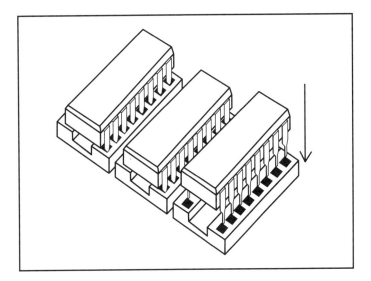

FIGURE 3.1
Typical DIP socket.

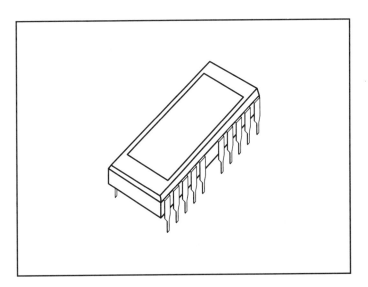

FIGURE 3.2
A DIP memory chip.

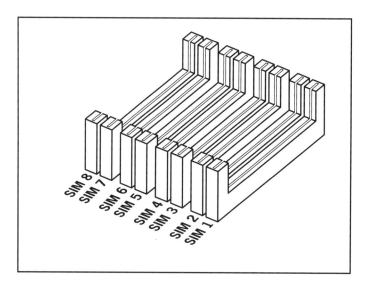

FIGURE 3.3
Typical SIMM sockets.

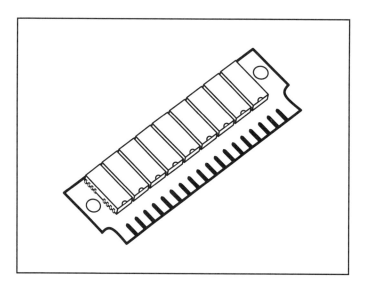

FIGURE 3.4
A memory SIMM.

For example, many PCs use 9 chips for each byte—with the last bit a parity bit for avoiding errors (as explained in Chapter 1). If each socket holds a 256Kb chip—256K bits—then 9 of them will make 256K. Similarly, if each holds a 1Mb chip, then 9 of them will make 1M.

Count the SIMM sockets. Refer to your manual to see what capacity the SIMMs are. You can typically add just one SIMM at a time. A 1M SIMM adds 1M to your computer, except—naturally there are lots of exceptions—when the SIMM you added replaces a previous SIMM. Some sockets let you replace lower-capacity SIMMs with higher-capacity SIMMs. You might replace a 1M SIMM with a 4M SIMM, effectively adding only 3M to the total.

Now you know how many DIPs or SIMMs you have sockets for. If that's enough space for the memory you need, then you're ready to buy that memory. If there aren't enough slots, then you'll want more. You'll need a new memory board or card (a circuit board). You have three choices:

▼ buy a new motherboard with more sockets (that's revolutionary, a lot of work, but probably will also give you a faster processor and faster bus), as shown in Figure 3.5

▼ buy an expanded memory board (make sure it's EMS 4.0, but only do this for an 8088, 8086, or 80286 PC), as shown in Figure 3.6

▼ buy an extended memory board (for 386, 486, and Pentium PCs), as shown in Figure 3.7

Motherboards typically have room for from 1M to 8M of memory. Recent motherboards all use SIMMs, which are easier to take out and put in than DIPs.

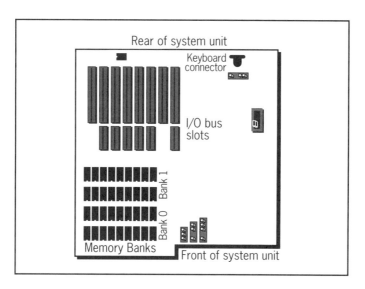

FIGURE 3.5
Example of a replacement motherboard.

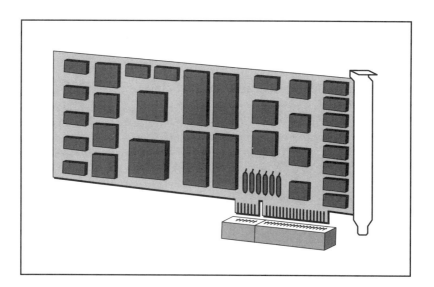

FIGURE 3.6
Example of an expanded memory board.

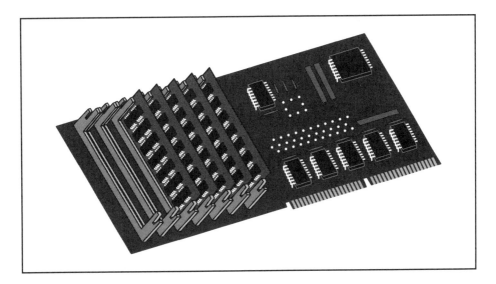

FIGURE 3.7
Example of an extended memory board.

 Many motherboards require a full bank of 4 SIMMS, not one at a time. Mixing SIMMS in a bank is also often not supported.

When buying an expanded memory board, ask if it has a daughter-board (a small board that connects to and becomes part of the memory board) option for adding yet more memory chips. You should get that option and fill it if you can afford. Two of the most famous makes are the AST Rampage and the Intel AboveBoard. Typically, they hold 2M and have daughterboards that hold 6M more. Some also come with a serial port, printer port, clock, or game port.

When choosing an extended memory board, make sure to ask first if your PC has a special, high-speed memory slot and board. If your PC is so equipped, choose this option. Then, use a standard extended memory board.

Buy a board with standard PC SIMM sockets because these are the easiest memory chips to install.

 Don't use an expanded memory board in a 386 or 486 PC. These two computers can use extended memory to emulate expanded memory and so get the most flexible use from extended memory.

Now you know how much memory you need, how many chips you need to buy, and where to plug in those chips. You're ready to buy chips and, if you need it, a memory board. Remember that if your memory is organized into banks, you may need to install chips of the same speed and capacity into those banks all at once.

 If you're comfortable installing chips, buy any new memory board *naked*—without any memory chips installed—or in *OK* configuration, because normally you can find the chips less expensively than those installed on the board by the manufacturer.

Sources for Buying Chips

RAM chips sell as DIPs or SIMMs (described in Chapter 1). There are many ways to buy them.

Source	Cost	Helpfulness
Computer store	Highest	Highest
Mail-order computer company	Middle	Middle
Chip company	Lowest	Lowest

The amount of help choosing and installing them varies directly with the price. For example, the computer store can charge 50% more than the chip company, but the service is better. In early 1994 SIMM prices had been fairly stable for some months at about $40 for 1 megabyte SIMMS, but you can get a feel for the current market price from the back pages of computer magazines, which often have ads for memory.

In such ads the $CALL$ means you should call for a price, either because it changes too often to print or because the company wants to be able to haggle over that price.

If you're a beginner, buy your chips at a retail store and pay to have them installed.

Portable PCs are often much harder to open and install chips in, so that even experienced computer users may want to pay someone to add memory to a portable.

When you buy chips, wherever you buy them, see if you can get an installation manual or even an installation video.

Identifying Chips

Chips have lots of information stenciled on their surfaces, as you can see in the example of Figure 3.8. This includes:

▼   *manufacturer*—by name or logo (stick to one maker)

▼   *capacity*—in a code for Kb, such as 1256 for 256K or 11000 for 1Mb (choose the capacity and number you need)

▼ *speed*—in a code for nanoseconds of access time, such as -15 for 150 ns or -70 for 70 ns (buy a chip that is fast enough for your PC, but no faster—buying faster chips won't make your PC work any faster)

▼ *orientation*—a dot or notch on the pin-one end to make sure that you correctly plug the chip in the socket, which also has a pin-one notch or dot, as shown in Figure 3.9.

FIGURE 3.8
Memory inscriptions.

Don't buy your chips from more than one manufacturer if you can help it. And make sure that all your chips have the same speed. Small changes in speed or even manufacturer can confuse some systems. OS/2 is especially vulnerable to this confusion.

A surge protector can save weak chips from actually breaking down, by conditioning the electric power fed to your PC.

Look for a memory upgrade kit that includes chips, instructions, and tips.

Installing the Board and Chips

Before you install anything, try to have a work area that is dry, dust-free, pet-free, smoke-free, and static-electricity-free (don't shuffle on a carpet, but do use anti-static spray, if you have it, and grounded cables).

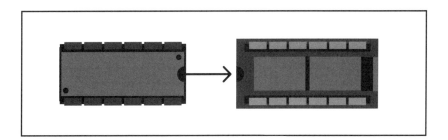

FIGURE **3.9**
Pin-one example.

Don't install a new motherboard unless you're fairly expert. It's a major operation.

Installing memory on a new expanded or extended memory board is not too complex, although beginners will want to have a pro do it for them. To get inside the computer case:

1. Ground yourself by turning off the PC and then touching the power supply so that there is no static charge on you.

2. Remove your new memory chips from their static-free containers and check that they are what you ordered.

3. Unplug the computer.

4. Open the computer case, as shown in Figure 3.10. There are several screws on the back of most PCs. Remove and save these screws.

5. Slide the case off, watching that you don't catch it on any cables inside.

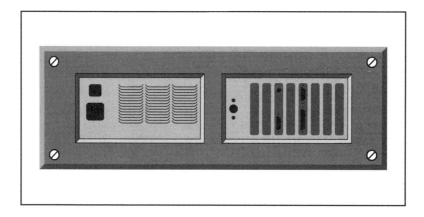

FIGURE **3.10.**

Opening the computer.

You should now see the motherboard. If that is where you'll add memory, find the sockets on it.

If you plan to add memory to an expanded or extended memory board that's already in the PC, identify this board (it should be plugged into a slot), remove the small screw that retains its back panel, and pry the board out, as shown in Figure 3.11. Then, place the board flat on your work area. Hold the board only by its back-panel edge. Don't touch the metallic connectors that slip into the slot.

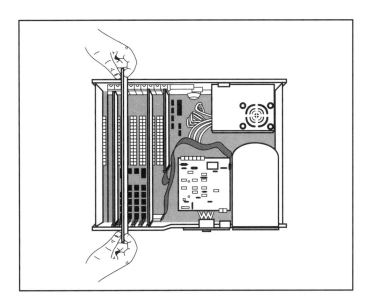

FIGURE 3.11
Removing an expansion board.

If you're adding memory to a new board, place that board flat on your work area. Hold the board only by its back-panel edge. Don't touch the metallic connectors that slip into the slot.

Line up your new memory DIPs or SIMMs but don't touch the legs. De-static yourself again. Now, remove any DIPs or SIMMs you're replacing. For DIPs, you'll want to slip the edge of a flat screwdriver gently under either end of the chip. Pry it up slowly, switching to the opposite end as it climbs out of the socket. If you need to remove a smaller capacity SIMM and replace it with a larger capacity, use your fingers to release any locks, then tilt the SIMMs away from the resting back side of the socket. Tilt them up to pointing straight away from the board. They should click out of their held place.

If the legs of a DIP are bent, straighten them gently with needle-nose pliers. For DIPs, hold the epoxy case—don't touch the legs— and press all the legs on one side sideways against the work area table top. You want to bend them in slightly so that the DIP is slightly "pigeon-toed." The legs will fit into the socket more easily.

Line up the DIPs or SIMMs you're going to install. Make sure that you're orienting them the right way—by pin-one markings on DIPs. SIMMs will fit in only one way, usually the chip-side is away from the hook on each side of the SIMM slot. Install the DIPs or SIMMs one at a time. Place the DIP or SIMM on the socket. Press a DIP into the socket, making sure each leg finds its own hole and doesn't bend up underneath the DIP. See Figure 3.12. Lightly press a SIMM straight into the socket and then tilt it until it clicks into place. If it isn't snapping in, catching on the hooks, turn it around and try again. See Figure 3.13.

Inspect your work. If the DIPs or SIMMs seem well seated, then its time to put the extended or expanded memory board into the PC. Replace the expansion board where you found it, pressing it firmly into the slot. If you're adding a new board, choose a slot for it and press it firmly into that slot. Hold the board only by its back-panel edge. Don't touch the metallic connectors that slip into the slot. Once the board is well-seated, screw it in with the single small screw at the back panel.

You could close the computer case at this point, but it's probably better not to. Instead, you can set the computer up and test it to make sure that the new memory is properly installed. Then, you can close the case.

To use the new memory, you must add any necessary software for it, such as an expanded memory manager that comes with the expanded memory board or an extended memory manager (see the board's manual and Chapters 6 through 8 for examples). Sometimes you must also tell this software about the memory change, but other memory managers recognize the change automatically.

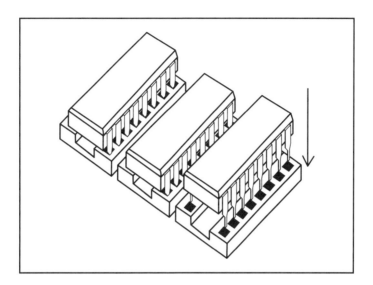

FIGURE 3.12
Pressing a DIP into a socket.

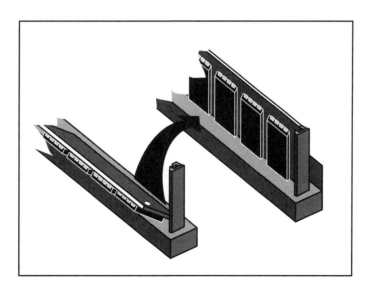

FIGURE 3.13
Pressing a SIMM into the slot.

Reconfiguring and Testing Your Added Memory

After installing memory, you'll need to configure that memory. Then, you should test your system to see that it and the new memory are working properly. You can just leave the computer case open when you do this.

When you add memory to a 286, 386, or 486 PC, you'll get an error message. The system remembers how much memory it had and now counts more. You'll need to run the PC's Setup program to change the entry for amount of memory. Check your manual—PCs do this differently, even though many will offer it as a choice immediately after such an error message. 8088 and 8086 PCs don't count memory in the same way and so won't give you a setup error.

If you see a Parity error message after installing more memory, then there's a bad chip. It could be bad internally, be broken, or just have a bent leg that isn't fitting into its socket. Check the chips. If a leg is out of place, carefully remove the chip, straighten the leg with needle-nose pliers, and *reseat* (push back in) the chip. Check too for a DIP that's backwards, with Pin 1 in the wrong place.

Finally, use the memory-measurement utilities of Chapter 2 to see the new memory active and usable. Then you're ready to manage it.

If you have leftover, removed memory chips, such as disabled DIPs or lower-capacity SIMMs, you could donate them to a school or other charitable organization that can always use more memory.

MEMORY MANAGEMENT

Manage Memory with DOS's Own Utilities

DOS sets the 640K restriction. That's all the conventional memory a PC can have, and most software must run in conventional memory. But the latest versions of DOS have some powers to elude that barrier, or to at least soften it. However, the best part of using DOS's own utilities to manage memory is that they're free. They come with DOS and are almost certainly already installed in your DOS directory, waiting to work. This chapter will tell you how.

Which DOS?

Wait a minute, though. In most of this book, I use the term *DOS* to mean MS-DOS 6, the latest version made by Microsoft, but the different versions of DOS have some different abilities and memory management options.

Different DOS Versions—3, 4, 5, 6, 6.0, 6.1, 6.2?

Programs are given version numbers as they change over time. Larger numbers mean more recent versions. A change in the first number means a large change; a change in the decimal point values means a smaller change.

DOS has grown from version 1 to version 6. Actually as this book goes to press, PC-DOS 6.1 and MS-DOS 6.2 are actually the most recent versions. But both of these versions of DOS have the same memory management abilities as MS-DOS 6 and so are lumped into that same term.

The previous version—DOS 5—had some of the memory management abilities of DOS 6, although it does not have all of them, especially not the automatic optimizer called *MemMaker*. This chapter mainly focuses on DOS 6, which you should get if you're interested in memory management. But some previous versions of DOS had memory management options. DOS 1 had no memory management abilities. DOS 2 had no memory management abilities, and even took up more conventional memory than DOS 1. DOS 3 added support for expanded memory, although you still needed to have expanded memory hardware, RAM, and software. DOS 4 added the **MEM** command for seeing what was in memory but took up even more conventional memory for itself. DOS 5 was the first version serious about memory management, with:

> **HIMEM.SYS** to manage extended memory
>
> **HIMEM.SYS** to create UMBs

DOS=HIGH to load part of DOS into the HMA

EMM386.SYS to manage expanded memory on 386 and 486 systems

LOADHIGH to load memory-residents into UMBs

DEVICEHIGH to load drivers into UMBs

DOS 6 kept all of those improvements, but:

▼ added new options for the **MEM** command

▼ added multiple configurations for **CONFIG.SYS** and **AUTOEXEC.BAT**

▼ permitted bypassing **CONFIG.SYS** and **AUTOEXEC.BAT** commands

▼ replaced **EMM386.SYS** with **EMM386.EXE**, still to manage expanded memory on 386 and 486 systems

▼ added MemMaker to install the **HIMEM.SYS**, **DOS=HIGH**, **LOADHIGH**, and **DEVICEHIGH** commands automatically

▼ took up less conventional memory as well

Get the latest version of DOS to have the best memory management choices.

DOS 6 is much easier to use for memory management than DOS 5.

Different DOS Sources—Microsoft, IBM, Novell

Microsoft created DOS and licensed it to IBM back when the PC was born. It was called *PC DOS* on IBM PCs and *MS-DOS* on most other

PC compatibles. (Some PC-compatible makers put their own abbreviations on it, such as Z-DOS or T-DOS.) It was all the same program. There were small differences between the PC-DOS and MS-DOS, such as PC-DOS's added *shell* (a menu for commands) for easier operation in version 4.0. But generally the differences weren't significant, especially for memory management.

A competing DOS from Digital Research—called *DR DOS*—introduced the ability to load drivers and memory-residents into upper memory. This change gave DR DOS lots of good publicity, although MS-DOS still remained by far the most popular DOS. Microsoft's memory management additions to DOS 5 were probably in part a response to the growing popularity of DR DOS.

Then Microsoft and IBM battled over which operating system would follow DOS: Windows or OS/2. (See Chapter 12 for more details on these two operating systems.) When DOS 6 came along, Microsoft and IBM parted ways.

Microsoft produced MS-DOS 6, with the memory management abilities of DOS 5 plus the automation of MemMaker. MS-DOS 6 also included anti-virus, defragmenting, and disk compression utilities. Later, when the *disk compression utility*—to make the disk fit more information—damaged information on some disks, Microsoft created MS-DOS 6.2. This version is almost identical to 6.0, even though it contains a few changes to make disk compression safer. Its memory management abilities are nearly identical. One change is to the **SMARTDrive** disk cache, which has new default settings to eliminate some of the data loss problems from users who turned their PCs off too soon for information to write through to disk. Version 6.2 also adds the ability to single-step through the **AUTOEXEC.BAT** file when starting the PC. This capability is explained later in this chapter.

IBM developed PC-DOS 6.1. This version had the memory management abilities of MS-DOS 5 and the **MemMaker** of MS-DOS 6. It differed from MS-DOS 6.0 and 6.2 mainly by having different utility programs for fighting viruses, defragmenting the disk, and compressing the disk. (It also didn't drop some old commands—not related to memory management—that MS-DOS 6 did drop from version 5.)

Meanwhile, the DR DOS program and its company were acquired by Novell, the networking software company. The result is an improved DOS called *Novell DOS*, with more advanced memory management (such as loading drivers and memory-residents even into extended memory, although only if the program is written to permit it) and even built-in simple networking software. Novell DOS does not have a memory management optimizer, unlike MS-DOS or PC-DOS.

Novell DOS has multitasking you don't find on MS-DOS 6. But because of MS-DOS's traditional popularity and the concern of current users for full compatibility with the past DOS versions and with current Windows, MS-DOS is and probably will remain by far the most popular DOS.

MEM and MSD—Measuring Memory

The first step in managing memory is to know how much you have and what it is used for. DOS comes with several commands for doing this, and a utility program for analyzing your PC in detail. Chapter 2 explored this program in detail.

The **MEM** command gives you a quick rundown on how much memory is in your PC. Just type:

```
mem
```

and you'll see a display similar to that in Figure 4.1.

MEM also has its own options to give detailed lists of what programs, drivers, and memory-residents are in memory. For example, if you type:

```
C:\>mem

Memory Type        Total =  Used +  Free
----------------   ------   ------   ------
Conventional        640K     121K     519K
Upper                 0K       0K       0K
Adapter RAM/ROM     384K     384K       0K
Extended (XMS)     3072K      64K    3008K
----------------   ------   ------   ------
Total memory       4096K     569K    3527K

Total under 1 MB    640K     121K     519K

Largest executable program size     519K  (531520 bytes)
Largest free upper memory block       0K       (0 bytes)
MS-DOS is resident in the high memory area.

C:\>
```

FIGURE 4.1

Use the MEM command to see how much memory you have.

```
mem /d
```

you'll see several screens full of such lists, as shown in the example in Figure 4.2.

```
Modules using memory below 1 MB:

  Name       Total       =  Conventional  +  Upper Memory
  --------   -----------    ------------     ------------
  MSDOS       13677  (13K)    13677  (13K)       0   (0K)
  HIMEM        1168   (1K)     1168   (1K)       0   (0K)
  COMMAND      2912   (3K)     2912   (3K)       0   (0K)
  SNAP       105872 (103K)   105872 (103K)       0   (0K)
  Free       531616 (519K)   531616 (519K)       0   (0K)

Memory Summary:

  Type of Memory      Total     =      Used      +      Free
  ----------------   -----------     -----------      -----------
  Conventional       655360  (640K)   123744  (121K)   531616  (519K)
  Upper                   0    (0K)        0    (0K)        0    (0K)
  Adapter RAM/ROM    393216  (384K)   393216  (384K)        0    (0K)
  Extended (XMS)    3145728 (3072K)    65536   (64K)  3080192 (3000K)
  ----------------   -----------     -----------      -----------
  Total memory      4194304 (4096K)   582496  (569K)  3611808 (3527K)

  Total under 1 MB   655360  (640K)   123744  (121K)   531616  (519K)

Press any key to continue . . .
```

FIGURE 4.2

MEM has options for listing what's in memory.

But you can learn even more about memory with the **Microsoft Diagnostics** utility or **MSD**. To run this program, get to the DOS directory and type:

msd

and you'll see, as shown in Figure 4.3, the overall memory statistics for your PC. If you press **M**, you'll see an overall memory map—as shown in Figure 4.4—or press **T** or **R** to see the details of memory-residents and drivers in memory.

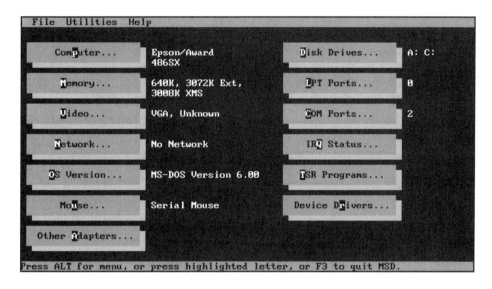

FIGURE 4.3
MSD's starting screen shows overall memory statistics.

CONFIG.SYS and AUTOEXEC.BAT— Directing Memory

When you turn on your PC, a small program in a ROM chip starts. This program tests some of the PC elements such as memory and then starts DOS. DOS starts and looks for a file called **CONFIG.SYS** in the root directory of your hard disk. If it does not find that file, it assumes some default values for configuring the PC, values such as the number of files that can be open at once and how many disk drives may be in the system. If DOS does find the **CONFIG.SYS** file, it reads the lines and overrides any defaults they change.

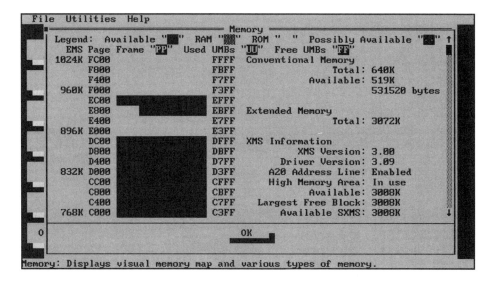

FIGURE 4.4
Map of memory in MSD.

CONFIG.SYS must be in the root directory and must be *pure text.* That is, you can't use just any word processor to create and save it but must use a processor that can save ASCII-only files. The DOS Editor program in MS-DOS 4, 5, and 6 can do this, as shown in Figure 4.5. Just type:

```
edit config.sys
```

to start the Editor with the **CONFIG.SYS** file on-screen.

Another job of the **CONFIG.SYS** file is to tell DOS where it can find the extra driver software it needs. These device drivers let DOS understand new hardware, such as a mouse or network. They also add software, such as memory managers, to DOS. Drivers load with lines such as:

```
device=himem.sys
```

as shown in the example in Figure 4.6, where a driver named **DRIVER.SYS** is in the root directory of your hard disk.

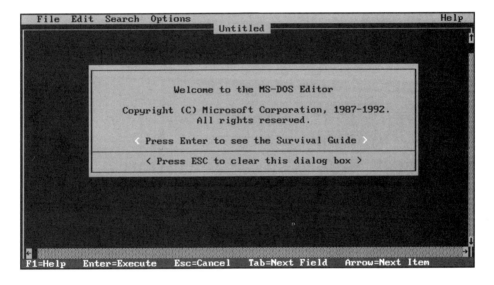

FIGURE 4.5
The DOS Editor program.

```
C:\>type config.sys
DEVICE=HIMEM.SYS
DOS=HIGH
BUFFERS=20
FILES=20

C:\>
```

FIGURE 4.6
A typical CONFIG.SYS file.

DOS 6 lets you interrupt the reading of **CONFIG.SYS**. If you press **F5** when you start your PC, **CONFIG.SYS** won't be read. However, if you press **F8**, DOS will let you step through the **CONFIG.SYS** file, choosing to use or ignore each line of commands in it. Starting with DOS 6, you can create *multiple configurations* in **CONFIG.SYS** as well. These configurations let you choose which set of commands to configure the PC with.

After reading **CONFIG.SYS**, DOS then runs the **AUTOEXEC.BAT** file. This is a *batch file*, a list of commands to execute in sequence. Figure 4.7 shows an example.

```
C:\>type autoexec.bat
@ECHO OFF
PROMPT $p$g
PATH C:\QEMM;C:\WINDOWS;C:\DOS;
SET TEMP=C:\DOS
CD C:\COLLDOS
SNAP
CD ..
CLS


C:\>
```

FIGURE 4.7
A typical AUTOEXEC.BAT file.

Some of the lines in **AUTOEXEC.BAT** concern memory management because they run memory-resident (TSR) programs. These programs load into memory and then wait for use later. For instance, the line:

    snap

runs a program called SNAP. Because it's a memory-resident, it stays in memory.

You can also bypass running **AUTOEXEC.BAT** by pressing **F5** when you start your PC. And in MS-DOS 6.2, you can step through **AUTOEXEC.BAT** by pressing **F8**.

Make and Use a Startup Disk

If you're going to change **CONFIG.SYS** or **AUTOEXEC.BAT** at all, you should first make a *startup disk* and work on the files there. This startup disk will be a floppy disk where you make your changes. Then, if the changes somehow disturb your PC into crashing or perhaps not even starting, you can just start from the hard disk and its original, unchanged configuration files. If you test and like the results of your changes to the **CONFIG.SYS** and **AUTOEXEC.BAT** on the startup disk, you can then copy those changed files to the root directory of the hard disk to make the changes permanent.

To make a startup disk, put a blank (or erasable) disk into the floppy disk drive (probably the A drive) and type:

```
format a: /s
```

After a while you should see the message:

```
System transferred
```

Remove the floppy disk and label it. Then, copy the important files to it with these commands:

```
copy c:\config.sys a:
copy c:\autoexec.bat a:
```

Then, make your changes to the files on the startup disk. Use the DOS Editor, like this:

```
edit a:\config.sys
```

or

```
edit a:\autoexec.bat
```

and save the results when you're done. Leave the startup disk in the drive and press **Ctrl+Alt+Del** to test your changes.

If you see a message such as:

> Bad or missing driver

then you probably didn't put the complete path name (drive and directory) of some driver. If you see:

> Bad command or filename

then perhaps there isn't a complete path for a program in **AUTOEXEC.BAT**.

CONFIG.SYS Commands

CONFIG.SYS is the system configuration file. It has two jobs: setting up the DOS environment and telling DOS what *device drivers* to load into memory. Drivers are small programs that extend DOS's abilities. Typically, each new peripheral you buy for your PC—a mouse, a scanner, a CD-ROM drive—comes with its own device driver. DOS doesn't know how to handle these peripherals. It needs help; it needs new instructions; it needs a device driver copied from floppy to the hard disk, stored there with DOS's built-in drivers and understandings, and then loaded into memory and linked to DOS when you start your PC. For example, if you want to use a mouse, you'll need a mouse driver called something like **MOUSE.SYS**. More important to us here, some drivers don't handle new hardware peripherals, they manage software and memory.

You don't need a **CONFIG.SYS** file to use DOS, but you do need a **CONFIG.SYS** file to get the most out of DOS. If you don't include any **CONFIG.SYS** file, DOS just assumes default settings for its own drivers. These settings almost certainly won't give you the best performance. Fine-tuning **CONFIG.SYS** is a favorite game of DOS fans.

Windows doesn't need all of those DOS drivers. It has some drivers of its own. Loading the DOS drivers is not only unnecessary, but it can also disturb and steal memory from the Windows drivers.

Consequently, the best **CONFIG.SYS** for DOS is not the best **CONFIG.SYS** for Windows.

> You'll want a different **CONFIG.SYS** when running DOS programs than when running Windows programs.

There are ten commands you can use in **CONFIG.SYS** that affect memory. Each sits on a single line of the file, by itself, and is no longer than that one line. Each starts with the command itself followed sometimes by an equals sign and any values you want to specify for that command. These values can be numbers or file names, as you'll see here. Only the **REM** command doesn't follow these conventions. It is put in front of any other command line to knock that line out of service temporarily. That option is explained here, too. It's also OK to have blank lines in a **CONFIG.SYS** file.

Here are the commands for **CONFIG.SYS** that affect memory, listed not in the order you'll see them appear but in alphabetical order. After these descriptions you'll find a summary of the best **CONFIG.SYS** to use for Windows.

BUFFERS

The **BUFFERS** command sets aside RAM memory to hold frequently accessed information from your disk drives. Storing such information in RAM speeds your PC. More buffers are better for performance, but adding more buffers eats up RAM. For Windows you could set **BUFFERS** to 20 with this command:

```
BUFFERS=20
```

but you would be better off if you used the **SMARTDrive** disk cache utility program that comes with DOS and Windows. **SMARTDrive** does the same job as **BUFFERS**, but it does it better. There's no reason to have both operating. If you do use **SMARTDrive**—and I'll tell you how later in this chapter—set **BUFFERS** to 10 with this command:

```
BUFFERS=10
```

 Unless you have a program that demands a higher setting, systems with 256K to 511K of RAM automatically get **BUFFERS=10** when you don't put any **BUFFERS** command into your **CONFIG.SYS** file. You could just live with that, but it's safer to explicitly say **BUFFERS=10** or whatever other **BUFFERs=** level you want in case you forget about the existence and size of your BUFFERS or you change your system's memory.

DEVICE

The **DEVICE** command loads a device driver into conventional memory (between 0K and 640K). You simply add an equals sign and the name of the device driver file, as in this example for a mouse driver:

```
DEVICE=MOUSE.SYS
```

Some drivers also let you set options with codes and numbers following the device driver name.

 Make sure that you either specify the full path (directory, subdirectory, file name) of your driver file in the **DEVICE** command line or that you include that path in your PATH statement, which is explained later.

DEVICEHIGH

The **DEVICEHIGH** command (explained in more detail later in this chapter) loads a device driver into a UMB (between 640K and 1024K), which saves on conventional memory. If **DEVICEHIGH** cannot fit the driver into a UMB—if none is available or they aren't ready to use—it will revert to loading the driver into conventional memory, just like **DEVICE**. Loading a typical mouse driver into a UMB could take a command such as:

```
DEVICEHIGH=MOUSE.SYS
```

DEVICEHIGH works only if you first load the **HIMEM.SYS** and **EMM386.EXE** memory management device drivers and you use the DOS command, as explained later.

 Don't use **DEVICEHIGH** unless you've already put commands to load **HIMEM.SYS** and **EMM386.EXE** into memory and the DOS command in **CONFIG.SYS**.

DOS

The **DOS** command loads DOS files into the HMA from 1024K to 1088K. It also lets the **DEVICEHIGH** command load drivers into UMBs and the **LOADHIGH** command load programs from the **AUTOEXEC.BAT** file into UMBs. The DOS command works only on a 386, 486, or Pentium system with memory management software such as **HIMEM.SYS** and **EMM386.EXE** loaded.

 Don't use the **DOS** command in **CONFIG.SYS** unless you have a 386, 486, or Pentium system with memory management software loaded.

FCBS

The **FCBS** command sets the maximum number of File Control Blocks DOS can use. This command is necessary only for programs that specifically request it (you'll be told in the manual or installation process), for networked PCs, or for PCs using the **SHARE** command in their **AUTOEXEC.BAT** file. A typical command line for **FCBS** could be:

```
FCBS=20
```

Before DOS 5 the **FCBS** command also specified how many of these File Control Blocks would be protected from closure. Then, the typical command line would be:

```
FCBS=20,8
```

where 8 would be protected.

 Don't bother with the **FCBS** command unless you're on a network—which will probably install it anyway, without your worry—or use the **SHARE** command in **AUTOEXEC.BAT**.

FILES

The **FILES** command tells DOS how many files you can have open at once. The higher the number, the less chance of running into any limit while working, but the result is that more memory is eaten up perhaps unnecessarily. A good setting for Windows is 30, as in this command line:

```
FILES=30
```

 If you see a message about *Insufficient file handles*, increase the value in the **FILES** line in **CONFIG.SYS**. For Windows you might need to increase to:

```
FILES=50
```

INSTALL

The **INSTALL** command loads memory-residents into memory, and it does this from inside the **CONFIG.SYS** file. Normally, they are loaded from the **AUTOEXEC.BAT** file. Don't bother with **INSTALL** with Windows.

 Don't use **INSTALL** to load the **FASTOPEN.EXE** program. In fact, don't use the **FASTOPEN.EXE** program at all. It conflicts with many other programs. And you don't need it—the **SMARTDrive** disk cache does all **FASTOPEN** promises and more.

LASTDRIVE

The **LASTDRIVE** command tells DOS the last letter that can be used to represent a disk drive (the way *A* is typically a floppy drive and *C* the main hard drive). To be able to use all the letters up to *Z*, use the command:

```
LASTDRIVE=Z
```

If you set a lesser **LASTDRIVE** value, say *G*, you'd save a few bytes of memory, but not much. If you have several drives and know you may add one or more RAM drives and then some network drives, just stick with *Z*.

Don't forget that RAM drives and network drives need a drive letter and that letter must fall within the **LASTDRIVE** specification.

SHELL

The **SHELL** command does two things. First, it tells DOS where to find the command interpreter, a necessary software element. Most PCs use the **COMMAND.COM** program that comes with DOS. Some use a replacement command interpreter, such as **4DOS** or **NDOS**, that is more powerful than **COMMAND.COM**. The second job of the **SHELL** command is to create an *environment space*—a small area in memory where DOS keeps commands about the PC's setup.

A typical **SHELL** command in **CONFIG.SYS** looks like this:

```
SHELL=C:\COMMAND.COM C:\ /E:2048 /P
```

The first part of this command tells where the **COMMAND.COM** program is, with the **C:** repeating the directory of **COMMAND.COM**. The second part sets the *environment size*, the amount of memory set aside for the environment. In this example, the /E:2048 says to make an environment of 2048 bytes, or 2K. This environment is larger than most DOS PCs need, but it is a good size for Windows. The **/P** makes **COMMAND.COM** the permanent command interpreter and tells **COMMAND.COM** to run the **AUTOEXEC.BAT** file stored in the root directory of the boot disk.

STACKS

The **STACKS** command tells DOS how much memory should be reserved for *stacks*, the areas DOS uses to keep track of the PC's hardware state when one part of the hardware interrupts another. The Windows Setup program automatically adds this **STACKS** command to **CONFIG.SYS**:

```
STACKS=9,256
```

which sets up 9 stacks of 256 bytes each. You can change this to:

```
STACKS=0,0
```

and you'll save about 3K of memory. That setting should work fine, although in some cases on some PCs you'll see the message:

```
Stack overflow
```

meaning that you should change the command back to:

```
STACKS=9,256
```

HIMEM.SYS—Extended Memory and the HMA

HIMEM.SYS is a device driver. It has two jobs. It controls extended memory by the XMS (Extended Memory Specification) rules and it creates the HMA from 1024K to 1088K. As discussed in Chapter 1, the HMA is a special part of extended memory that can hold some drivers and programs—even part of DOS—that normally fit only within conventional and upper memory.

Don't bother with **HIMEM.SYS** on PCs that don't have at least a 286, 386, or 486 processor.

Load **HIMEM.SYS** first, near the beginning of the **CONFIG.SYS** file, before loading any other drivers except those for hard disk configuration. Typically, it loads in the **CONFIG.SYS** file with a command (often the first command in that file) of:

```
device=himem.sys
```

Here is an unusually full command for it:

```
DEVICE=PATHNAME\HIMEM.SYS /A20CONTROL:ON|OFF
/CPUCLOCK:ON|OFF /HMAMIN=M /INT15=XXX
/MACHINE:XXX /NUMHANDLES=N /SHADOWRAM:ON|OFF
```

and what each part means:

DEVICE says load this driver.

PATHNAME tells where the **HIMEM.SYS** file is, typically in the **C:\WINDOWS** or **C:\DOS** directories.

\HIMEM.SYS finishes telling where the **HIMEM.SYS** file is.

/A20CONTROL:ONIOFF tells **HIMEM.SYS** whether it has control of the A20 line and so has control of the HMA. Use **ON** to give it control, even if some other device already has control. Use **OFF** to take control away. The default is **ON**.

/CPUCLOCK:ONIOFF helps **HIMEM** handle clock speed changes. The default is **OFF**. Use this option and **ON** only if you've been advised so.

/HMAMIN=M tells **HIMEM** the minimum program size to put into the HMA. Only one program can go into the HMA at a time. To make the most of memory, this value should be equal to the largest program that needs relocation and will fit there. You can use a value from 0 to 63, meaning K, with 0 as the default (meaning the first program that wants the HMA gets it). If you use **/HMAMIN=63**, then only programs that will use all 63K of the HMA will get it. At this setting you run the risk of no program being large enough and so no program using the HMA.

/INT15=XXX tells **HIMEM** that **XXX** bytes of memory, from 64 through 65535, should be set aside for the Interrupt 15. This command is for programs such as the **Vdisk** program that uses extended memory through the Interrupt 15. 0 is the default.

/MACHINE:XXX tells **HIMEM** which A20 line handler to use, which depends on the particular PC you're using. **HIMEM** will try to pick the right one, but if you question this, or a tech support person does, here's a list of possible values:

Abbreviation	Value	PC
at	1	IBM PC/AT or compatible
ps2	2	IBM PS/2
pt1cascade	3	Phoenix Cascade BIOS
hpvectra	4	HP Vectra PC A and A+
att6300plus	5	AT&T 6300 Plus PC
acer1100	6	Acer 1100 PC
toshiba	7	Toshiba 1600 and 1200XE
wyse	8	Wyse 286PC at 12.5 MHz
tulip	9	Tulip SX
		continued

Abbreviation	Value	PC
zenith	10	Zenith ZBIOS machines
at1	11	IBM PC/AT (alternative delay)
at2	12	IBM PC/AT (alternative delay)
css	12	CSS Labs
at3	13	IBM PC/AT (alternative delay)
philips	13	Philips
fasthp	14	Hewlett-Packard Vectra
ibm7552	15	IBM 7552 Industrial Computer
bullmicral	16	Bull Micral 60
dell	17	Dell XBIOS PCs

/NUMHANDLES=N tells **HIMEM** the number of simultaneous extended memory blocks it can use, from 1 to 128, with 32 as the default.

/SHADOWRAM:ON|OFF tells **HIMEM** if your PC uses Shadow RAM. The default is **OFF** for PCs with less than 2M of RAM.

HIMEM.SYS should be the first memory management driver in **CONFIG.SYS**, preceded only by hard disk drivers.

You'll rarely need any of the **HIMEM.SYS** options.

DOS=HIGH Command

Remember that the **DOS** command is listed as one of the things you can do in **CONFIG.SYS** (check discussion earlier in this chapter). Once you've installed **HIMEM.SYS**, you may use the **DOS** command like this:

```
DOS=HIGH
```

on the next line of **CONFIG.SYS**. This command puts 50K of DOS into the HMA, opening 50K more of conventional memory for other uses. You can also add the UMB option to this, as in:

```
DOS=HIGH,UMB
```

or on two lines as:

```
DOS=HIGH
DOS=UMB
```

The full command is:

```
dos=[high|low],[,umb|,noumb]
```

With the options in square brackets, the choices are separated by the vertical line (called a *broken pipe*).

> **DOS=HIGH** puts 50K of DOS into the HMA.
>
> **DOS=LOW** keeps DOS entirely in conventional memory.
>
> **DOS=UMB** prepares the PC for **EMM386.EXE** to make UMBs for **DEVICEHIGH** and **LOADHIGH** to use.
>
> **DOS=NOUMB** doesn't let **EMM386.EXE** make UMBs. The default is **dos=noumb**.

> You must have UMBs to later use **DEVICEHIGH** and **LOAD-HIGH**.

EMM386.EXE—Expanded Memory and UMBs

EMM386.EXE is a device driver, and a program. You specify it on the next line after **DOS**= in **CONFIG.SYS**.

When **EMM386.EXE** is working as a device driver, it does three things: manages expanded memory; converts extended memory to expanded on 386, 486, and Pentium PCs; and creates UMBs. Here's the full command for the **EMM386.EXE** driver:

```
DEVICE=PATHNAME\EMM386.EXE MODE [NOHIGH] MEMORY
A=ALTREGS B=ADDRESS D=NNN FRAME=ADDRESS
H=HANDLES I=MMMM-NNNN L=MINXMS MX /P=ADDRESS
PN=ADDRESS W=ON|OFF X=MMMM-NNNN
```

Here's what each part of the command means:

DEVICE= says load this driver into memory.

PATHNAME tells where the **EMM386.EXE** file is, typically in the **C:\WINDOWS** or **C:\DOS** directories.

\EMM386.EXE finishes telling where the **EMM386.EXE** file is.

MODE tells **EMM386** to turn its expanded memory support on or off or automatic. The default is **ON**. When you choose **AUTO**, **EMM386** creates expanded memory only when a program asks for it.

 You can use **EMM386.EXE** as a program to change the **MODE**. If **EMM386.EXE** is already loaded in the **CONFIG.SYS** file, then type:

```
EMM386
```

and then **OFF** or **ON** or **AUTO**, all at the DOS prompt. Press **Enter** and you'll see a report that the **MODE** has changed.

NOHIGH tells **EMM386** not to load the 3K part of itself into a UMB, which it would normally do.

MEMORY tells **EMM386** the amount of extended memory to convert to expanded memory, ranging from 16 to 32768, with the default of 256 (all referring to kilobytes). Don't specify more memory than is in your PC. In fact with Windows, don't specify any at all. Use the **MODE** command to keep conversion off, unless you have a DOS program that needs expanded memory within a Windows window.

A=ALTREGS tells **EMM386** how many alternate register sets to use, from 0 to 254, with 7 as the default.

B=ADDRESS tells **EMM386** the bottom address to use for LIM EMS 4.0 expanded memory banks to swap in and out of the page frame. Values range from 1000h to 4000h, with the default of 4000h meaning bank 4 of memory. You needn't worry about this; with Windows you don't want to use expanded memory anyway.

D=NNN tells **EMM386** how much RAM to use for DMA buffering, with values from 16K to 256K and a default of 16.

FRAME=ADDRESS tells **EMM386** the expanded memory (EMS specification) page frame address, chosen from these options:

1 means C000

2 means C400

3 means C800

4 means CC00

5 means D000

6 means D400

7 means D800

8 means DC00

9 means E000

10 means 8000

11 means 8400

12 means 8800

13 means 8C00

14 means 9000

for example, **FRAME=9** means put the page frame at E000.

Don't use more than one of the FRAME, M, or P options for EMM386.EXE. All refer to the page frame address.

H=HANDLES tells **EMM386** how many handles to use for expanded memory, with values ranging from 2 to 255, with 64 as the default. (*Handles* are the names DOS uses to know which piece of expanded memory it is talking about.)

I=MMMM-NNNN tells **EMM386** which area of upper memory to use as a UMB or for an EMS page. **EMM386**'s default is to convert to UMBs all areas of upper memory that it thinks are unused. It might miss an area, which you can then specify with **I**. **MMMM** and **NNNN** are the hexadecimal addresses for the start and end of the block.

L=MINXMS tells **EMM386** how much extended memory to preserve from conversion into expanded, with the value specified in kilobytes. Default is 0.

MX tells **EMM386** the address of the page frame for expanded memory, with values the same as for the **FRAME=ADDRESS** option above.

/PMMMM tells **EMM386** the address of the page frame for expanded memory, using the same address choices as for the **FRAME=ADDRESS** option.

PN=ADDRESS tells **EMM386** the address of a specific page in the page frame. The **N** tells which page, from 0 to 255. Pages 0, 1, 2, and 3 must be contiguous in memory (the specification says so). For **ADDRESS** use the same choices as for the **FRAME=ADDRESS** option.

W=ON|OFF tells **EMM386** to turn Weitek coprocessor support on or off. (This is a math coprocessor chip found in some PCs.) Default is **OFF**.

X=MMMM-NNNN tells **EMM386** to exclude an area of upper memory from being converted into UMBs. When **EMM386** automatically converts what it thinks is unused upper memory into UMBs, it may convert memory that was actually in use, perhaps by some unnoticed network interface card or other peripheral device. Using the exclusion, with **MMMM** and **NNNN** being the hexadecimal address for the start and end of this area of upper memory to protect, can save you from ruining the operation of the device that needs that memory.

NOEMS tells **EMM386** to create UMBs without converting any extended memory to expanded memory. Use this command with Windows.

NOEMS is the option you want when running Windows, because it makes **HIMEM.SYS** create UMBs (that's good for Windows, because they can save your conventional memory) but not convert extended memory to expanded (which would be bad, because Windows wants extended memory).

RAM=mmmm-nnnn creates UMBs and converts extended memory to expanded. Don't use this command with Windows.

Don't use both **NOEMS** and **RAM**—they contradict each other. For Windows you just want **NOEMS**.

You must install **HIMEM.SYS** after **EMM386.EXE**.

Don't use the **NOEMS** or **RAM** switches with DOS versions before DOS 5.0.

EMM386.EXE also operates as a program, giving you the status of the **EMM386.EXE** driver and changing that status in a few ways. Here's the complete command:

```
EMM386 state weitek
```

and what each part of the command means:

EMM386 identifies the program itself.

state tells the **EMM386** driver to turn **ON** or **OFF** or **AUTO** the conversion of extended memory to expanded. The default is **ON**.

You cannot turn **EMM386**'s conversion of extended to expanded **OFF** after UMBs have been created.

weitek tells the **EMM386** driver to turn **ON** or **OFF** support for the Weitek math coprocessor chip. **OFF** is the default.

If you use neither the **state** nor **weitek** options when typing **EMM386** as a program, you'll see the status of the driver, as shown in Figure 4.8. Few use any of these options. Even advanced users tend to stick with **RAM**, **NOEMS**, **X**, and **I**.

```
C:\>emm386

MICROSOFT Expanded Memory Manager 386   Version 4.44
Copyright Microsoft Corporation 1986, 1991

Expanded memory services unavailable.

EMM386 Active.

C:\>
```

FIGURE 4.8

Using EMM386 as a program to see the status of EMM386's
memory management.

DEVICEHIGH—Moving Drivers to Upper Memory

Device drivers are small pieces of software that let DOS understand and work with added hardware or software in your PC. They provide the software link to expanded memory, extended memory, scanners, a mouse, and other additions.

Traditionally, you load drivers into conventional memory by putting their names on device lines in the **CONFIG.SYS** file, like this:

```
device=c:\driver.sys
```

But if you move drivers out of conventional memory, there's more conventional memory left for your programs. DOS 5 introduced the **DEVICEHIGH** command to do this. DOS 6 also has this command.

To use **DEVICEHIGH**, you first must have UMBs. Use **EMM386.EXE** and the **DOS** command or some other memory manager to map extended or expanded memory into upper memory addresses, as mentioned above. Then, you just replace any mention of **device** in the **CONFIG.SYS** file with a **devicehigh**, like this:

```
devicehigh=c:\driver.sys
```

When you restart your PC and DOS reads the **CONFIG.SYS** file, it will try to load the driver into a UMB, an upper memory address. If it cannot, that driver will load into conventional memory.

You can use the **MemMaker** utility in DOS 6 to convert your **device** lines into **devicehigh** lines automatically in CON-FIG.SYS.

To test if a driver loaded high and how much memory it occupies, use the mem /c /p command, as shown in Figure 4.9.

```
Conventional Memory Detail:

  Segment          Total          Name        Type
  --------      ----------------  --------    --------
   00000          1039    (1K)                Interrupt Vector
   00040           271    (0K)                ROM Communication Area
   00050           527    (1K)                DOS Communication Area
   00070          2656    (3K)    IO          System Data
                                  CON         System Device Driver
                                  AUX         System Device Driver
                                  PRN         System Device Driver
                                  CLOCK$      System Device Driver
                                  A: - C:     System Device Driver
                                  COM1        System Device Driver
                                  LPT1        System Device Driver
                                  LPT2        System Device Driver
                                  LPT3        System Device Driver
                                  COM2        System Device Driver
                                  COM3        System Device Driver
                                  COM4        System Device Driver
   00116          5072    (5K)    MSDOS       System Data
   00253          8352    (8K)    IO          System Data
                   1152    (1K)    XMSXXXX0    Installed Device=HIMEM
  Press any key to continue . . .
```

FIGURE 4.9
Testing to see where drivers load.

You could use the information from the **MEM** command to specify loading a driver into a specific UMB. Here's the full command for that:

```
devicehigh=[/L:region[,size1][;region2[,size2][/S]]]
```

and what each part of the command means:

> **devicehigh=** loads the driver high.
>
> **/L** puts the driver into a specific region.
>
> **region** indicates the region, from 1 through 4.
>
> **size1** identifies the size of the driver in memory in bytes.
>
> **region2** indicates a second region for use by the driver, if it is the type that can split in memory.
>
> **size 2** identifies the size of the second part to load into a second region, in bytes.
>
> **/s** shrinks the UMB to the smallest size that will hold the driver.

If you have a driver you don't want to load high, make sure to list it in the **MEMMAKER.INF** file so that **MemMaker** won't automatically try to relocate it. Although the RAM disk driver **RAMDrive** loads high, the RAM disk itself must be in conventional, extended, or expanded memory. It's too big for UMBs. The **SMARTDrive** disk cache was a device driver in DOS 5 but became a memory-resident in DOS 6. If not all of your drivers load into UMBs, then try changing the order in which they load (by changing the order of their **devicehigh** lines in **CONFIG.SYS**.) Try loading the larger drivers first. DOS resources such as **FILES** and **BUFFERS** occupy conventional memory, but some memory managers can load most or all of them into upper memory.

LOADHIGH—Moving Memory-Residents to Upper Memory

Memory-resident programs are programs that load into memory and stay there, even after they're not running. These programs can be anything from simple calculator utilities to disk cache controllers. Although they're often useful, sitting in memory they reduce the conventional memory you have left for other purposes.

In the **AUTOEXEC.BAT** file that runs when you start DOS, you can load memory-residents simply by typing their names on a line, such as this (for a program called *memres*):

```
c:\utils\memres
```

and the program would load into conventional memory. (That **C:\UTILS** part is the full path name for this particular program, which is in the **UTILS** directory.)

DOS 5 added a new command for **AUTOEXEC.BAT** that could instead try to load the memory-resident into a UMB. That command saves conventional memory for other uses. To use this new **LOADHIGH** command, you first must have UMBs. Use **EMM386.EXE** and the **DOS** command or some other memory manager to map extended or expanded memory into upper memory addresses, as mentioned above. Then, just put the **LOADHIGH** command before any of the memory-resident lines in **AUTOEXEC.BAT**, like this:

```
loadhigh memres
```

or just:

```
lh memres
```

If a UMB is large enough for the program (**memres** in this case), it will load high. Otherwise, it will just load into conventional memory.

 You can automatically add **LOADHIGH** to memory-resident lines in **AUTOEXEC.BAT** by running the **MemMaker** utility mentioned in the next section.

After you make any **AUTOEXEC.BAT** changes, restart your PC to see them take effect. Then run the **mem** program:

```
mem /c
```

to see where the memory-residents end up. Figure 4.10 gives an example. If they are in upper memory, you'll have more conventional memory free. If they are not in upper memory, you'll see them in conventional memory still. In that case, you can try changing the order in which you load memory-residents (by the order of their lines in **AUTOEXEC.BAT**).

```
                       3104    (3K)      EMMQXXX0   Installed Device=EMM386
                        896    (1K)                 FILES=20
                        256    (0K)                 FCBS=4
                        512    (1K)                 BUFFERS=20
                        448    (0K)                 LASTDRIVE=E
                       1856    (2K)                 STACKS=9,128
         0045D           80    (0K)      MSDOS      System Program
         00462         2640    (3K)      COMMAND    Program
         00507           80    (0K)      MSDOS      -- Free --
         0050C          272    (0K)      COMMAND    Environment
         0051D          128    (0K)      MEM        Environment
         00525        88608   (87K)      MEM        Program
         01AC7       545664  (533K)      MSDOS      -- Free --

      Upper Memory Detail:

        Segment  Region      Total       Name        Type
        -------  ------  ----------------  ------------  --------
         0C13A      1         128    (0K)    SNAP        Environment
         0C142      1      105744  (103K)    SNAP        Program
         0DB13      1       20144   (20K)    MSDOS       -- Free --

         0E901      2       28656   (28K)    MSDOS       -- Free --

      Press any key to continue . . .
```

FIGURE 4.10

Use MEM to see if LOADHIGH actually put a memory-resident into UMBs.

 If you load a memory-resident high and your PC starts to have problems, change the memory-resident back to conventional memory—it just may not run right up high.

 Some applications may be predicted on others loading first. For example, you can't load a program that runs an application on CD-ROM without first loading the CD-ROM pile **MSCDEX**.

If you want to load a memory-resident into a specific UMB, then use the **MEM /C** command to view the UMBs and then use the **/L** switch with **LOADHIGH** and a region number—from 1 through 4—to specify where to put it.

Although you can specify loading the **DOSKEY** utility more than once in **AUTOEXEC.BAT**, if you're using later mentions to create macros, use **LOADHIGH** only with the initial **DOSKEY** line.

MemMaker—Automatic Customizing

The great innovation in DOS 6 for memory management is the utility called **MemMaker**. This utility automates memory management. Where DOS 5 users had to learn all about the **DEVICEHIGH**, **LOADHIGH**, **HIMEM.SYS**, **EMM386.EXE**, and **DOS=** commands, DOS 6 owners can just type:

```
memmaker
```

to see all those commands automatically put to work. The **MemMaker** utility:

▼ analyzes what processor, memory, and software is in your PC

▼ automatically adds the commands to **CONFIG.SYS** and **AUTOEXEC.BAT** to load memory management drivers such as **HIMEM.SYS** and **EMM386.EXE**

▼ puts those memory managers to work making UMBs

▼ tests all the drivers and memory-residents in conventional memory to see where they'll best fit in UMBs

▼ adds the necessary **DEVICEHIGH** and **LOADHIGH** lines to **CONFIG.SYS** and **AUTOEXEC.BAT** to load those drivers and memory-residents into UMBs

▼   and then returns your PC control to you, with more conventional memory ready for your programs.

The complete **MemMaker** command is:

```
memmaker
[/b][/session][/swap:drive][/t][/undo][w:n,m]
```

and the parts of the command mean:

memmaker is the command.

/b runs it in black-and-white display.

/batch runs unattended, with the default settings.

/swap:c tells **MemMaker** that there's a compressed hard drive—from **DoubleSpace**, **Stacker**, or some other utility—with *c* as the drive letter of the original or uncompressed drive.

/t disables detection of IBM Token-Ring networks, in case they conflict with **MemMaker** in your PC.

/undo reverses the changes **MemMaker** made to your **AUTOEXEC.BAT** and **CONFIG.SYS** files.

/w reserves a portion of upper memory for Windows.

 MemMaker uses the **SIZER.EXE** program and the **CHK-STATE.SYS** driver in the DOS directory, so don't delete them.

Start **MemMaker** with the command above. You'll see a display similar to that shown in Figure 4.11. Then, follow the instructions on-screen. You can quit at any time by pressing **F3**.

You'll choose whether to run a **Custom** or an **Express** optimization. If you're going to choose **Express**, you could just as well have chosen the **/batch** option mentioned above. This option runs through the entire process without asking you any questions. **Custom** optimization is for the more experienced user. It provides a list of choices, which are shown in Figure 4.12. It pauses after each question, waiting for your **Yes** or **No** answer. Give a **Yes** only to those you understand and are sure of. **Custom** options could set your memory up with conflicts and be ready to cause crashes.

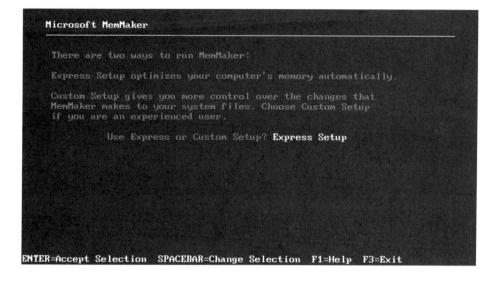

```
Microsoft MemMaker

    There are two ways to run MemMaker:

    Express Setup optimizes your computer's memory automatically.

    Custom Setup gives you more control over the changes that
    MemMaker makes to your system files. Choose Custom Setup
    if you are an experienced user.

            Use Express or Custom Setup? Express Setup




ENTER=Accept Selection   SPACEBAR=Change Selection   F1=Help   F3=Exit
```

FIGURE 4.11
MemMaker gets going.

Keep a "boot floppy" nearby, a floppy with the basic DOS software, to restart your PC if memory management changes crash it.

Don't let **MemMaker** use **B000-B7FF** if you use Windows, even though you know this monochrome display adapter region is rarely used. Using it diminishes extended memory because that memory is mapped into those addresses.

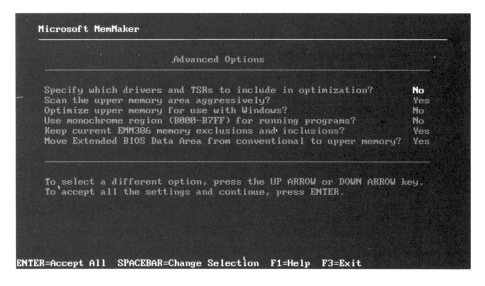

FIGURE 4.12
Custom choices for MemMaker.

Still, **Custom MemMaker** can open more memory than batch **MemMaker**, if you understand memory well enough. The choices (and my suggestions for your answers) are:

Specify drivers and TSRs to include? Answer **Yes** if you know what is and isn't a memory-resident program and you want to choose those to be loaded into UMBs.

Scan upper memory aggressively? Answer **Yes**, even though this can make your PC unstable and you may have to undo **MemMaker**.

Optimize upper memory for Windows? Answer **Yes**, if you use Windows.

Use monochrome memory region for running programs? Answer **No** if you use Windows; answer **Yes**, otherwise.

Keep EMM386 Excludes and Includes? Answer **Yes** if you use **EMM386.EXE**'s **X** or **I** options.

Move extended BIOS area to upper memory? Answer **Yes**, even though this choice could crash some PCs and may need to be undone.

If you see an error message about a particular memory-resident or driver after using **MemMaker**, run **MemMaker** again and choose **Specify Which Drivers and TSRs to Include**. Then say **No** to the one that makes trouble.

To undo **MemMaker's** choices, you type:

```
memmaker /undo
```

and the backup copies of your previous **CONFIG.SYS** and **AUTOEXEC.BAT** files will be restored to the root directory. Then, you need to reboot.

If you know particular programs or drivers you don't want **MemMaker** to play with, list them in the **MEMMAKER.INF** file.

MemMaker can handle only DOS 6 multiple configurations. If you separate the configurations, optimize them singly and then combine them again. Some other memory managers can handle multiples without that much trouble. Nor can **MemMaker** always optimize memory-residents in batch files called by lines in **AUTOEXEC.BAT**. Some competitors can.

The **MEMMAKER.STS** file contains details on what size your memory-residents and drivers are (you must run **MemMaker** to create this file). You could use the information in it to customize your loading order and placement. There's a **FinalSize** and a **MaxSize**. Load the programs with the largest difference first.

SMARTDrive—Using a Disk Cache

If you've managed memory well, you should have some left over. If you have at least 256K left over, you should definitely put it to work as a disk cache—to improve your PC's disk speed reading and writing.

SMARTDrive is a disk cache program. It creates a disk cache in expanded or extended memory (only in extended memory in DOS 6). That is, it sets aside a section of expanded or extended memory to hold the information most recently and frequently asked for from disk. Then it routes all program requests for disk information first to the cache. If the wanted information is there, it can be supplied far faster than from disk. Caching improves performance tremendously. It is very important for using Windows.

SMARTDRV.EXE is the name of the file for **SMARTDrive** in Windows 3.1. You use it by adding it as a line in **AUTOEXEC.BAT**. (Previous versions of Windows started **SMARTDrive** from the **SMARTDRV.SYS** device driver, which loaded from a line in **CONFIG.SYS**.) Here's the full command line for **SMARTDRV.EXE**:

```
SMARTDRV.EXE drive+-/e:elementsize init win
/b:buffsize /c /r /l /q /s /? /double_buffer
```

And here's what each part means:

> **SMARTDRV.EXE** is the name of the program you're running from **AUTOEXEC.BAT**.
>
> **drive** is the letter of the drive you want to cache. If you don't specify the drive, all drives are cached.
>
> **+** tells to cache reads and writes. If you don't use the **+**, just reads are cached.
>
> **–** disables caching, which you should do for network, **Stacker**, and RAM drives.
>
> **/e:elementsize** tells how many bytes should be in each element of the cache. For example, **/e:2048** means 2048 bytes in each element. Your choices are 1024, 2048, 4096, or the default of 8192.

init tells the initial and maximum size for the cache in kilobytes. For example, **256** means make a cache of 256K and have that as the maximum size. (Note that you don't have to type **init**.)

In **SMARTDRV.EXE** the default size of the cache is based on the amount of memory in your PC.

win specifies the minimum size for the cache in kilobytes, the size that Windows can reduce the cache to if it is short on memory. For example, you might use 128 meaning that if Windows needs more memory it can reduce the cache to 128K. (Note that you don't have to type **win**.)

/b:buffsize tells **SMARTDrive** how far to read ahead. That is, it tells **SMARTDrive** how much to grab from the disk, gambling that the information currently accessed will soon be followed by requests for consecutive information on the disk. By reading ahead, the cache can improve performance even more, although if you read ahead too far you increase the probability of wasting memory space (read-ahead buffer space) and processor time grabbing information from disk that won't be asked for soon. The default value for **buffsize** is 16, which means 16 bytes. You can use any value that is a multiple of the **element-size** value mentioned above.

/c tells **SMARTDrive** to clear the write cache. You'll use this command before turning off your PC to make sure any information that hasn't yet been saved to disk will be, and so won't be lost when you shut off power. The command can simply be:

```
smartdrv /c
```

/r tells **SMARTDrive** to clear the cache and restart. Use this option only after **SMARTDrive** is already loaded and not until you've either assured yourself that write caching is not active or that you've used the **smartdrv /c** command to save write cache information to disk.

/l tells **SMARTDrive** to load into conventional memory, not upper memory.

/q tells **SMARTDrive** to run in its *quiet* mode where no information is displayed on-screen when you load **SMARTDrive**.

/s tells **SMARTDrive** to show its status. Use this option only after **SMARTDrive** is already loaded.

/? tells **SMARTDrive** to give you help by explaining its various options and commands on-screen.

/double_buffer tells SMARTDrive that you have a hard drive with a SCSI or ESDI controller using physical memory addresses that conflict with memory from 386-Enhanced mode of Windows or the **EMM386.EXE** memory manager. Those systems need a double buffer to work properly. You can know if you have such a hard drive by opening a DOS window inside Windows and then typing:

```
smartdrv
```

You'll see a display as shown in Figure 4.13.

If any item has *yes* in the Buffering column, then you need the **double_buffer** option. You enter this option as a separate line in **CONFIG.SYS**. (Remember that the rest of the **SMARTDrive** command is in **AUTOEXEC.BAT**, because this is DOS 6 we're talking, not DOS 5 and before where the **SMARTDrive** was all in **CONFIG.SYS**.) Just put:

```
DEVICE=C:\WINDOWS\SMARTDRV.EXE /DOUBLE_BUFFER
```

in **CONFIG.SYS**.

```
C:\>smartdrv
Microsoft SMARTDrive Disk Cache version 4.0
Copyright 1991,1992 Microsoft Corp.

Cache size: 1,048,576 bytes
Cache size while running Windows: 524,288 bytes

              Disk Caching Status
drive   read cache    write cache    buffering
----------------------------------------------
  A:       yes            no            no
  B:       yes            no            no
  C:       yes            yes           no

For help, type "Smartdrv /?".

C:\>
```

FIGURE 4.13

Checking to see if your SMARTDrive disk cache needs double-buffering.

You probably don't need to worry about any of **SMARTDrive**'s options because it will try to set itself up automatically in the best way.

Don't use a **LOADHIGH** command to put **SMARTDrive** into upper memory UMBs. If loading high is possible, **SMARTDrive** will do so automatically.

Always run `smartdrv /c` before rebooting perhaps, by putting it into a **poweroff.bat** file to prevent losing write-cached information.

The /**a** switch used by **SMARTDrive** in DOS 5 is no longer an option in DOS 6 because the DOS 6 **SMARTDrive** cannot load into expanded memory.

Remember that you can test to see if **SMARTDrive** is in memory, and even what its *hit* rate (a measurement of efficiency) is by typing:

```
smartdrv /s
```

You'll see a report similar to that in Figure 4.14.

```
C:\>smartdrv /s
Microsoft SMARTDrive Disk Cache version 4.0
Copyright 1991,1992 Microsoft Corp.

Room for 128 elements of 8,192 bytes each
There have been 90 cache hits
     and 24 cache misses

Cache size: 1,048,576 bytes
Cache size while running Windows: 524,288 bytes

                Disk Caching Status
drive    read cache    write cache    buffering
-------------------------------------------------
  A:         yes           no            no
  B:         yes           no            no
  C:         yes           yes           no

For help, type "Smartdrv /?".

C:\>
```

FIGURE 4.14
SMARTDrive cache report.

Don't bother with the DOS **Fastopen** command. This command caches file locations but is incompatible with many hard disk utilities, and is obsolete if you use **SMARTDrive**.

Before you use **SMARTDrive**, clean up your hard disk by removing unneeded files, running **chkdsk** to eliminate unallocated clusters, and defragmenting with a utility such as DOS 6's **DEFRAG**.

RAMDrive—Using a RAM Disk

RAMDrive is a device driver. It makes a RAM disk. That is, it makes an area of memory act like a disk drive, a very fast disk drive. If you have enough memory to use **RAMDrive**, it can make your PC and Windows work faster.

As mentioned in Chapter 1, a RAM disk works just like any other disk drive, except that you don't format it, its information disappears when you turn off the computer's power, and it is many times faster than a rotating disk drive.

 For running DOS programs, a RAM disk is always a good idea, if you've already satisfied all other needs for memory and have at least 512K or more left over. For running Windows programs you're often better off leaving the memory to Windows for its direct use, instead of putting it into a RAM disk.

RAMDrive works in conventional, expanded, or extended memory. You load it with a command in **CONFIG.SYS**. The full command to use it is:

```
device[high]=pathname\ramdrive.sys size sec-
tor entries [/e|/a]
```

Here's what all those parts mean:

>**device=** means that you use the start with the **device** command to load this device driver into memory.

>**[high]** means that you can use **devicehigh** instead of **device** to try to load the driver into upper memory instead of in conventional memory.

>**pathname** tells the location of your **RAMDRIVE.SYS** file, which typically means the WINDOWS or DOS directories, such as **C:\WINDOWS**.

\RAMDRIVE.SYS just finishes the job of telling where the **RAMDRIVE.SYS** file is.

size tells how large the RAM drive should be in kilobytes, ranging from 4 to 32767. Don't specify more memory than is in your PC, or even most of the memory in your PC. Any memory put into a RAM drive isn't available for any other use. The default is 64, meaning 64K, if you don't specify a size. A typically good size for Windows on a PC with 8M of extended memory is 2048 (or 2M), although if you have a full 16M in your PC and want to put more of your Windows files into the RAM drive you could pump that up to 8096 (or 8M). For DOS you can do well even with a small RAM disk, just large enough to fit your batch files.

sector tells the size of the sectors on the RAM drive in bytes. This can be 128, 256, or 512. The default is 512, which is typical for floppy and hard disks and is just fine for your uses. If you don't bother specifying sector size, the default will set up.

entries tells how many directories and files can be in the root directory of the RAM drive, ranging from 2 to 1024. The default is 64, which is fine unless you're making a large RAM disk with lots of files.

/e tells DOS to make the RAM drive in extended memory, instead of the default of conventional memory. Don't use this option and the **/a** option together.

For Windows, you should put the RAM disk in extended memory.

/a tells DOS to make the RAM drive in expanded memory, instead of the default of conventional memory. Don't use this option and the **/e** option together.

You can use **RAMDRIVE.SYS** to create as many RAM disks as your memory can hold. You use the statement once for each RAM disk you want.

The **RAMDRIVE.SYS** statement in **CONFIG.SYS** assigns a drive letter to your new RAM disk drive. It uses the next available drive letter after those in your system already, including networked drives and compressed drives.

You need to restart your PC after adding the **RAMDRIVE** statement to **CONFIG.SYS**. Then, you can test to see if the new RAM disk is working. Check it with the **CHKDSK** command. Type:

```
chkdsk
```

followed by a space and the drive's letter. You should see a confirmation along with the size of the drive.

If you use the **MEM** command, you can discover that the **RAMDRIVE.SYS** driver itself takes up only 1184 bytes of conventional memory.

To make your RAM disk as safe to operate as possible—so you won't lose its information when the PC loses power accidentally—you should copy applications only to your RAM disk (because they don't change anyway).

You'll get the most from a RAM disk by copying to it programs that frequently use the disk.

If you specify more memory for the RAM disk than is available in your PC, **RAMDRIVE.SYS** will just make a smaller RAM disk.

Files suitable for RAM disks include:

▼ applications that keep the disk drive active and show it by flashing the hard drive light frequently

▼ applications with overlay files

▼ graphics applications that work on large images in memory

▼ temporary and overflow files

Files not suitable for RAM disks include:

▼ applications that rarely use the disk

▼ copy-protected software (which often conflicts with a RAM disk)

 Add your RAM disk to the path command in **AUTOEXEC.BAT** for better performance.

 For some programs—such as Ventura Publisher and WordPerfect—you must specify within the program where the **TEMP** files are or they won't be put on the RAM disk.

 A small sector size, such as 128 byte sectors, is most efficient for a RAM disk.

You can compress a RAM disk with DOS 6's **DoubleSpace** disk compression utility, if that disk is larger than 650K, but it isn't simple. Have an expert do this for you, or be an expert.

Summary

Here are some summaries of the basic, best approaches to managing memory. What you do depends on your PC's processor. All of these summaries assume you start with DOS.

For an 8088 or 8086-based PC:

1. Buy a new 386 or 486 PC if you can.

2. If you cannot afford a 386 or 486 system, consider buying a 386/486 motherboard replacement. Then follow the 386/486 rules. Find an LIM EMS 4.0 memory card for your 8088/8086.

3. Put as much expanded memory on that card as you can. 1M is good; 2M is better.

4. Install the **EMM** device driver that came with the LIM card (add the command to the **CONFIG.SYS** file).

5. Disable all but 256K of conventional memory and backfill to the 256K address with expanded memory.

6. Install a third-party memory manager such as **QEMM**, **386MAX**, or **Netroom**.

7. Use any extra memory for a disk cache and perhaps for a RAM disk.

For an 80286-based PC:

1. Buy a new 386 or 486 PC if you can.

2. Install memory management drivers such as **HIMEM.SYS** or drivers from third-party memory managers such as **QRAM**, **MOV'EM**, or **Netroom**.

3. Use DOS memory commands to load DOS into the HMA.

4. Load drivers and memory-residents into UMBs (there should be at least 384K of extended memory on almost any 286 PC).

5. Add extended memory, either on the motherboard or on an extended memory board. Get at least 1M, preferably 2M or more.

6. If you have programs that use expanded memory, then add LIM EMS 4.0 expanded memory on an expanded memory card. Backfill as much conventional memory as possible with this expanded memory.

7. Use any extra memory for a disk cache and perhaps for a RAM disk.

For a 386-, 486-, or Pentium-based PC:

1. Install memory management drivers such as **HIMEM.SYS** and **EMM386.EXE**, or drivers from third-party memory managers such as **QEMM**, **386MAX**, or **Netroom**.

2. Use DOS memory commands to load DOS into the HMA, unless there are third-party drivers that would do better there.

3. Load drivers and memory-residents into UMBs (there should be at least 384K of extended memory on almost any 286 PC).

4. Load DOS resources high if you can (some memory managers let you).

5. Add extended memory, either on the motherboard, on a special 32-bit high-speed memory card, or on an extended memory board. Get at least 1M, preferably 2M or more.

6. Use extended memory to simulate expanded memory if you have any programs that want expanded memory.

7. Use any extra memory for a disk cache and perhaps for a RAM disk.

In general, get a 386 or 486 with 4 to 8MB of RAM, install a memory manager, run its optimizer, and create a large disk cache.

Manage Memory
for Microsoft Windows

DOS is the fundamental software (or operating system) that runs on nearly all PCs. Microsoft Windows is a software environment that sits on top of DOS. It changes your PC's screen appearance from that of Figure 5.1 to that of Figure 5.2.

Windows needs lots of memory. Get at least 4M, 8M is better, 16M is fantastic.

```
    Volume in drive C has no label
    Volume Serial Number is 3338-14EB
    Directory of C:\

    DOS          <DIR>      06-12-93    1:35p
    WINDOWS      <DIR>      06-12-93    1:36p
    NETROOM      <DIR>      01-01-94   10:47a
    COMMAND  COM      52925 03-10-93    6:00a
    WINA20   386       9349 03-10-93    6:00a
    386MAX       <DIR>      01-01-94    3:18p
    RAMEXAM      <DIR>      01-01-94    5:22p
    CONFIG   NET        197 01-08-94   12:11p
    AUTOEXEC NET        138 01-08-94   12:11p
    CONFIG   QEM        298 01-08-94   10:16a
    HSG2         <DIR>      09-07-93   10:09a
    CONFIG   MAX        335 01-08-94   10:54a
    QEMM         <DIR>      09-07-93   10:38a
    AUTOEXEC QEM        112 01-08-94   10:11a
    AUTOEXEC MAX        171 01-08-94   11:06a
    CONFIG   SYS        132 01-26-94   10:55a
    AUTOEXEC BAT        122 01-26-94   10:55a
    GT!          <DIR>      01-10-94    9:54a
    TRIAL    GIF       4408 01-10-94   10:15a
    Press any key to continue . . .
```

FIGURE 5.1
What DOS looks like on-screen.

The Windows look is generally thought to be easier to understand and use than the DOS look. The menus across the top of the Windows screen keep commands where you can easily find them, as you can see in Figure 5.2. The *icons* on the screen—those small pictures—represent common commands or important files. Again, look at Figure 5.2. You can choose commands from menus or select icons with a *mouse*, a device you connect to the computer and then slide around on your desk to choose commands on screen. (Figure 5.3 shows a typical mouse.) As you move the mouse, the *mouse-cursor*—a small arrow or similar pointing device—moves on the screen. The arrow in Figure 5.2 shows a typical mouse cursor. When the cursor is on the menu or command you want to use, you are *pointing* the mouse at it. To activate that command, you press the left button on the mouse, which is called *clicking* the mouse. When you point at an icon, you need to *double-click* the mouse to start the program or open the file that the icon represents. You can also press the **Enter** key to make your selection.

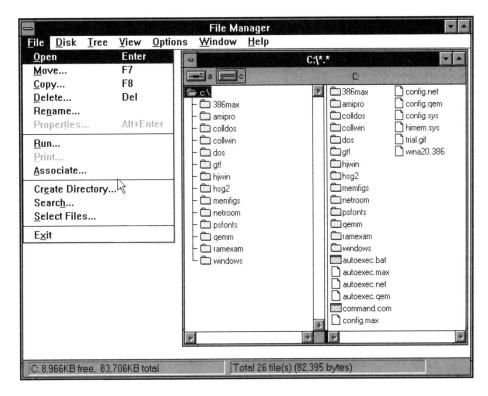

FIGURE 5.2
What Windows looks like on-screen.

But Windows does more than just change the look of your PC's screen. It changes the way programs interact with each other and with your PC. It forces programs to cooperate with each other and to share the screen and other computer parts.

DOS programs don't automatically run the Windows way. They don't automatically have the menus and icons that make Windows easier. You can run DOS programs inside Windows, but they'll still look like DOS programs. To get the full Windows feel, you'll need programs written specifically for Windows.

Windows memory management is different from DOS memory management. The same memory chips are still in your computer, and DOS is still underneath, with its memory-use restrictions (as explained in Chapter 4), but you need different rules and tools when managing memory for best Windows performance. That's what this chapter is about.

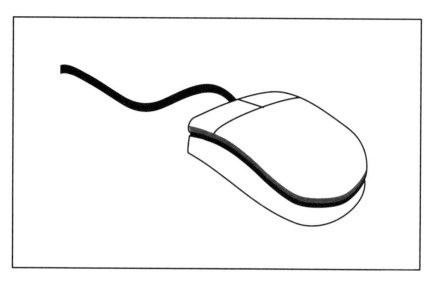

FIGURE 5.3
A mouse, used for pointing and clicking on menus and icons in Windows.

Versions and Modes

Windows has been around for years. Early versions were slow, buggy, and difficult to use. Windows 3.0 was the first widely popular version. It had three operating modes—Real mode, Standard mode, and 386-Enhanced mode. Real and Standard modes were designed for PCs with slower processors and less memory. Enhanced mode required a 386 processor chip and several megabytes of memory. As you read back in Chapter 1, a 386 chip is not only faster than previous chips such as the 286, it also has special circuits for managing memory. The latest version of Windows has two modes—Standard and Enhanced. Standard mode is fine for running a single program; Enhanced mode is more flexible and is the mode of choice for running more than one program at a time.

 Windows will automatically start in Enhanced mode if it can, falling back to Standard mode if there isn't enough memory or the 386/486 processor for Enhanced mode. You can force it to start in Standard mode by adding a space and **/S** after the **WIN** command you normally use.

Because Windows 3.1 is faster, smoother, and better than Windows 3.0 in every way, we will assume in this book that you've upgraded to 3.1 or will do so shortly. (Doing so is the first important memory management step for Windows.)

Windows for Workgroups is a networking version of Windows 3.1. Use it if you want to share disk drives and printers and send messages from one Windows-equipped PC to another on a local area network. Memory management for Windows for Workgroups is the same as for Windows 3.1.

If Windows is running, you can see how much memory is available and so which mode Windows finds, by choosing **About Program Manager** from the Program Manager's Help menu. Figure 5.4 shows an example.

If you want Enhanced mode and you don't have it, perhaps you don't have enough memory. Windows can sense this and won't run in Enhanced mode. First make sure there's enough extended memory installed—at least 2M. Then check your **CONFIG.SYS** file to ensure that **EMM386.EXE** isn't using all of extended memory as expanded.

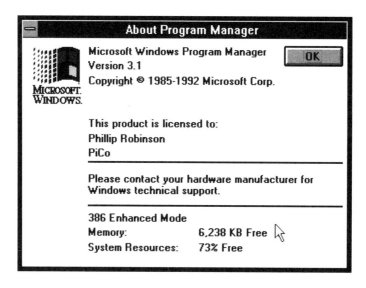

FIGURE 5.4
About Program Manager tells you how much memory is in your system and what mode Windows is in.

If you are surprised by the large size of the memory free in About Program Manager, remember that this includes virtual memory—disk masquerading as memory—which you can adjust as explained later in this chapter. For a more accurate estimate of memory, get to DOS and use the **MEM** command.

You can get advice on how to use the memory—and other resources in your PC—from utilities such as SoftLogic Solutions' WinSense or Landmark Research's WinProbe. They'll show you what memory is doing and give detailed advice on making it do more.

Hardware

To run well, Windows needs more hardware power than plain DOS PCs have. Whereas DOS will run quickly on a 286 or slow 386 processor chip with 1 or 2M of RAM and a 20 to 40M hard disk, Windows needs a 486 processor chip with 4 to 8M of RAM and a 100 to 200M hard disk to run as well. Handling all those graphic images—the menus and icons—and keeping more than one program running at a time means greater demand for processor speed, memory, and disk space.

To run Windows well, get a system with a 486 processor with at least 4M of RAM and a 100M hard disk. Better yet, get a fast 486 or Pentium processor with 8M and a 200M hard disk.

Windows is also infamous for slow printing and slow video. You will enjoy Windows time more if you buy a printer accelerator and a video accelerator. These are special boards with special chips that get pages of information to the printer faster (your printer's own speed will still determine how fast they pop out) and splash images onto the screen faster (this is a necessity for comfortable Windows use).

Use a utility such as **Microsoft Diagnostics**, called **MSD**—described in Chapter 2—to learn what is in your PC already. MSD comes with DOS 6, and if you have that version of DOS you can use MSD just by changing to the DOS directory and typing:

```
msd
```

The first display, which is shown in Figure 5.5, will tell you the basics. There's detail in the categories.

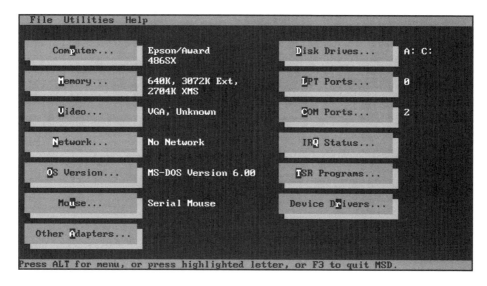

```
 File  Utilities  Help

   Computer...      Epson/Award        Disk Drives...     A: C:
                    486SX

    Memory...       640K, 3072K Ext,   LPT Ports...       0
                    2704K XMS

    Video...        VGA, Unknown       COM Ports...       2

   Network...       No Network         IRQ Status...

  OS Version...     MS-DOS Version 6.00    TSR Programs...

    Mouse...        Serial Mouse       Device Drivers...

 Other Adapters...

 Press ALT for menu, or press highlighted letter, or F3 to quit MSD.
```

FIGURE 5.5
Use MSD to see what's in your PC already.

MSD is also included with some Microsoft applications.

Memory

To get more memory, add as many RAM chips as you can to your PC. Configure them all as extended memory, as explained back in Chapters 1 and 3. Windows can't use expanded memory. If you have a 386, 486, or Pentium PC (anything later than a 286, which you shouldn't really be running Windows on anyway), add as much of the memory as possible to the motherboard of the computer or to any high-speed memory card. These add-ons will help the memory run as fast as possible. Have at least 4M of RAM. 8M is better and 16M is best. Hold off on any more than that since more confuses some PC systems.

Windows can use four kinds of memory:

▼ conventional (but only when it is loading or for DOS programs)

▼ extended (throughout its operation)

▼ virtual (borrowing hard disk to get more memory)

▼ expanded (but only emulated and only for DOS programs that need it)

The memory management techniques you use for DOS are only vital in Windows when you want to run DOS programs. You need only carefully conserve conventional memory—loading memory-residents and drivers high, using the HMA—if you're going to run DOS programs under Windows. That's explained in more detail later in this chapter. For running Windows programs, you need only XMS extended memory—and an XMS memory manager such as Windows' own **HIMEM.SYS** to handle it. Of course, you'll need lots of XMS memory. Windows does need some free conventional memory to start, but even a cursory management—with say 500K free—will do the trick.

Processors

Windows crawls on a 286, walks lamely on a typical 386, strides on a 486, and runs on a Pentium processor. Get a system with the fastest processor chip you can to run Windows; with more speed, your programs that use graphics (games, desktop publishing, and design can take the most processor power) will move along quickly. If your PC has a slow processor, consider buying a new PC with a faster chip. This purchase can sometimes be cheaper than buying a processor upgrade or new motherboard, especially when you consider that you'll probably get a faster and larger hard disk, faster video, and other improved elements in the bargain. You will also get the comfort of a new warranty.

The 286 chip is not only slow but also lacks the memory management circuits of all later PC chips (386, 486, Pentium). If you have a 286 PC, don't bother with Windows.

For some PCs you can buy a chip or board that will replace or take over from a slower processor, but the possibility and success of this type of memory expansion depends on your particular PC and your experience with hardware fixes. You might see an ad to upgrade a 286 PC to 486 status, but I suggest that you buy a new 486 instead. Due to basic design differences, such an upgrade can only deliver a small part of the advantages of a true 486 system.

Hard Disk Space

Windows needs lots of space on your hard disk. It needs it for the Windows program itself, for text fonts, for graphic images, and for the programs you run under Windows. Altogether, a fairly basic Windows installation can take up 40M or more. To get more disk space you can buy another disk drive; replace your disk drive with a larger, faster disk drive; or use disk compression to double the effective space of your current drive.

MS-DOS 6 and 6.2 include disk compression as a utility program called **DoubleSpace**. IBM's PC-DOS 6.1 also has a disk compression utility. Or you can buy a separate compression utility from a company such as Stac or AddStor. Compression utilities add a slight element of danger, however. They're often complicated to learn and install and occasionally damage files. Unless you're experienced and dedicated to making regular backup safety copies of everything on your disks, I wouldn't use compression.

Another scheme to get more disk space is to delete files you don't need. Naturally, it's a good idea to rid yourself of your own document files that are out of date. But this is dangerous.

Mistakenly erasing important files could crash your PC. Know what your deleting!

Incidentally, you'll have more usable hard disk if you periodically delete unneeded files, remove unused subdirectories, and use:

```
chkdsk /f
```

before starting Windows to fix any lost clusters of memory on disk. Also use the **DEFRAG** utility of MS-DOS 6 (or some other defragmentation utility) occasionally to keep the files on your disk well organized. To use **DEFRAG**, just change to the DOS directory and type:

```
defrag
```

and press **Enter**. You'll see a display similar to that shown in Figure 5.6. Here you can use the **F1** key to get help or just press **Alt+B** to start.

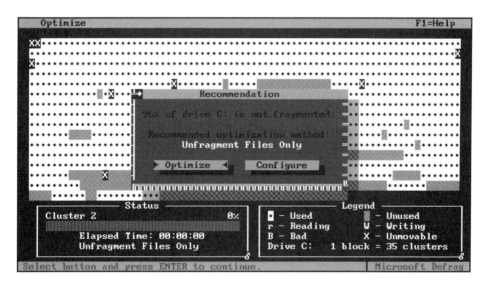

FIGURE 5.6
Using DEFRAG to free disk space and improve disk performance.

Don't use **CHKDSK** or **DEFRAG** from inside Windows.

Then, after you run Windows, delete any Windows temp files in the hard disk's root directory with a command such as:

```
if exist c:\~*.* del c:\~*.*
```

Printer Memory

This book is about the memory in your computer. But there is also memory in your printer, especially if you have a laser printer. Printer memory determines how fast your printer operates, how quickly the computer finishes sending information to the printer (and so is ready again for other work), and how large or graphic the pages are you can print. 512K isn't much printer memory, but 3 or 4M is usually plenty. You buy this memory as special printer-memory circuit boards, known as *cards*, that plug into the printer. To save money, buy the cards without memory chips, buy the memory chips separately, and install them yourself (assuming you're comfortable installing memory chips, as described in Chapter 3).

Video Memory

There is also memory on your video card. Video memory helps determine how fast your video works—how fast you can scroll through a page of text on-screen, how quickly new drawings appear on-screen, how quickly you can switch programs, and so on. 512K is the typical minimum on today's standard video card for Windows, called Super Video Graphics Array or SVGA. 1M is better for SVGA, and the 2M some cards can hold is even better. This memory installs right on the video card itself and is completely separate from the megabytes of memory for the PC. You don't need to manage this memory, other than to get more if you want higher resolution or more color. Read your video adapter manual to see just how much.

Video memory is related to other memory since part of upper memory is set aside for use by video. Typically, this is only 2K to 32K— less for text mode and more for graphics mode. If you choose to use only text mode programs, some memory manager utilities—such as **QEMM** and **386MAX**—let you "borrow" the unused upper memory addresses. These addresses can be combined with standard conventional memory to make as much as 736K or even more conventional memory that is usable by most standard programs. Chapter 1 explained this technique. Remember that the amount of video memory used from upper memory is not affected by how much memory is on your video card, only by the graphics mode your program uses.

Multitasking in Windows

Multitasking means running more than one program at a time. It's one of the key reasons to use Windows. In fact, Windows is always multitasking because the Program Manager that shows you your files and documents is itself a program running alongside whatever application you start. When multitasking, you can *minimize* programs so that they appear as icons only. The program you're viewing in the *foreground* can be operating, but so can the programs in the *background*, continuing to print, sort, calculate, or perform other chores that don't require input from you.

 You can switch from one running program to another in Windows by pressing **Alt+Tab**.

Sharing Information with DDE and OLE

Windows programs not only run simultaneously but they can also share information directly with each other. You can cut and paste information between them, and you can use the *OLE* and *DDE* technologies.

DDE is Dynamic Data Exchange. In it you dynamically cut and paste information. This creates a link between two programs. When information changes in the original you cut from, it is also then changed automatically in the destination it was pasted to. You'll know DDE is available if there is a command such as **Paste Special** or **Paste Link**, probably in the Edit menu of the program.

OLE (pronounced *olé* as though in a bullfight) is Object Linking and Embedding. Information doesn't just cut and paste from one program to another, but rather is *embedded* from one program into another. When you double-click on that information in the destination document, the original program automatically starts (or is switched to, if it has already started). You edit the embedded information using its originating program. Look for an **Insert Object** menu command to know if your program supports OLE.

DOS Programs in Windows

You can run DOS programs within Windows. They won't get any Windows features—such as DDE and OLE, not even the standard menus of Windows—and they'll use their own printer drivers, instead of printing through Windows. Still, if you can't find or don't want to pay for a Windows program to replace your DOS software, then you'll be glad to run your DOS program in Windows.

Why not run it without Windows? It's easier to start and stop DOS programs inside Windows than it is to quit Windows, start the DOS program, quit the DOS program, start Windows again, and so on. In

Windows Enhanced mode you can just leave the DOS program or programs running alongside Windows programs.

DOS runs only one program at a time, except when aided by an additional environment utility such as **DESQview**. Windows in Standard mode can run only one DOS program at a time. Other Windows programs that are loaded in the Standard mode "freeze" when the DOS program is active. In Enhanced mode, though, Windows can run multiple DOS programs at once.

In Standard mode the **DOSX.EXE** program of Windows lets it run only one DOS program in extended memory at a time. When you leave that DOS program, the **DSWAP.EXE** utility runs, freeing memory by saving most of the DOS program to disk and reloading Windows. The Enhanced mode sets up a separate virtual 8086 machine for each DOS program, so they can run simultaneously.

To start a DOS program, you either use the File menu's **Run** command—which gives a command line where you can type the program's command and options—or you can start a DOS session. To get such a session started, you double-click on the **DOS** icon, which is shown in Figure 5.7.

You'll see a DOS window open. In that window you can use DOS commands and start DOS programs. The memory you have available in that window will depend on the DOS memory management you ran before starting Windows. In other words, this is where you still need to study DOS memory management, even if you're otherwise a Windows regular. As you'll see in Chapters 6-8, the third-party memory managers cater to Windows, with special utilities to free even more than 640K in some cases. Be sure to move part of DOS into the HMA, if possible, move DOS resources out of conventional memory, relocate drivers and memory-residents to upper memory, if possible, and tell any optimizing utility to think Windows.

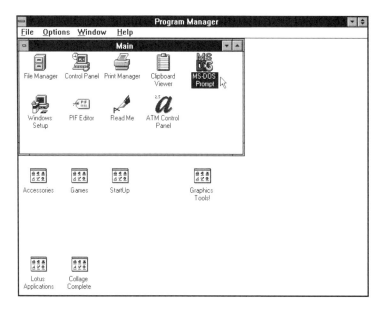

FIGURE 5.7
The DOS session icon.

For example, when you run the **MemMaker** optimizer for DOS 6's own memory management commands, you can optimize for Windows. Choose the Custom Setup, Advanced Options screen, which is shown in Figure 5.8. In this display, choose:

> **No** in answer to *Specify which drivers and TSRs to include in optimization?*
>
> **Yes** in answer to *Scan the upper memory area aggressively?*
>
> **Yes** in answer to *Optimize upper memory for use with Windows?*, if you're using DOS programs and Windows programs, or
>
> **No** in answer to *Optimize upper memory for use with Windows?*, if you're using Windows programs only
>
> **Yes** in answer to *Use Monochrome region (B000-BFFF) for running programs?*, if you have an EGA or VGA display or

No in answer to *Use Monochrome region (B000-BFFF) for running programs?* if you have a monochrome or SVGA display,

No in answer to *Keep current EMS386 memory exclusions and inclusions?*

Yes in answer to *Move Extended BIOS Data Area from conventional to upper memory?*

```
Microsoft MemMaker


                        Advanced Options


    Specify which drivers and TSRs to include in optimization?     No
    Scan the upper memory area aggressively?                       Yes
    Optimize upper memory for use with Windows?                    No
    Use monochrome region (B000-B7FF) for running programs?        No
    Keep current EMM386 memory exclusions and inclusions?          Yes
    Move Extended BIOS Data Area from conventional to upper memory? Yes



    To select a different option, press the UP ARROW or DOWN ARROW key.
    To accept all the settings and continue, press ENTER.




    ENTER=Accept All   SPACEBAR=Change Selection   F1=Help   F3=Exit
```

FIGURE 5.8
Customize for Windows with MemMaker's Custom Setup, Advanced Options display.

How much memory you have for DOS program sessions also depends on what memory-resident programs and drivers you load. If you loaded your regular complement of these before starting Windows, then they would occupy space in every DOS session. If, instead, you load them only in the DOS session you start, they will occupy memory only in that session. And if you run them in separate windows or replace them with Windows equivalent programs, they won't occupy any DOS memory. Later in this chapter you'll read more about memory-residents and Windows.

Don't load your mouse driver before loading Windows. Windows has its own mouse software, and your DOS mouse driver will waste memory space. If you need it for a DOS program, load it in that DOS session.

PIF Memory Settings

You specify how much extended and expanded memory (converted from extended or especially laid aside as expanded before starting Windows) each DOS program gets. To do this, you create a PIF (Program Information File) for that program. Windows comes with a PIF editor, which is installed in the Main group in Windows, to help you do this. Figure 5.9 shows this editor.

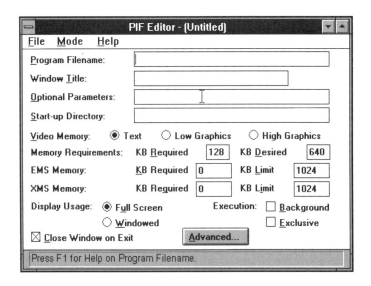

FIGURE 5.9
PIF editor in Windows.

The PIF has settings for how much memory a program can have and for how the program looks and behaves as it runs. You can just use the default PIF that comes with Windows, but you can get more from your programs if you customize your PIFs. The PIF lets you start a program with any COM, EXE, BAT, or other PIF file to run and with any command-line options. You can even create your own icons and then start DOS programs by double-clicking on them—which activates their PIF. If you're dealing with a DOS program that can load a file by placing that file's name after the program command on the command line, then you can *associate* a file type with that program. In other words, you can automatically load files of that type when starting the DOS program under Windows.

These are the memory settings in the PIF:

> **Video Memory**. Tells Windows if your application runs in any graphics modes. The higher the mode, the more memory Windows sets aside for it.

> **Memory Requirements**. Tells Windows how to give conventional memory to your DOS application. KB Required is the minimum memory to give; KB Desired is the maximum memory to give.

Set KB Required and KB Desired to -1 to give all RAM to the program.

> **EMS Memory**. Tells Windows the settings for expanded memory. KB Required is normally set to 0, and KB Limit is set to whatever the program needs.

> **XMS Memory**. Tells Windows the settings for extended memory. KB Required is typically set to 0 (this is for extended memory outside what Windows uses for itself), and KB Desired is set to a minimum of 1024.

The Advanced PIF editor options, which are shown in Figure 5.10, also affect that use of extended and expanded memory.

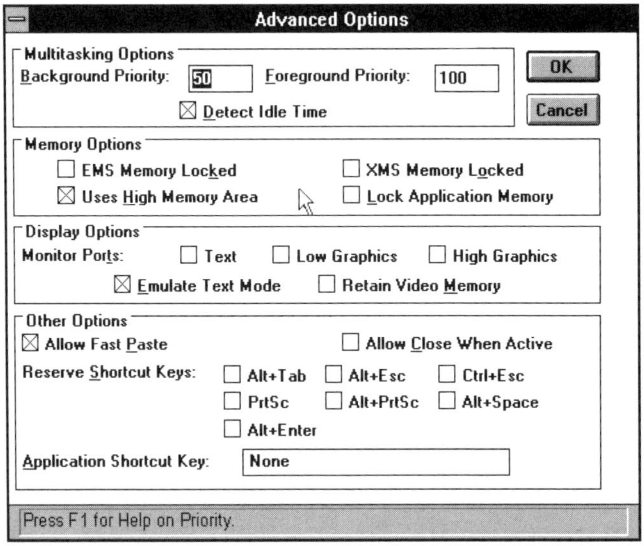

FIGURE 5.10
PIF editor's Advanced options.

EMS Memory Locked. Checking this option can speed the individual program by preventing any expanded memory used by this program from being swapped to hard disk. It can slow the rest of the system though, so leave it unchecked.

Uses High Memory Area. Checking this option lets the application use the HMA. Check it.

XMS Memory Locked. Checking this option can speed the individual program by preventing any extended memory used by this program from being swapped to hard disk. It can slow the rest of the system though, so leave it unchecked.

Lock Application Memory. Checking this option prevents the application from releasing any conventional memory it has used but isn't using now—because it has swapped to disk. It can speed the individual program but slow the system. Don't check it.

You must launch the program with the PIF instead of from its EXE file to use the memory management choices you've made.

WIN.INI and SYSTEM.INI

The **WIN.INI** and **SYSTEM.INI** files are Windows' own configuration files, much like **CONFIG.SYS** and **AUTOEXEC.BAT** for DOS. They contain commands that cover all Windows programs, not just those you individually set options or PIF for. In fact, they can override the details of a PIF.

Both INI files are divided into sections, set off by square brackets. The **SYSTEM.INI** file has a [NonWindowsApp] section where you can place lines that set policy for DOS applications under Windows. You'll rarely edit this section, instead depending on programs to set them automatically. The possible memory management commands for this section include:

>**CommandEnvSize=**, which tells the DOS environment byte size. The default equals the size set by the /E:nnnn option for the **COMMAND.COM** when that started. Set this to 0 to disable.

>**GlobalHeapSize=**, which dictates the kilobyte size of the memory area for sharing information between DOS programs in Standard mode, with a default of 0.

>**LocalTSRs=**, which names the TSRs loaded each time a DOS program runs in Windows.

In the [Standard] section you can find this command:

>**Stacks=**, which tells how many internal stacks Windows passes to DOS programs that run in the Standard mode. The

default is 12, the choices are 8 through 64. Don't mess with this unless you see a *Stack Overflow* error message when running the DOS program. In that case, choose a higher value.

And in the [386enh] section, devoted to Enhanced mode, you can use these commands (most are set automatically):

AllEMSLocked=, locks all EMS memory so that it can't swap to disk. It overrides the EMS Memory Locked setting in any particular DOS program's PIF. Set to either on or off. The default is off.

AllXMSLocked=, locks all XMS memory so that it can't swap to disk. It overrides the XMS Memory Locked setting in any particular DOS program's PIF. Set to either on or off. The default is off.

EMMSize=, determines the amount of expanded memory that Windows makes available to programs that request it. Set to the number of kilobytes of expanded memory available. Use this and **NoEMMDriver=Off** for applications to use expanded memory.

NoEMMDriver=, turns Windows expanded memory on or off. When it is on, no program can use expanded memory. Set to either on or off. The default is off.

ReservePageFrame=, sets up an EMS page frame in conventional memory for DOS programs. Set to either on or off. Turn this off to give DOS programs more conventional memory.

ReserveVideoROM=, protects video memory. Try this if text in a DOS program becomes corrupted. Set to either on or off. The default is off.

VideoBackgroundMsg=, warns you if the suspended or video memory runs low, when this is on and a DOS program runs in the background. Windows will warn you. Set to either on or off. The default is on.

Memory Resident Programs in Windows

Memory-resident programs—also known as *TSRs* or *pop-up programs*—sit in memory waiting to be used. They were described in Chapter 1. Chapter 4 then explained how DOS can relocate them from conventional memory to upper memory—*loading high*—to conserve conventional memory. *Device drivers*, software for controlling peripherals such as mice, work in a similar way. There are several ways to run device drivers with Windows.

First, you can load them before Windows, from **CONFIG.SYS** and **AUTOEXEC.BAT**, just as you always would for DOS. The disadvantage here is that they will occupy memory for any DOS program you start under Windows. This may waste memory. Also, they may not be necessary. For example, Windows has its own built-in mouse control. It doesn't need a separate **MOUSE.SYS** or **MOUSE.COM** driver. (Nor does Windows need the **PRINT**, **GRAPHICS**, **APPEND**, or **ANSI.SYS** programs—unless you specifically need them for a DOS session. Windows has pieces for all these needs.) The advantage of this approach is simplicity—the drivers are there for any DOS programs that need them, and you don't have to load them specially after quitting Windows. In summary, use this approach only if you run lots of DOS programs, even quitting Windows to do so, and need the same set of memory-residents for all.

Second, run them in their nonresident mode as independent DOS programs under Windows. Most have an option that lets them run without remaining in memory. If so, you can just run them as DOS programs under Windows, losing no memory and making it easy to switch back and forth from them to other programs. Make a PIF for the program and use the Optional Parameters text box for whatever code tells the program to start in nonresident mode. Figure 5.11 shows an example for SideKick (with its /G switch).

Create a batch file to load these memory-resident programs when you leave Windows, and a separate batch to unload them before you start Windows.

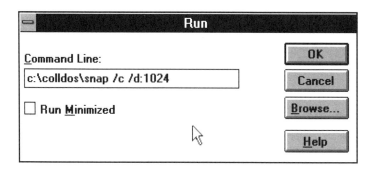

FIGURE 5.11

Example of using options when starting a program as nonresident in Windows.

Running a memory-resident program as a DOS program under Windows and leaving it in its resident mode could make Windows unstable.

Third, find a Windows program that does what the DOS memory-resident does and give up the DOS memory-resident. To use this option, you must find the time to look for a new program and the money to buy it—if it exists—but it is the most stable and Windows-compatible solution.

Fourth, check the memory-resident program's manual to see if it is compatible with Windows. If it is, add it to the list in the **SYSTEM.INI** file's [NonWindowsApp] LocalTSRs entry. These are programs Windows will start each time it runs a DOS program.

Don't load the **ANSI.SYS** and **MOUSE.SYS** drivers with Windows unless you need them for every DOS program running under Windows. If so, put them in the **CONFIG.SYS** file as device lines.

Expanded Memory and EMM386.EXE

Windows doesn't need the **EMM386.EXE** for creating expanded memory. Windows doesn't use expanded memory and has its own ability to convert extended to expanded for DOS programs that need it.

If you have a DOS program that needs expanded memory, you can tell Windows to allocate some in the PIF for that DOS program—it will convert that memory from extended. Check the PIF editor, which is shown in Figure 5.12, and the **SYSTEM.INI** settings mentioned earlier in this chapter.

```
┌─────────────────────────────────────────────────────────┐
│ ─         PIF Editor - (Untitled)              ▼ ▲        │
├─────────────────────────────────────────────────────────┤
│  File   Mode   Help                                       │
│                                                           │
│  Program Filename:    [                              ]    │
│  Window Title:        [                              ]    │
│  Optional Parameters: [                              ]    │
│  Start-up Directory:  [                              ]    │
│                                                           │
│  Video Memory:   ● Text    ○ Low Graphics  ○ High Graphics│
│  Memory Requirements:  KB Required [128]  KB Desired [640]│
│  EMS Memory:           KB Required [256]  KB Limit  [1024]│
│  XMS Memory:           KB Required [0]    KB Limit  [1024]│
│  Display Usage: ● Full Screen    Execution: ☐ Background   │
│                 ○ Windowed                  ☐ Exclusive    │
│  ☒ Close Window on Exit       [ Advanced... ]             │
├─────────────────────────────────────────────────────────┤
│  Press F1 for Help on EMS Memory.                         │
└─────────────────────────────────────────────────────────┘
```

FIGURE 5.12
You can set expanded memory in the PIF for a DOS program. Windows will convert the given amount of extended memory into expanded memory just for that program.

EMM386.EXE is useful for creating UMBs that let you move drivers and memory-residents out of conventional memory, to maximize free conventional memory for DOS programs that run under Windows.

A Permanent Swap File

Windows makes use of *swap files*, areas on disk that items in memory can be copied to and then copied back from. Swap files are a form of virtual memory that is built into Windows. By temporarily removing things from chip memory, it makes that chip memory available for other uses. Two kinds of swap files in Windows are temporary and permanent.

The *temporary* swap file lasts only as long as Windows is running. When Windows starts, it creates such a temporary file on the hard disk and then deletes it when you exit Windows. Stick with this automatically created temporary swap file if you don't have much free hard disk space.

Enhanced mode lets you create a *permanent* swap file. This is faster than the temporary swap file because it remains on disk permanently. The information within it is contiguous instead of spread to whatever nooks and crannies of the disk Windows can happen to find. If you have the space to set aside for a permanent swap file, do so.

To create a permanent swap file, use the Windows Control Panel—double-click on the Control Panel icon in the Main group of the Program Manager, as shown in Figure 5.13. Within the Control Panel, double-click on the Enhanced icon, which is shown in Figure 5.14. Click on the **Virtual Memory** button in the dialog box that appears, shown in Figure 5.15. Then, in the Virtual Memory dialog box that opens, click on the **Change** button, as shown in Figure 5.16.

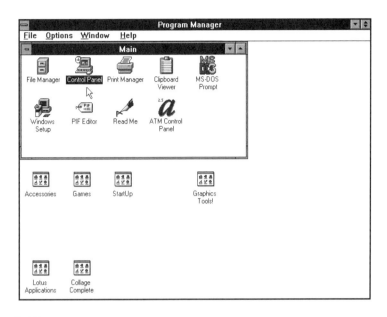

FIGURE 5.13
The Control Panel icon.

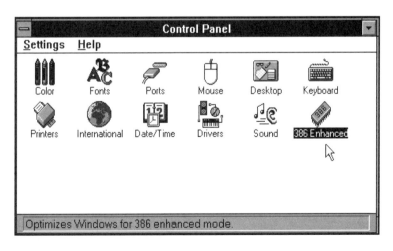

FIGURE 5.14
The 386 Enhanced icon.

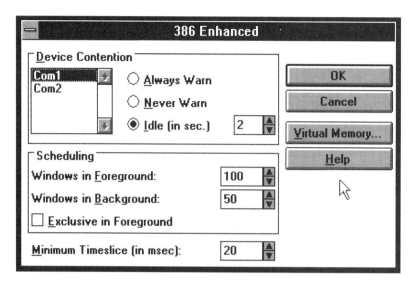

FIGURE 5.15
The 386 Enhanced dialog box.

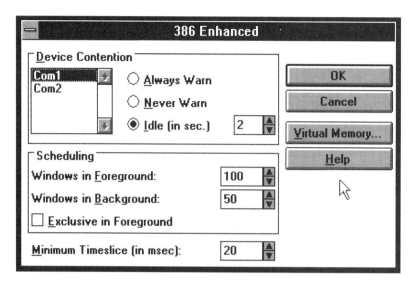

FIGURE 5.16
The Virtual Memory dialog box.

You needed to do some drilling to get this far, but now you have a larger Virtual Memory dialog box, as shown in Figure 5.17. Here you can choose the drive, the type of swap file you want, and its size. (Or you can just view the current settings.) If you need help in this pursuit, a **Help** button is handy.

```
┌─────────────────────────────────────────────────┐
│ ─         Virtual Memory                          │
├───────────────────────────────────────────────────┤
│ ┌─Current Settings──────────────────┐  ┌────────┐ │
│ │ Drive:    C:                      │  │   OK   │ │
│ │ Size:     7,792 KB                │  └────────┘ │
│ │ Type:     Temporary (using MS-DOS)│  ┌────────┐ │
│ └───────────────────────────────────┘  │ Cancel │ │
│                                         └────────┘ │
│                                         ┌────────┐ │
│                                         │Change>>│ │
│                                         └────────┘ │
│ ┌─New Settings──────────────────────┐  ┌────────┐ │
│ │                                   │  │  Help  │ │
│ │ Drive:   [▭ c:              ] [▼] │  └────────┘ │
│ │ Type:    [Temporary        ] [▼] │             │
│ │ Space Available:        11,304 KB │             │
│ │ Recommended Maximum Size: 5,652 KB│             │
│ │                                   │             │
│ │ New Size:              [5652] KB  │             │
│ └───────────────────────────────────┘             │
└─────────────────────────────────────────────────┘
```

FIGURE 5.17
Changing settings in the Virtual Memory dialog box.

Best of all, you'll see a Recommended size for the swap file. Go with that size unless you're sure you know better. But give it at least 4M if you can (2M is the real minimum). Don't use a larger swap file unless you often run several large applications at once. You'll just waste disk space. You can't create a permanent swap file on a network or compressed drive.

> Quit to DOS; then use a defragmentation utility such as the DOS 6 **DEFRAG** before setting up your permanent swap file, in order to create additional contiguous space on your hard disk.

When you're done with the swap file settings, just OK your way back to the Program Manager (click on **OK** repeatedly).

The SMARTDrive Disk Cache

A *disk cache* sets aside a section of expanded or extended memory to hold the information most recently and frequently asked for from disk. Then, it routes all program requests for disk information first to the cache. If the wanted information is there, it can be supplied much faster than from disk. This rerouting improves performance tremendously and is very important for using Windows.

SMARTDrive is a disk cache program that comes with DOS and Windows. It is explained in more depth in Chapter 4 on DOS. SMARTDrive can create a disk cache in expanded or extended memory.

SMARTDRV.EXE is the name of the file for SMARTDrive in Windows 3.1. You use it by adding it to **AUTOEXEC.BAT**. (Previous versions of Windows started SMARTDrive from the **SMARTDRV.SYS** device driver, which loaded from a line in **CONFIG.SYS**.) Here's a typical AUTOEXEC.BAT command line for SMARTDRV.EXE:

```
device=c:\windows\smartdrv.exe /double_buffer
```

Some caching, SCSI, and ESDI controllers use physical memory addresses that can make trouble with Windows Enhanced mode and its virtual memory. For these addresses you'll want to use the **double_buffer** option, which is shown in the command line. Windows Setup adds this buffer automatically if needed. You can check to see if its needed by typing:

```
smartdrv
```

at the DOS command prompt and seeing if *Yes* appears in the Buffering column, as shown in Figure 5.18.

You probably don't need to worry about any of SMARTDrive's options because it will try to set itself up automatically in the best way.

```
C:\>smartdrv /s
Microsoft SMARTDrive Disk Cache version 4.0
Copyright 1991,1992 Microsoft Corp.

Room for 128 elements of 8,192 bytes each
There have been 12,881 cache hits
      and 4,409 cache misses

Cache size: 1,048,576 bytes
Cache size while running Windows: 524,288 bytes


             Disk Caching Status
drive    read cache   write cache    buffering
-----------------------------------------------
  A:        yes           no            no
  B:        yes           no            no
  C:        yes           yes           no

For help, type "Smartdrv /?".

C:\>
```

FIGURE 5.18
Testing to see if double-buffering is necessary for SMARTDrive.

Don't use a **LOADHIGH** command to put SMARTDrive into upper memory UMBs. If loading high is possible, SMARTDrive will do it.

When SMARTDrive sets up, it automatically allocates extended memory for the disk cache by noting the amount of memory in your PC. Here's the table it uses:

Extended Memory	Cache Size	Cache in Windows
up to 1M	all	0K
up to 2M	1M	256K
up to 4M	1M	512K
up to 6M	2M	1M
more than 6M	2M	2M

As you can see, when Windows starts, the SMARTDrive disk cache automatically shrinks if it thinks Windows would be better off using the extended memory directly. You can adjust the size of this shrink—the initial and the Windows size—with SMARTDrive options, as explained in Chapter 4.

The RAMDrive RAM Disk

If you have 12M or more extended memory, consider using a RAM disk to make Windows run faster. The RAMDrive device driver can create a RAM disk. That is, it makes an area of memory act like a disk drive, a very fast disk drive. It comes with DOS and Windows and is explained in more depth in Chapter 4 on DOS.

 Using a RAM disk with Windows is controversial. Some say it helps, some say you should just leave the memory to Windows for its direct use. If you have time, experiment on your system and see which works best.

RAMDrive works in conventional, expanded, or extended memory. For Windows you should put it in extended memory. A typical Windows command is:

```
device=c:\windows\ramdrive.sys size /e
```

with *size* telling how many kilobytes are in the RAM disk. The size can range from 4 to 32767 with a default of 64. A good size for Windows on a PC with 8M memory is 2048 (for 2M). If your PC has 16M, you might try 8096 for an 8M RAM disk. The /e puts the RAM disk into extended memory.

If you have the full 8M RAM disk, you can put entire Windows applications into it. If you don't have that much memory for the RAM disk, however, at least store Windows temporary files on it. For this you need a 2M RAM disk. Then, put this line in **AUTOEXEC.BAT**:

```
set temp=d:\
```

if the RAM disk is drive D. DOS will put its own temporary files on the RAM disk as well.

 If you see an error message such as *Can't open temporary file*, you may have an application that does not want a backslash at the end of its TEMP environment variable. Try changing the **AUTOEXEC.BAT** line to:

```
set temp=d:
```

and reboot.

CONFIG.SYS and AUTOEXEC.BAT Guidelines for Windows

Windows needs DOS. It can't start your PC without DOS. And the way you set up DOS affects the way Windows works.

As explained back in Chapter 4, you set up DOS, that is you tell DOS how to run, with commands in the **CONFIG.SYS** and **AUTOEXEC.BAT** files. DOS automatically reads these two files when it starts the PC to learn what you want done and how. Both are text files: they don't have any special control characters and must be created or changed with a utility that can save files as plain-text or ASCII. The DOS Editor can do this. So can the Windows Notepad. Both files are also stored in the root directory of your hard disk. If they are stored elsewhere, DOS won't find and use them when it starts.

The best **CONFIG.SYS** and **AUTOEXEC.BAT** files for Windows are rarely the same as the best for DOS. As you can see throughout this chapter, Windows doesn't need the same drivers, memory-residents, and memory management techniques as DOS.

What does Windows need? In **CONFIG.SYS** you'll want (and you'll want them pretty much in this order):

▼   drivers that set up your disk drives (if you have special drives that must be configured before use, which few PCs do)

▼   memory management drivers (only **HIMEM.SYS** is necessary for Windows, not **EMM386.EXE**, although you may get another driver if you install a memory management package such as **386MAX** or **QEMM**)

▼   **EMM386.EXE** allowed to create UMBs with the NOEMS option

▼   the command **DOS=HIGH** to load part of DOS into HMA on 386

▼   the command **FILES=** set to 30 or less

▼   the command **BUFFERS=** set to 20 or 15, if you're using SMARTDrive

▼   the command **Stacks=0,0** but changed to 9,256 if Windows locks up

▼   all **INSTALL** commands in **CONFIG.SYS** changed to **LOADHIGH** commands in **AUTOEXEC.BAT** (**INSTALL** uses conventional memory)

▼   sound and CD-ROM drivers (on a multimedia PC)

▼   SMARTDrive to create a disk cache

▼   network drivers

▼   virus-scanning drivers

▼   DOS version fooling driver (such as **SETVER.EXE**)

▼   disk-compression drivers (also known as disk-doubling drivers) (put these at the end of the **CONFIG.SYS**)

If you have an EGA video adapter, you might want to add:

```
device=c:\dos\ega.sys
```

to give Windows help when switching from a DOS application back to Windows graphics. Don't use this option with a VGA display.

What should be in **AUTOEXEC.BAT**?

▼ The Windows subdirectory should be in the PATH.

▼ Necessary memory-residents should be loaded into UMBs with **LOADHIGH**.

▼ You could start Windows automatically by putting **win** as the last line.

Include the **WINA20.386** driver when running Windows 3.0 with DOS 5, to keep the 386-Enhanced mode compatible with the DOS use of HMA.

With Windows 3.1 you don't need the **WINA20.386** file. Change its attributes and then erase it if you want less clutter on your disk.

Always use the latest version of **HIMEM.SYS, EMM386.EXE, RAMDRIVE.SYS,** and **SMARTDRV.EXE.** Check file dates to see.

System Resources

Windows isn't perfect, and one example is the way it releases resources. *Resources* are memory areas and other internal data structures Windows needs to start programs, remember what it's doing, and keep track of documents. Each program that starts takes some resources. Then, each program is supposed to release those resources again when it quits, but many programs don't let go of everything they were given in a way that other programs can get at the resources. Because of this glitch, if you start and stop lots of programs as you use Windows, your resources will diminish. Eventually the PC will slow down and you may run into errors and perhaps even lose the ability to start a new Windows program. See Figure 5.19 to see the resources gauge in the About the Program Manager window.

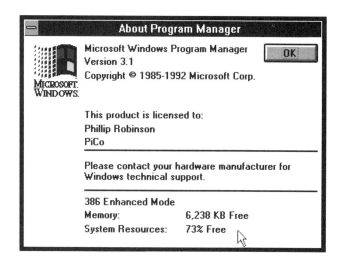

FIGURE 5.19
About the Program Manager tells you what percent of system resources are still available.

If your free resources approach 25% or less, it's time to quit Windows and then start it again. Restarting will collect all the resources together and get them ready again for any new program you start. Now you can turn to Chapters 6, 7, and 8 for utilities that can manage memory even more efficiently than DOS, and have special provisions for Windows.

Manage Memory with the QEMM Utility

Quarterdeck's **QEMM** (Quarterdeck Expanded Memory Manager) does a lot more than manage expanded memory. It also:

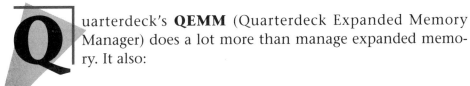

- ▼ analyzes the memory in your PC
- ▼ manages extended memory
- ▼ creates UMBs (replacing **HIMEM.SYS** and **EMM386.EXE**)
- ▼ loads drivers and memory-residents into UMBs
- ▼ moves DOS to the HMA
- ▼ moves DOS resources to UMBs
- ▼ copies ROMs to RAM for faster performance
- ▼ supports the DPMI and VCPI standards for sharing memory between DOS Extender programs

QEMM is the best-selling memory manager. The latest version of **QEMM** is Version 7, which is compatible with DOS 6 and Windows 3.1. It needs a 386, 486, or Pentium PC with at least 1M total memory—meaning at least 384K extended memory. It supports VCPI for handling DOS extender programs. You can get this utility from:

>Quarterdeck Office Systems
>150 Pico Boulevard
>Santa Monica, CA 90405
>800-354-3222
>310-392-9851
>310-314-4217 fax

Quarterdeck also makes **QRAM**, a memory manager for 8088, 8086, and 80286 PCs with expanded memory hardware, and **DESQview**, a multitasking utility for 386 PCs and other software utilities. **DESQview** lets you run many programs at once, each in its own window, and you don't need new versions of those programs to do so—an advantage over competitor Microsoft Windows.

DESQview-386 comes with a copy of **QEMM** because multitasking requires good memory management. Because it is so popular, **QEMM** has spawned classes and books devoted to better use of it and **DESQview**.

Install QEMM

To install **QEMM**, you insert the floppy disk it comes on and type:

```
a:install
```

After the display telling you how long installation will take and how much disk space it will occupy, **QEMM** asks you if you want

Express installation   (press **Enter** for this)
or
Advanced installation   (press **A** for this)

Choose **Express** for fast installation without questions. **QEMM** uses its own best judgment in copying necessary files to your hard disk. This option is the choice for beginners. When installation is complete, **QEMM** asks you if you want to run **Optimize**, a **QEMM** utility that tailors memory management to your hardware and software. Say **Yes** by removing the floppy disk and then pressing **Enter**. Then, follow the instructions for running **Optimize** in the next section of this chapter.

 Throughout the installation you may press:

F1   for help

Esc   to quit installation

Choose **Advanced** if you're an expert who wants to dictate the details of the memory management. You'll see a series of questions on the screen about which directory to put **QEMM** in, what to do with conflicting drivers **QEMM** finds in your **CONFIG.SYS** file, and so on. When you have a choice of changes, the installation tells you what it's about to do and then lets you press **R** to review or change the plan. When you press **R**, you'll see a display similar to that in Figure 6.1.

To choose any of these change categories, press the first letter shown for it. Then you'll see another screen for actually making changes, such as the list of **QEMM** parameters shown in Figure 6.2. Again you choose a specific item on the screen by pressing its first letter and then change the setting for that item by following the further instructions on the screen.

Finally, **QEMM** asks you if you want to optimize. Say **Yes** by removing the floppy disk and pressing **Enter**. Read the next section to see what you have done.

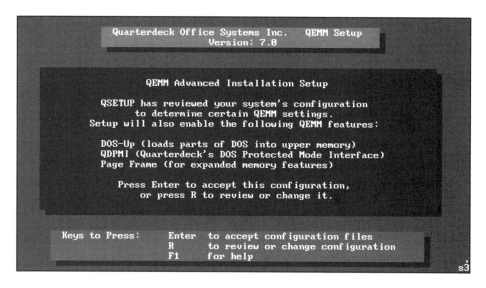

FIGURE 6.1

You may review planned changes when using the Advanced installation of QEMM.

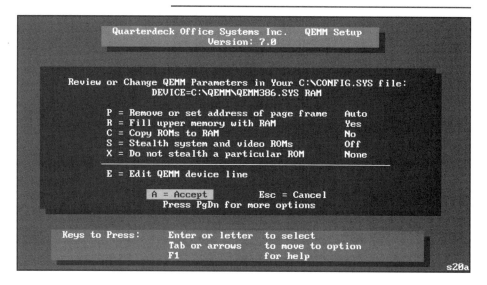

FIGURE 6.2

QEMM parameters you may change during installation.

Optimize

Optimize automatically applies the many possible QEMM memory management options to your particular PC. It will test thousands or even millions of ways that software can be loaded into one or another part of memory to find the most efficient solution. Along the way it will reboot your PC several times (and on some PCs you may need to turn power off and then on again for the rebooting).

You should run **Optimize** when you first get **QEMM** and then again every time you add a new program or peripheral to your system.

Optimize also has **Express** and **Custom** approaches. **Express** is for quick, no-questions optimization. It is best for almost everyone, and certainly for beginners. **Custom** is for experts who think they can do a better job, or who need to insist on some particular detail that **QEMM** and **Optimize** may have overlooked, or who require drivers loaded in a specific order.

Choose **Express** and you'll hear your disk spin as optimization starts. You'll also notice that your old **CONFIG.SYS** and **AUTOEXEC.BAT** files are saved as **CONFIG.QDK** and **AUTOEXEC.QDK**. Now you still have them in case you want to return to your original, pre-**QEMM** setup. Figure 6.3 shows one of the steps in optimization, where **QEMM** is comparing millions of possible memory schemes. This step alone could take 10 or 15 minutes, maybe more.

 When **Optimize** finishes, it deletes both .**QDK** files. It is safer to back up **Autoexec** and **Config**. Copy them, using the date as an extension, *i.e.*, Autoexec.212 and Config.212. This way, changes can be undone.

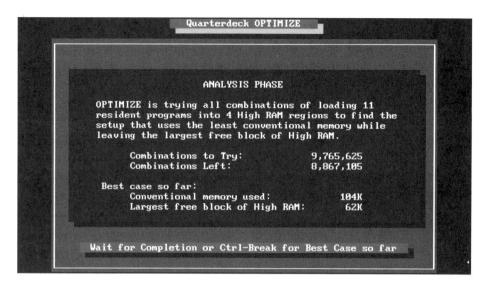

FIGURE 6.3

Optimize compares millions of possible memory management schemes to find the best.

The last phase of optimization is the **Stealth** check. **Stealth**, as explained later in this chapter, is **QEMM**'s most advanced feature. It's a way of borrowing ROM memory addresses while those ROMs aren't in use and then giving them back when a program needs the ROM. It can add lots of upper memory to your PC, but it risks using memory that isn't completely available—and so crashing programs or the system. Before using **Stealth**, **Optimize** wants to test your system to see if it will be OK. You can choose, naturally, **Express** or **Custom** checking. For **Custom** checking, press **F3**, but be sure that you know what you're doing. Follow the instructions on the screen. If **Stealth** will work on your PC, **Optimize** will have more memory for relocating drivers and memory-residents, and so may want to run the previous phases over again.

Eventually you should see a report similar to the one shown in Figure 6.4 telling you what installing **QEMM** and optimizing accomplished.

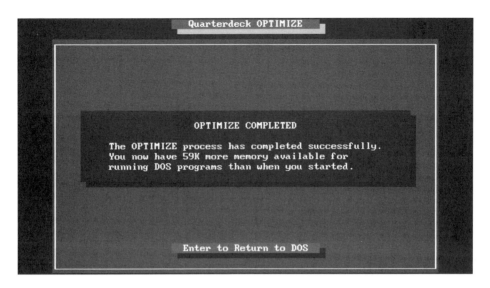

FIGURE 6.4
Final report from installing and optimizing QEMM.

If you want to make any changes, press **O** for options. Then you can see maps or layouts showing what **Optimize** saw and why it made the decisions, as shown in Figure 6.5. This is also the place to change the order in which memory-residents are loaded into memory, if you think you have a better idea than **Optimize** could find.

If you accept the decisions, **Optimize** will put them into your **CONFIG.SYS** and **AUTOEXEC.BAT** files. **QEMM** is at work, and you won't even know it's there except that you'll have more memory to use.

Check your **CONFIG.SYS** file and you'll see that **QEMM386.SYS** has replaced **HIMEM.SYS** and **EMM386.EXE**. You'll also see the **LOADHI.SYS** driver used to load other drivers into UMBs.

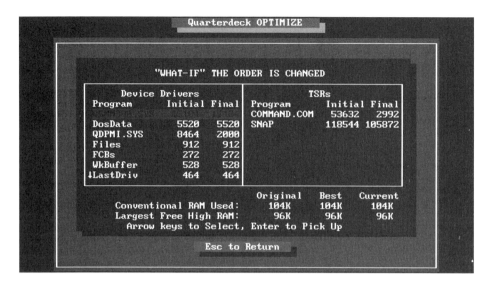

FIGURE 6.5
Viewing Optimize's analysis and decisions.

To run **Optimize** again later, after changing software or hardware, just switch to the QEMM directory and type:

```
optimize
```

Add the **/stealth** option on the same line if you want to try the advanced **Stealth** technique.

Manifest

Manifest is a system and memory testing utility that comes free with **QEMM**. It installs automatically when you install **QEMM**. To use it, type:

```
mft
```

and you'll see the main display, as shown in Figure 6.6.

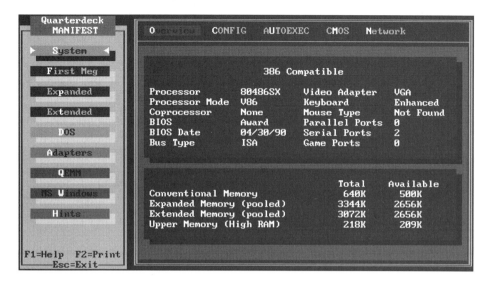

FIGURE 6.6
Manifest, a system analysis utility that comes with QEMM.

Manifest will tell you about the hardware and software in your PC. Besides the summary of memory on this first display, you can also look at other, more specific kinds of memory:

▼   First Meg—conventional memory in the first megabyte (from 0K to 1024K)

▼   Expanded

▼   Extended

Choose any of these categories by pressing the highlighted letter of the category. For example, you would press **F** for the First Meg. You'll see a map similar to that shown in Figure 6.7.

Look at the top of the screen. There are other options to tell you more about the First Meg. You could press **r** to see details on the programs in the First Meg, for example. See Figure 6.8.

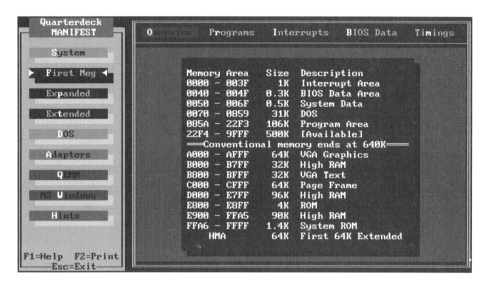

FIGURE 6.7

First Meg memory map in Manifest.

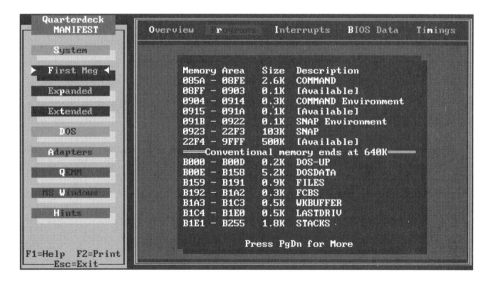

FIGURE 6.8

Programs in the conventional memory, from Manifest.

A unique feature in Manifest is Hints, a category that suggests ways you can save on memory. After I ran **Optimize**, there wasn't much left to do. All Hints could suggest was:

Stop DOS from allocating its interrupt stacks.

Press **F3** when quitting Manifest to keep it resident, ready to tell you about memory use as programs move and change in memory.

What's in QEMM

QEMM is a bundle of programs. It starts with the automatic **Install** utility. Then comes the **Optimize** utility to find the best way to use all of **QEMM**. Next is **Manifest**, a system analysis utility that can tell you how your memory is used and how much is there to use.

Then comes the main **QEMM386.SYS** driver, the software that replaces **HIMEM.SYS** and **EMM386.EXE** from DOS, creates UMBs, and manages expanded and extended memory. There are scores of **QEMM386.SYS** options for fine-tuning its memory management, telling it just which areas to use and ignore, what special circumstances to watch out for, and more.

LOADHI.SYS and **LOADHI.COM** utilities can load drivers and memory-residents into UMBs, saving conventional memory. DOS-UP (new to version 7 of QEMM) can load part of DOS in the HMA while **BUFFERS.COM**, **FILES.COM**, **FCBS.COM**, and **LAST-DRIV.COM** can load DOS resources high.

VIDRAM can steal unused video memory and make it part of conventional memory. **QEMM.COM** can report on memory use from the command prompt, as shown in Figure 6.9. **QSetup** is a utility for changing memory configuration, any time after installing and optimizing **QEMM**.

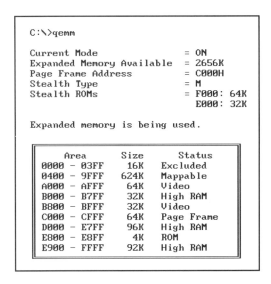

```
C:\>qemm

Current Mode                = ON
Expanded Memory Available   = 2656K
Page Frame Address          = C000H
Stealth Type                = M
Stealth ROMs                = F000: 64K
                              E000: 32K

Expanded memory is being used.

    Area         Size        Status
 0000 - 03FF     16K      Excluded
 0400 - 9FFF    624K      Mappable
 A000 - AFFF     64K      Video
 B000 - B7FF     32K      High RAM
 B800 - BFFF     32K      Video
 C000 - CFFF     64K      Page Frame
 D000 - E7FF     96K      High RAM
 E800 - E8FF      4K      ROM
 E900 - FFFF     92K      High RAM
```

FIGURE 6.9

Type qemm *at the prompt to see a QEMM report on memory.*

Stealth and Squeeze

Squeeze and **Stealth** are special techniques **QEMM** uses to free more memory than DOS and MemMaker can.

Squeeze depends on the difference between initialization size and resident size for memory-residents in UMBs. Many memory-residents need more, sometimes much more, memory as they load into a UMB than after they're loaded. The drop could be from 70K down to 7K. Memory managers used to be stuck, unable to load such memory-resident programs into a UMB unless there was a full 70K available. **QEMM's** Squeeze feature is smarter, borrowing memory from an area such as the page frame addresses just long enough to let these bloated-at-first-sight memory-residents load and then giving that memory back to the page frame. After all, the page frame and its expanded memory won't use those addresses during initialization. The result is that more memory-residents fit into UMBs, and so free more conventional memory.

Stealth, or **Stealth ROM** in its full name, can create 48K to 115K more high memory on most PCs. It depends on the fact that some memory addresses hold ROM chips that aren't frequently called upon. **Stealth** maps RAM into those same addresses and manages whether the processor is talking to the ROM or to the RAM. In essence, **Stealth** puts two memories in the same space but neatly routes requests to the relevant memory. That trick makes more high memory space available, more UMBs possible, and so less conventional memory is lost. There are two disadvantages. First, **Stealth** uses some of your extended memory for the RAM at those addresses; this is extended memory that you cannot use for other purposes. Second, **Stealth** doesn't work on some PCs. It will crash them by not routing requests to the proper place. **QEMM** tries to avoid putting **Stealth** on such PCs, but sometimes it makes mistakes, especially if you are manually fiddling with options so that you can include **Stealth**.

 Optimize will automatically suggest using **Stealth** if it thinks your PC is up to it and will test to see if **Stealth** works on your PC. Leave the decision to **Optimize** unless you're an expert.

QSetup

QSetup lets you change your **QEMM** configuration after installation. Type:

```
qsetup
```

and you'll see the display in Figure 6.10. Here you can change parameters, edit configuration files, and read from the bundle of technical notes and tips Quarterdeck installs with **QEMM**. Figure 6.11 shows just the start of the list that you can choose from.

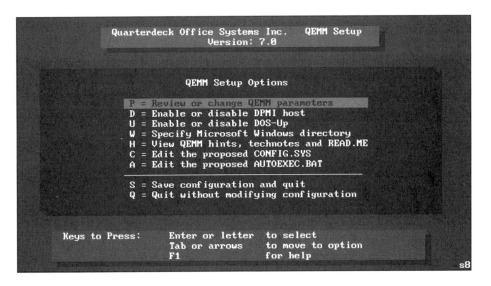

FIGURE 6.10

Qsetup display for changing QEMM configuration.

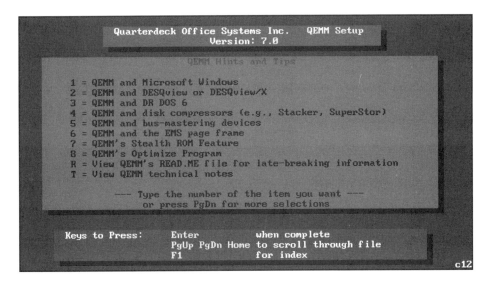

FIGURE 6.11

Technical notes for QEMM, in Qsetup.

QEMM and Windows

QEMM is compatible with Windows 3.0 and Windows 3.1 and gives DOS programs running in Windows 8K to 24K more memory. In fact, the **VIDRAM** utility could even give DOS sessions in Windows up to 96K more memory.

If you install Windows after **QEMM**, you'll need to run the **QSetup** utility to tell **QEMM** about the change. In it use the **Select Microsoft Windows directory** choice and type the name of the directory.

 You can automatically tell **QEMM** about a new Windows installation by typing

```
qwinfix
```

at the DOS command prompt.

The next chapter is about QEMM's greatest competitor: 386 Max.

CHAPTER
7

MEMORY MANAGEMENT

Manage Memory with the 386Max Utility

Along with **QEMM**, **386MAX** from Qualitas is one of the best memory managers. It needs at least a 386 or later PC with at least 256K of extended memory. If you have less, you can use the MOVE'EM program that Qualitas makes. This is described in Chapter 10.

If you have an IBM PS/2 computer, choose BlueMAX instead of **386MAX**. It includes special abilities to avoid the rarely used ROM BASIC in the PS/2s and to compress the ROM BIOS, leaving more upper memory addresses free. Otherwise, it is identical to **386MAX**.

386 MAX can:

▼ manage expanded memory

▼ manage extended memory

▼ create UMBs

▼ load drivers and memory-residents into UMBs

▼ put DOS resources into UMBs

▼ put DOS into the HMA

▼ analyze your PC's memory use

It also doles out memory to programs as they need it, without explicit advanced configuration of amounts of extended, expanded, and so on.

Version 7, the most recent version of **386MAX**, works with DOS 6 (including compressed drives) and Windows 3.1. You can get this utility from:

Qualitas
7101 Wisconsin Avenue
Suite 1386
Bethesda, MD 20841
800-733-1377
301-907-6700
301-907-0905 fax
BBS 301-907-8030
MCI Mail 336-2907
CompuServe 75300,1107

Install

To start **386MAX**, slip its floppy disk into the drive and type:

```
install
```

You'll soon see a notice indicating that **386MAX** is ready to load. Press a key or click the mouse button to make it load. Enter your serial number when asked (it's on the bottom of the box). You'll see the progress as files are copied. The screen will let you know what **386MAX** detects as it runs. Unless you're an expert who knows differently, accept its defaults by pressing **Enter** at each question. An example of such a question is shown in Figure 7.1.

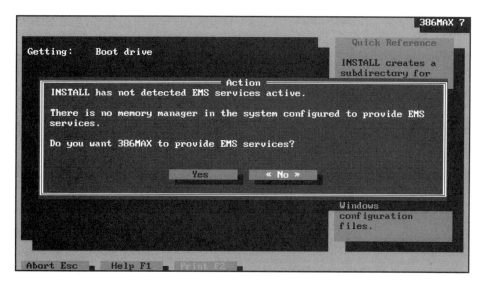

FIGURE 7.1
An example question 386MAX asks as it installs.

If you want to see the changes to the various configuration files—such as **CONFIG.SYS**, **AUTOEXEC.BAT**, **386MAX.PRO**, and **SYSTEM.INI**, you can do so during installation.

Finally, you'll be asked if you want to run **MAXIMIZE**, a utility that will automatically analyze your PC and try to figure the best way to set commands in the configuration files.

MAXIMIZE

The **MAXIMIZE** utility analyzes the software and hardware in your PC and looks for the best, most appropriate way to manage memory. It will add commands to **CONFIG.SYS** and **AUTOEXEC.BAT** to give you the most free conventional memory.

You can run **MAXIMIZE** as just part of the installation process, or you can run it from the command prompt. (You should run it whenever you change the drivers or memory-residents in your PC.) To run it, type:

```
maximize
```

You'll see that there are two modes in **MAXIMIZE**: **Quick** and **Full**. **Quick** is for those who don't want to answer questions. From Figure 7.2 choose **Yes** for **Quick**. **Full** is for experts who want to second-guess **MAXIMIZE**'s suggestions. As indicated in Figure 7.2, choose **No** for **Full**.

Quick will soon reboot your PC (take any floppy disks out of the drives), and it could reboot more times. You'll see reports during the process about the relocation of drivers and memory-residents. Figure 7.3 shows an example. When the process is complete, you'll see just the DOS prompt.

If you choose **Full MAXIMIZE**, you'll first be told that Phase 1 is inspecting your **CONFIG.SYS** and **AUTOEXEC.BAT** files.

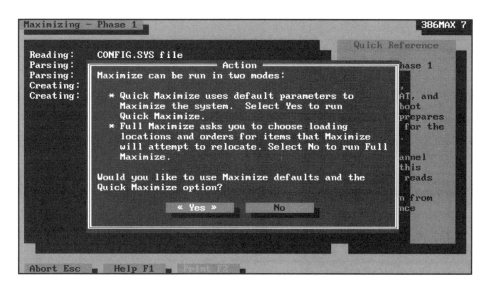

FIGURE 7.2
Choosing Quick or Full when running MAXIMIZE.

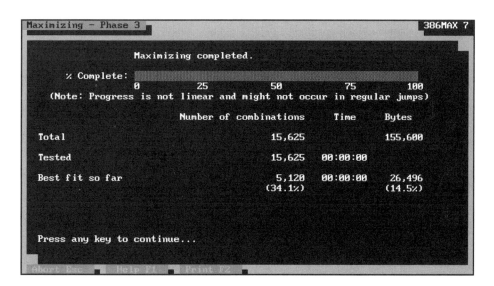

FIGURE 7.3
A report on the process of MAXIMIZE.

Throughout the process you'll see these commands on the screen:

Enter   when you're done

F1   for help

F2   to print

F6   to turn something on or off (toggling)

F7   to see the previous screen

F8   to see the next screen

Esc   to stop **MAXIMIZE**

One line at a time, you'll be presented with the changes to **CONFIG.SYS** and **AUTOEXEC.BAT**. Press **F6** to change the setting; press **F6** again to see more possibilities for the setting. Stick with the setting you want to use to load drivers high or low. Figure 7.4 is an example for **CONFIG.SYS** and Figure 7.5 is for **AUTOEXEC.BAT**.

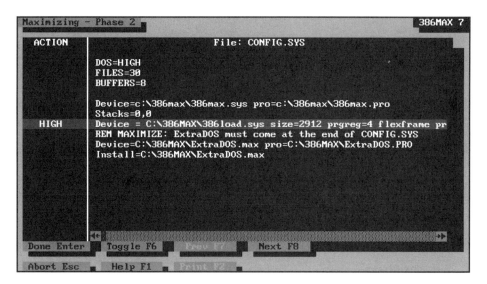

```
Maximizing - Phase 2                                           386MAX 7

  ACTION                          File: CONFIG.SYS

              DOS=HIGH
              FILES=30
              BUFFERS=8

              Device=c:\386max\386max.sys pro=c:\386max\386max.pro
              Stacks=0,0
   HIGH       Device = C:\386MAX\386load.sys size=2912 prgreg=4 flexframe pr
              REM MAXIMIZE: ExtraDOS must come at the end of CONFIG.SYS
              Device=C:\386MAX\ExtraDOS.max pro=C:\386MAX\ExtraDOS.PRO
              Install=C:\386MAX\ExtraDOS.max




 Done Enter      Toggle F6                      Next F8

 Abort Esc        Help F1
```

FIGURE 7.4
Example of toggling CONFIG.SYS options in Full MAXIMIZE.

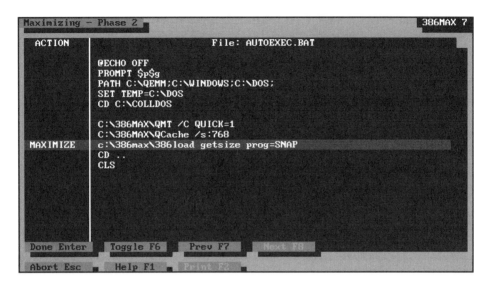

FIGURE 7.5
Example of toggling AUTOEXEC.BAT options in Full MAXIMIZE.

Then the PC will reboot several times. On the way you'll see progress measurements as shown in Figure 7.6. The final result will be a simple DOS prompt. To see what was done, you can always check the **386MAX.PRO** file, as in the example shown in Figure 7.7, which lists the actions.

ASQ

386MAX comes with the **ASQ** analysis program that tells you what hardware and software is in your PC. To run it, type:

    asq

You'll see the menus shown in Figure 7.8.

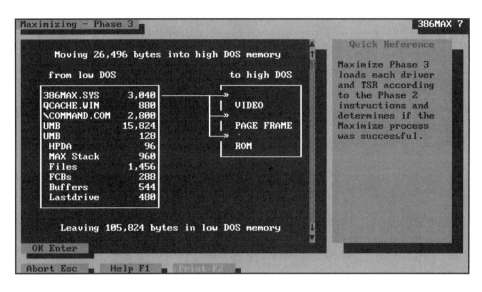

FIGURE 7.6
Progress measured during Full MAXIMIZE.

```
C:\386MAX>type 386max.pro
    ; This profile created automatically by INSTALL
SWAPFILE=C:\386MAX\386MAX.swp /S=8192    ; INSTALL ==> Create an 8192 KB temporar
y DPMI swap file
NOWIN30   ; INSTALL ==> Windows 3.0 support code not needed
USE=B000-B800    ; INSTALL ==> Recover RAM in MDA region
VGASWAP              ; MAXIMIZE ==> Relocate video ROM.
USE=F500-F600        ; MAXIMIZE ==> ROMSRCH recovers  4 KB.
USE=F800-FE00        ; MAXIMIZE ==> ROMSRCH recovers 24 KB.
PRGREG=3  ; Load 386MAX.SYS into this program region
HPDAREG=80,3       ; MAXIMIZE ==> Move DPMI Host Private Data Area to region 3 for
 80 bytes
STACKREG=944,4      ; MAXIMIZE ==> Move Stack Overflow Protection to region 4 for
 944 bytes
; Previous memory manager line removed by STRIPMGR:
; DEVICE=c:\qemm\QEMM386.SYS ST:M RAM R:1

C:\386MAX>
```

FIGURE 7.7
The 386MAX.PRO file shows what MAXIMIZE has done.

The commands are organized in menus. Each menu has a name: To see the commands in a menu, point the mouse at the menu's name and click or press **Alt** and the first letter of the menu name.

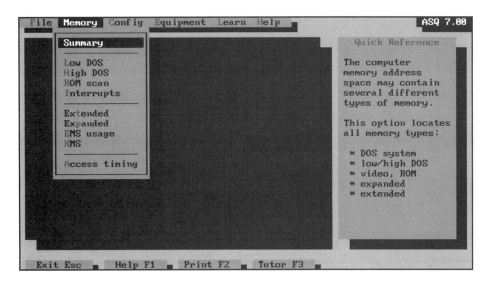

FIGURE 7.8
ASQ's main menus for analyzing your PC.

▼ *File* lets you save or load files with system analysis information.

▼ *Memory* is the most important menu here, as explained later.

▼ *Config* lets you view configuration files such as **CONFIG.SYS**.

▼ *Equipment* details the video, drives, and BIOS.

▼ *Learn* is full of tutorials on PC hardware—including memory.

▼ *Help* has help information on using ASQ.

Also, you can always press:

F1 for help

F2 to print

F3 for a tutorial on what you're viewing

Esc to quit **ASQ**

To choose commands from any one menu, click on it with the mouse or press the highlighted letter of the command name. When you do, the command will do its work. For example, the Memory menu's **Summary** command will give you a display similar to that of Figure 7.9.

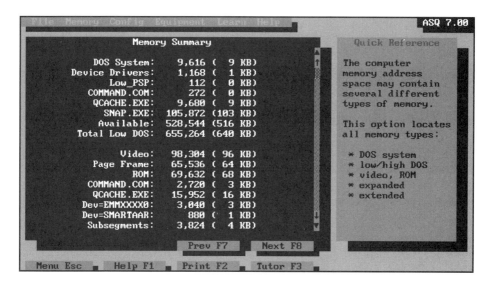

FIGURE 7.9
Memory Summary from ASQ.

To see more memory reports, you can choose them from the Memory menu (press **Esc** to get rid of the Summary and then choose a new command) or press **F8** to see the next report in order. **Low-DOS** is conventional memory; **High-DOS** is upper memory; **ROM-scan** tells you where the ROMs are in memory; **Extended** and **XMS** tell you about extended memory; **Expanded** and **EMS** tell you about expanded memory; and **Access timing** tests memory speed.

Figures 7.10 and 7.11 show the Low-DOS and High-DOS reports. Figure 7.12 shows the ROM-scan report. Figure 7.13 shows an example XMS report, and Figure 7.14 shows the memory access timing report. Figure 7.15 shows what a tutorial is like, this example telling about the access timing of Figure 7.14.

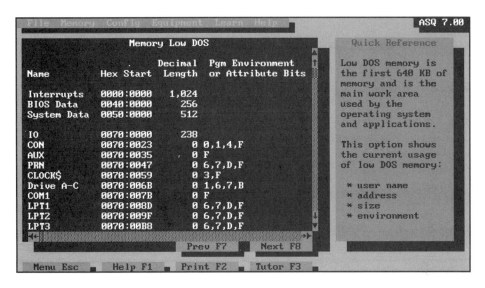

FIGURE 7.10
Low-DOS report from ASQ.

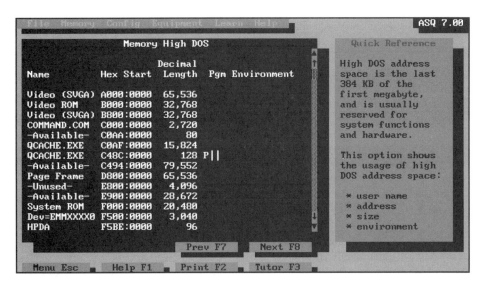

FIGURE 7.11
High-DOS report from ASQ.

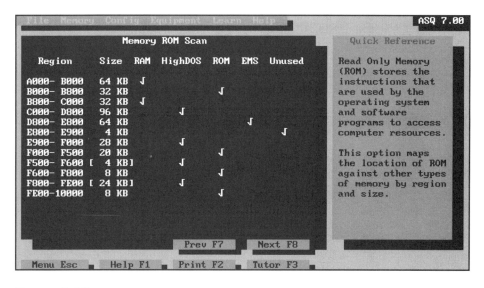

FIGURE 7.12
ROM-scan report from ASQ.

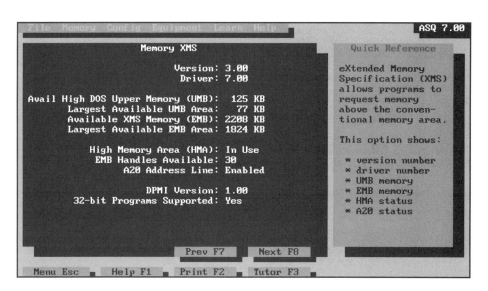

FIGURE 7.13
XMS report from ASQ.

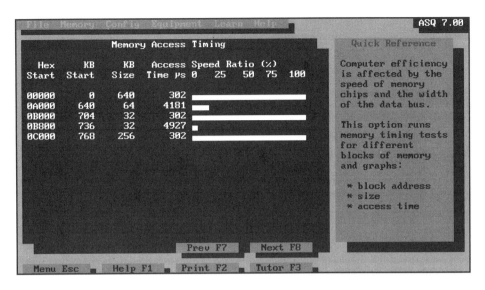

FIGURE 7.14

Access timing report from ASQ.

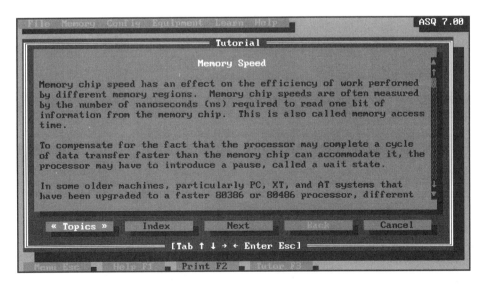

FIGURE 7.15

Tutorial example on access timing.

ASQ's Config menu lets you view important configuration files, including the obvious **CONFIG.SYS** and **AUTOEXEC.BAT** but also lesser-known files such as **SYSTEM.INI** for Windows (as shown in Figure 7.16) and files detailing your **386MAX** installation such as:

▼ **MAX PROfile**, which tells what **386MAX** has done

▼ **ExtraDOS PRO**, which tells what the utility **ExtraDOS** has done to relocate DOS resources

▼ **Qualitas**, which tells which parts of **386MAX** are at work (as shown in Figure 7.17)

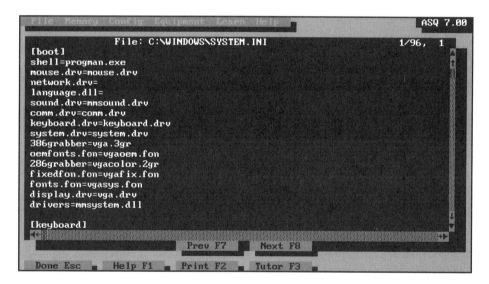

FIGURE 7.16

SYSTEM.INI example file shown in ASQ's Config menu.

You can also see some of these reports in the MAX shell.

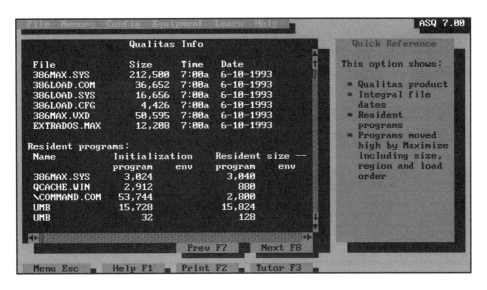

FIGURE 7.17

The Qualitas command in ASQ's Config menu tells you what parts of 386MAX are at work.

MAX—the 386MAX Shell

386MAX comes with a *shell* program that puts all of its various utilities under a single set of menus. This menu looks a lot like ASQ, as you can see in Figure 7.18. Here you can not only view the Configuration files but also edit them—under the File menu. In the ASQ menu you can get at the basic Memory, Configuration, and Equipment summaries from ASQ, or start ASQ itself. In the Maximize menu you can start that utility in Full or Quick modes. In the Info menu you can get an Overview of the 386MAX setup, as shown in Figure 7.19, and you can get details on resident programs (Figure 7.20), device drivers (Figure 7.21), how large those residents and drivers are when loaded into a UMB (Figure 7.22), and more.

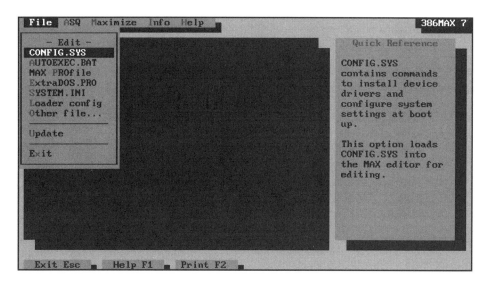

FIGURE 7.18
MAX—the 386MAX shell.

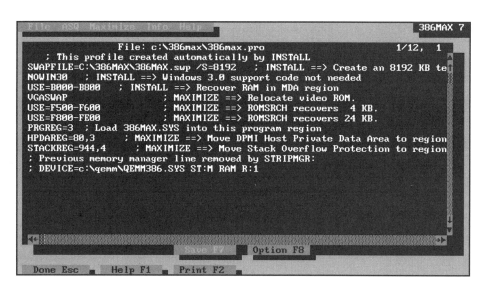

FIGURE 7.19
Overview of the 386MAX setup from the MAX shell.

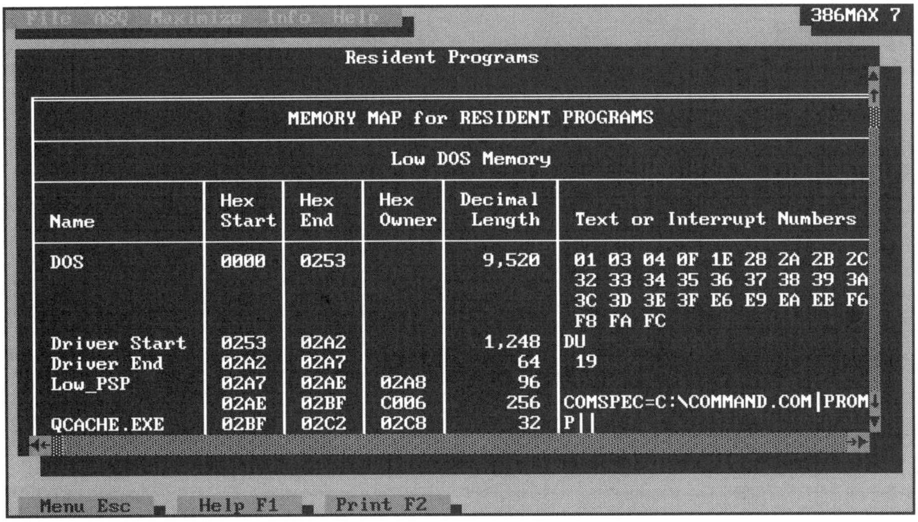

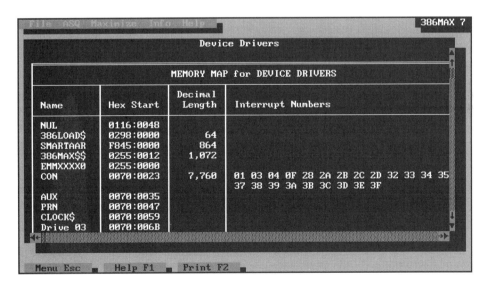

FIGURE 7.20

Resident program details from the MAX shell.

FIGURE 7.21

Device driver details from the MAX shell.

```
File  ASQ  Maximize  Info  Help                           386MAX 7
                          Load Sizes

        RESIDENT PROGRAM MEMORY SUMMARY

                   Size Parameters    Allow
                                      Flex
  Device or                          Frame?  Suggested Action
  Program Name    Initial   Resident

  386MAX.SYS        3,024     3,024    No    No SIZE parameter needed
  QCACHE.WIN        2,912       864    Yes   No SIZE parameter needed
  \COMMAND.COM     53,744     2,784    No    Continue with SIZE=53744
  UMB              15,728    15,808    No    No SIZE parameter needed
  UMB                  32       112    No    No SIZE parameter needed

  All programs/environments fit        Prog/env in use        22,
  into high DOS memory                 Available             132,

  Menu Esc      Help F1      Print F2
```

FIGURE 7.22
Loading size of drivers and memory-residents from the MAX shell.

If at any time you want to know what you're doing in MAX, read the quick reference on the right or press **F1**. If you want to print something you see on screen, press **F2**.

RAMExam

With the latest **386MAX** you get **RAMExam**. This program is a limited version of the new Qualitas **Memory Tester** program, which you could buy separately. It will test the memory chips in your PC. Not only will it find broken chips—where an address here or there has already failed—but it will also find unstable chips— with parts that are about to or could soon fail. There's no way to do this with DOS or with most other system analysis utilities that come with memory managers.

To install **RAMExam**, put its disk (for now its on a separate disk) into the drive and type:

```
rsetup
```

Its files will copy to your hard disk. You can set **RAMExam** to run every time you start your PC, at least in a quick version, by answering **Yes** to that question when it appears on the screen. Running **RAMExam** will add several seconds to startup time. Then, you can tell **RAMExam** to run automatically every day, week, or month, as shown in Figure 7.23.

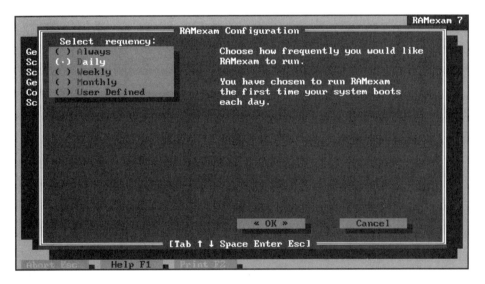

FIGURE 7.23
RAMExam setup for automatic, interval testing.

After installation, you can also run **RAMExam** at any time by changing to its directory and typing:

```
ramexam
```

You'll be asked if you want Quick (5 seconds on my 486 with 4M) or Full testing (about 10 minutes on my system). As testing runs, you'll see how much time has elapsed and how much longer **RAMExam** thinks it will run.

Press **Esc** twice to stop the Full testing.

Press **Alt+Tab** and you'll see more detailed choices for testing, such as for which faults. Figure 7.24 shows an example after some testing.

```
    Qualitas RAMexam          Choose the number      Stuck-At Faults      [   0]
    Version 7.01              of times to run        Transition Faults    [   0]
      (c) 1988-93             each test or C          Linked Inversion     [   0]
   All rights reserved.       to run a test          Unlinked Inversion   [   0]
                              continuously.          Linked Idempotent    [   1]
    Press F1 for Help         Press Ctl-Enter        Unlinked Idempotent [   1]
    Press Esc to Quit         to run test once.            START


 Memory To Test              Status  Elapsed  0:00:00      Estimated  0:00:00
                          │  Wr 0s                         239 K to     640 K
       0 K-    239 K   239   Rd 0s/Wr 1s                   239 K to     640 K
     239 K-    640 K   401   Rd 1s/Wr 0s                   239 K to     640 K
     640 K-   1876 K  1236   Rd 0s/Wr 1s                   640 K to     239 K
    1876 K-   3632 K  1756   Rd 1s/Wr 0s                   640 K to     239 K
    3632 K-   4096 K   464   Rd 0s                          640 K to     239 K
               Total  2157   Wr 0s                         239 K to     640 K
                             Rd 0s/Wr 1s                   239 K to     640 K
                             Rd 1s/Wr 0s                   239 K to     640 K
   Gray = in use/not tested  Rd 0s/Wr 1s                   640 K to     239 K
                          │  Elapsed time   0:00:03

 Alt-TAB for basic display              Press H to display hexadecimal addresses
```

FIGURE 7.24
Detailed choices in RAMExam.

RAMExam has a special utility called **MAKEBOOT** that will help you make a boot floppy disk. Just put a disk you don't mind erasing into the A: drive and then type:

```
makeboot a: c:
```

You want to to this because **RAMExam** only tests RAM not in use—RAM used for drivers and TSRs is not tested.

What's in 386MAX

386MAX has the **ASQ** and **Memory Tester** utilities you read about previously. These utilities analyze what's in your PC so that **386MAX** can best manage memory.

Its ROMsearch feature finds all BIOS functions that aren't being used and eliminates them—leaving more high memory free. Another feature, the MAX shell, lets you get at all **386MAX** features. The **386LOAD.SYS** driver manages extended and expanded memory, while the **386LOAD.COM** utility can load memory-residents and drivers into UMBs. ExtraDOS loads DOS resources into UMBs.

The **MAXIMIZE** utility compares the thousands or even millions of ways of managing memory to find the best for your particular combination of software and hardware. Then, it implements that scheme automatically. This utility can even work with embedded batch files in **AUTOEXEC.BAT** and DOS 6 multiconfigurations.

VGAswap steals video memory, and relocates the video BIOS in the process, to get at as much video memory as possible. In addition, DOSMAX for Windows helps free even more memory for DOS sessions in Windows than would be open in plain DOS. WinSmart grabs 24K of high memory for DOS use until Windows needs it and then gives it back. DOS 6 just leaves that memory always set aside for Windows.

The FlexFrame technology lets programs use the page frame area during installation, without eliminating the page frame. The ROM caching feature copies ROM software into faster RAM for better performance. The PIF editor makes creating and changing PIF files for running DOS programs inside Windows easier.

386MAX is currently the only manager that supports DOS 6 multiconfiguration.

The QCache disk cache is optimized to work with Windows and is commonly thought to offer better performance than SMARTDrive. **386MAX** supports both VCPI and DPMI for sharing memory among DOS Extender programs.

386MAX and Windows

386MAX has several features to attune it to working with Windows.

First, the DOSMAX for Windows comes in two flavors: Full Screen and Windows. If you double-click on its icon, as shown in Figure 7.25, you'll open a DOS session under Windows with more memory—as much as 736K—than you could get via the normal DOS icon.

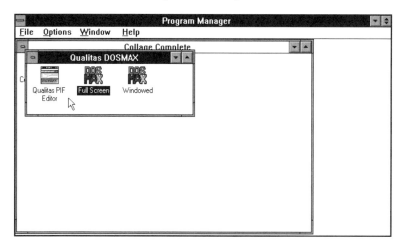

FIGURE 7.25
Double-click on either DOSMAX icon to open a DOS session with more memory under Windows.

WinSmart prevents DOS 6 from wasting 24K of high memory set aside for Windows, then gives that memory back to Windows when it needs it.

The Virtual High DOS and TSR Instancing features let you run memory-residents inside Windows that wouldn't normally survive there.

Finally, the PIF editor makes creating and changing PIF files for running DOS programs inside Windows easier. Figure 7.26 shows what this looks like.

386MAX and 8088, 8086, and 80286 PCs

386MAX used to include the MOVE'EM utility. MOVE'EM could manage memory in 8088, 8086, and 80286 PCs with some expanded memory. It no longer does this, although you can get this product separately, as detailed in Chapter 10.

Now on to... Chapter 8 describes Netroom, another popular memory manager.

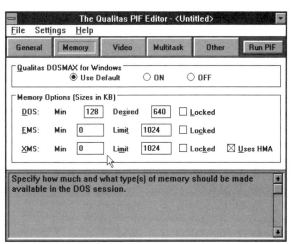

FIGURE 7.26
The PIF editor.

CHAPTER

8

MEMORY MANAGEMENT

Manage Memory with the Netroom Utility

Netroom can do more to manage memory than DOS can alone. Although the name evokes networking, this utility is actually for any PC. It is true, however, that networks are major RAM-crammers. They come with drivers and shells that can occupy lots of conventional memory. Therefore, those responsible for setting up networking-PCs would be especially hungry for memory managers such as **Netroom** that can:

▼   manage expanded memory

▼   manage extended memory

▼   create UMBs

▼   load drivers and memory-residents into UMBs

▼   put DOS resources into UMBs

▼   put DOS into the HMA

▼   analyze your PC's memory use

▼   replace an old BIOS with a newer one (on 386s)

Netroom Version 3 is the newest version (at press time). You can get this utility from:

Helix Software Company
47-09 30th Street
Long Island City, NY 11101
(718) 392-3100
(718) 392-4212 fax
(718) 392-3735 voice tech support
(718) 392-4054 computer bulletin board support

Besides the voice and fax tech support, Helix offers its own bulletin board as listed above and maintains a 24-hour forum for answering questions on the CompuServe on-line service.

Helix Software made the MemMaker utility that comes with DOS6.

Netroom works on pretty much any PC: 8088, 8086, 80286, 386sx, 386, 486sx, 486, Pentium, and compatibles. It is compatible with the following operating systems: MS-DOS, PC-DOS, and DR DOS (or Novell DOS—the new name). It needs some expanded or extended memory to work. Expanded memory can meet the older EMS 3.2 or EMS specifications or the new EMS 4.0 specification. On 8088, 8086, and 80286 PCs, **Netroom** needs EMS 4.0 hardware. The *cloaking* features need a 386, 486, or Pentium PC. This lets you squeeze even more into upper memory by using ROM addresses while those ROMs aren't being called upon.

Installing Netroom

Netroom comes on a single floppy disk. To install it you simply start your PC, insert the floppy disk, and type:

```
a:setup
```

Then follow the instructions on the screen. (The serial number is on the 5.25″ floppy disk.) You can choose the various options with the mouse or by pressing keys. You press the **Tab** key to move from one option to the next. Press **Enter** to accept the option as is.

Then you'll see the files copied to the hard disk. The screen will tell you when that's done. The **Netroom** commands will be in your **CONFIG.SYS** and **AUTOEXEC.BAT** files. In case you need to un-install **Netroom** later, your original **CONFIG.SYS** and **AUTOEXEC.BAT** files have been saved under the names **CONFIG.B4** and **AUTOEXEC.B4**.

If you have the **STACKS** command of DOS in your **CONFIG.SYS** file, you'll next be asked if you want to install the **STACKS.EXE** utility program that comes with **Netroom**. This is faster and smaller than DOS's own **STACKS** command. It is also safer to use if you choose one of **Netroom**'s cloaked utilities. Go ahead and say **OK**, unless you have some specific reason to avoid **STACKS.EXE**. You can always install it later—you'll even be asked automatically if you installed a cloaked utility.

Finally, you'll get a chance to read the **README.TXT** file. It contains the latest notes on troubles you might have using **Netroom** with some specific hardware and software. Scroll through this file with the **Down Arrow** key to see if something you're using shows up on the list. Choose **OK** when you're through.

The last step of installation offers you a choice of: **Help**, **Exit**, **Discover**, and **Customize**. **Help** just tells you how to select options and **Exit** dumps you back to the DOS prompt. **Discover** is a utility that comes with **Netroom**. It can search through your PC to see what's in it, including how much memory. **Customize** is another **Netroom** utility. It can automatically tailor **Netroom** commands to make the best use of your PC's memory.

Discover

The **Discover** utility that comes with **Netroom** can tell you all about your PC. From it you can learn not just what memory is in your PC and how it is used, but also what processor you have, what disk drives you have, and more.

To start **Discover** from the **Netroom** directory, type:

```
discover
```

You'll see the main Discover screen as shown in Figure 8.1.

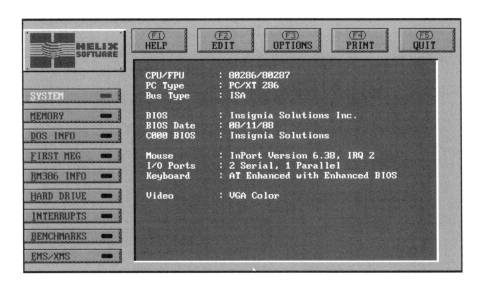

FIGURE 8.1
The Discover utility program.

As you can see, the function keys are as follows:

F1 to get help information

F2 to edit a file (such as **CONFIG.SYS** or **AUTOEXEC.BAT**)

F3 to see options (such as how to print and how to show the cursor)

F4 to print any of the information categories

F5 to quit **Discover** and get back to DOS

Down the left side of the screen you'll see the information categories that **Discover** can report on. Choose any one by **Tab**bing to it and pressing **Enter** or by pressing **Alt** plus the first letter of the category name.

System tells you about the *processor, bus, BIOS* (Basic Input Output System software inside the computer), *ports, keyboard,* and *video adapter* type.

Memory summarizes how much *conventional* and *upper* memory are available in the PC. Then it lists the programs that use conventional memory—which is vital information for finding drivers and memory-residents that you can relocate to upper memory. Figure 8.2 shows an example. This is vital, as you know, because freeing conventional memory is the prime goal of PC memory management.

DOS Info is also useful for memory management, as it gives details on the DOS resources in your PC—such as Files, Buffers, FCBs, and Stacks. See Figure 8.3 for an example.

First Meg is a natural place for memory managers to look. **Discover** maps the first megabyte of memory for you and shows you (as in Figure 8.4) where the Video RAM, ROMs, Page Frame for expanded memory, mapped UMBs from expanded (EMS) memory, mapped UMBs from extended (XMS) memory, and mappable conventional memory are.

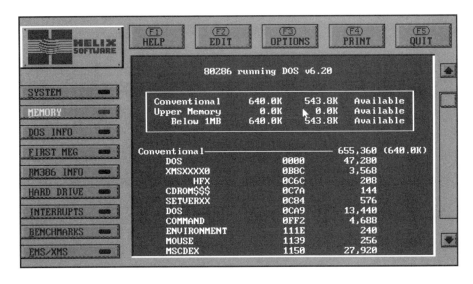

FIGURE 8.2

The Memory information from the Discover utility—showing the drivers and memory-residents in conventional memory.

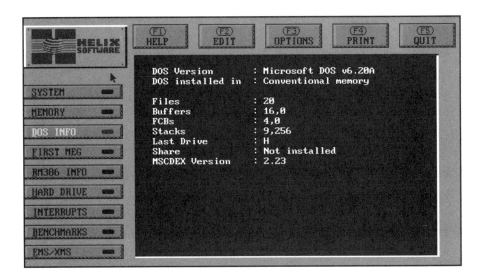

FIGURE 8.3

DOS Info in Discover tells you about DOS resources in your PC.

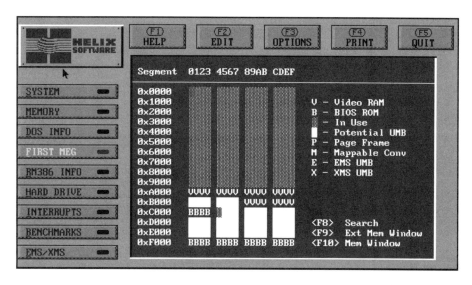

FIGURE 8.4
First Meg report from Discover.

RM386 deals with the RAM-MAN memory manager component of **Netroom**. **Hard Drive** tells about the disk drives—both floppy and hard—on the PC. **Interrupts** is for real PC experts. It lists all the addresses and uses of the places the PC keeps track of overlapping programs and peripherals. **Benchmarks** tests the speed of memory, as you can see in Figure 8.5. You may also see this as a graph, as shown in Figure 8.6.

EMS/XMS details how much expanded memory and extended memory are in your PC. The example PC in Figure 8.7 has only 3M of extended memory—and no expanded memory. The Extended half of the screen even tells you about the HMA (High Memory Area) that's part of extended memory.

When you're done with the category, press **Esc** to return to the main Discover screen. You may run **Discover** from Windows. There's even an **ICO** file to let you give **Discover** its own icon.

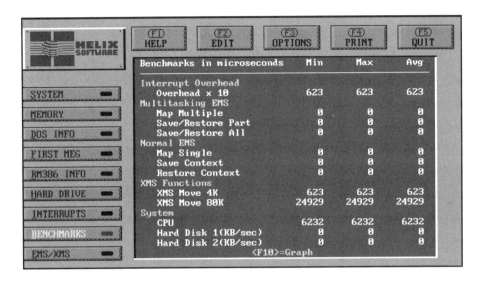

FIGURE 8.5
Benchmarks in Discover tests the speed of memory.

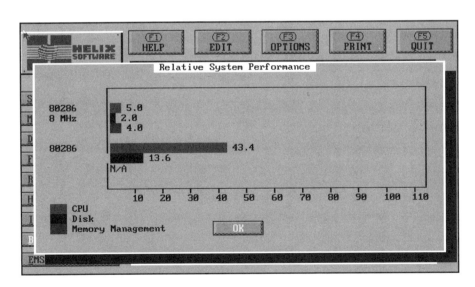

FIGURE 8.6
Benchmarks from Discover as a graphic measure of memory speed.

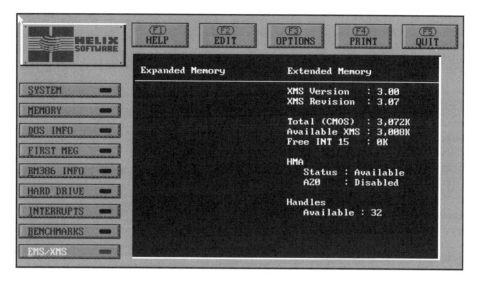

FIGURE 8.7
EMS/XMS in Discover tells how much expanded and extended memory you have.

Customize

Memory-management commands aren't enough for most people. They also need help putting those commands to use. **Customize** does that for **Netroom**. It analyzes your PC to decide the best way to apply memory management to your particular specifications, and then it adds the necessary lines to your **CONFIG.SYS** and **AUTOEXEC.BAT** files.

Start **Customize** by typing:

```
customize
```

You'll be asked if you want to make new backups of your **CONFIG** and **AUTOEXEC** files (which you should do unless you're running **Customize** to fix some **Netroom** problem). If Windows is on your

PC, you'll also get a backup of **SYSTEM.INI**. Then you must choose from three Customize approaches: **Conservative**, **Aggressive**, or **Custom**.

Conservative gives the least memory but avoids possible conflicts that could disrupt your programs or even crash your system. **Aggressive** can yield more usable memory but takes a chance on making trouble with programs and peripherals. (**Aggressive** even replaces your PC's regular BIOS with its own **Netroom** BIOS.) **Custom** is for those experts who think they can do better by choosing commands and options themselves. Press the **Spacebar** to change the setting. When you have the approach you want, press **Enter**.

If you choose **Custom**, you'll see the list of options shown in Figure 8.8.

 Always make backup copies of all your configuration files before customizing. Copy them on the hard disk with new filename extensions, perhaps using the current date, such as AUTOEXEC.330 and CONFIG.330 for March 30 files. Also, copy them to a bootable floppy disk.

If you choose **Conservative** or **Aggressive**, you'll be notified as **Customize** works through a series of possibilities, booting and rebooting your PC on the way. It will ask you a few questions, to which you can just assent by pressing **Enter**. If you have any trouble with your PC, you should choose **No** when asked if things are *OK*, and you can then have **Customize** undo its changes.

Figure 8.9 shows the typical changes made in a **CONFIG.SYS** file by **Netroom**'s aggressive approach. Figure 8.10 shows the changes to **AUTOEXEC.BAT**.

```
Customize v3.0
───────────────────────────────────────────────────────────────────

Set aside upper memory for EMS page frame?                      Yes
Create High-DOS memory in the monochrome region (B000-B7FF)?    No
Utilize Video BIOS CLOAKING?                                    Yes
Utilize System BIOS CLOAKING?                                   Yes
Utilize the BIOS area as High-DOS?                              Yes
Specify which drivers and TSRs to include during optimization?  No
Optimize upper memory for use with Windows?                     No
Relocate FILES to High-DOS memory?                              Yes
Shadow the BIOS?                                                Yes
Test the system RAM in protected mode?                          Yes
Virtualize the interrupt controller?                            Yes
Virtualize the keyboard controller?                             Yes
Buffer disk I/O locally?                                        No
Move the Extended BIOS Data Area to High-DOS memory?            Yes
Check for a PS/2 system?                                        Yes

To move to a different option, press the UP ARROW or DOWN ARROW key.
To accept all the settings and continue, press F10.

 F10=Accept All  SPACEBAR=Change Selection  F1=Help  F3=Exit
```

FIGURE 8.8

Custom setup options for Netroom.

```
C:\>type config.b4
DEVICE=HIMEM.SYS
DOS=HIGH
BUFFERS=20
FILES=20


C:\>type config.sys
DEVICE=C:\NETROOM\RM386.EXE AUTO X=B000-B7FF XMS=F800-FDFF


DEVICE=C:\NETROOM\XLOAD.SYS -O
DOS=HIGH
DOS=UMB
BUFFERS=8,0
FILES=20
LASTDRIVE=E
FCBS=4,0
STACKS=9,256
SHELL=C:\NETROOM\XLOAD.EXE -SC001 -M57021 -E C:\COMMAND.COM /E:256 /P

C:\>
```

FIGURE 8.9

CONFIG.SYS changes from Netroom's Aggressive approach.

```
C:\>type autoexec.b4
@ECHO OFF
PROMPT $p$g
PATH C:\QEMM;C:\WINDOWS;C:\DOS;
SET TEMP=C:\DOS
CD C:\COLLDOS
SNAP
CD ..
CLS


C:\>type autoexec.bat
C:\NETROOM\XLOAD.EXE -SF801 -M2864 C:\NETROOM\SETCFG.COM -F30
@ECHO OFF
PROMPT $p$g
PATH C:\WINDOWS;C:\DOS;
SET TEMP=C:\DOS
CD C:\COLLDOS
SNAP
CD ..
CLS


C:\>
```

FIGURE 8.10

AUTOEXEC.BAT changes from Netroom's Aggressive approach.

Customize comes with many options, including the very useful **Undo** option to reverse work. Just type:

        customize /undo

To see more options, type:

        customize /?

Netroom Version 3 can work with disk compression utilities such as **DoubleSpace**, **DoubleDisk**, **Stacker**, and **SuperStor**.

What's in Netroom

Netroom has a variety of utilities, commands, and options to manage memory.

The heart of **Netroom** is RAM-MAN, a memory-management driver. Another is XLOAD, which is a driver that can load other drivers and memory-residents into UMBs. DEVLOAD is one that loads drivers high from the command prompt. The **CUSTOMIZ.INF** file can hold names of drivers and memory-residents you don't want to load high. **CUSTOMIZ.STS** can tell you just how much space each could take, as shown in Figure 8.11.

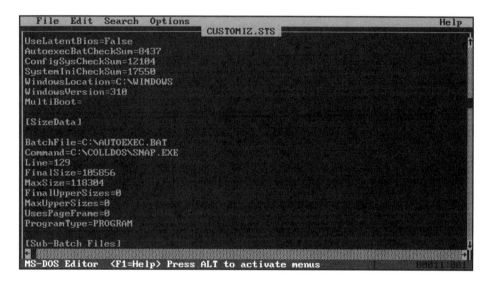

FIGURE 8.11
The CUSTOMIZ.STS file keeps track of the memory needs of drivers and memory-residents.

SETCFG can load DOS resources high. You can also use it at the command prompt to show the status of DOS resources, as shown in Figure 8.12.

STACKS.EXE replaces DOS **STACKS** and uses less memory. DOSUMB loads DOS into XMS upper memory when it won't fit into the HMA. HMALOAD loads COM files into the HMA, and NETHMA loads network software there.

```
C:\NETROOM>setcfg

SETCFG v3.00 - DOS Tables Extender
Copyright (c) 1990,91 Helix Software Company, Inc.
All rights reserved.

FILES=30
FCBS=4,0
BUFFERS=8,0

C:\NETROOM>
```

FIGURE 8.12

Type setcfg *at the DOS prompt to see the status of resources such as files and buffers.*

STRETCH steals video memory and can even do so for Windows in some circumstances. MOVEBIOS copies the Video BIOS to the monochrome region and lets you increase the size of the UMB at C000. This is only for those who can't use video cloaking, and those who can handle manual management. Cloaking is the latest, most sophisticated feature of **Netroom**.

Cloaking Memory

Cloaking is a new technology in **Netroom** Version 3. It lets 32-bit protected mode programs run under DOS and Windows. This process frees memory that would normally hold drivers, memory-residents, and BIOSs for the Video and System. Programs must be adapted to work with cloaking. The CLOAKING driver loads into 1K of conventional memory while the rest of it loads into extended memory. Its BIOS takes up only 8K of memory instead of 96K. The freed 88K can be UMBs. Also, this new BIOS improves performance for PCs with old BIOS software. And there's a virus protection feature as well and a screen accelerator, for DOS programs.

Cloaking doesn't work with Windows 3.0, only with Windows 3.1.

The **CACHECLK.EXE** disk cache utility and **DRIVECLK.EXE** RAM disk utility work with cloaking. There's a screen saver that works with cloaking as well.

 Use the **CACHECLK** and **DRIVECLK** utilities to get the most from cloaked memory.

Helix supplies an *API* (application programming interface) that software developers can use to adapt their programs for cloaking.

Netroom and Networks

Netroom may be the best memory manager for networked PCs. Not only does it have the standard abilities to load drivers and memory-residents high, but it also has a special **NETSWAP** utility to create *virtual machines*. **NETSWAP** is something like the **Stealth** of **QEMM** or the **Cloaking** of **386MAX**. It lets you create batches of drivers and memory-residents that load as groups into high memory, which makes working with network drivers such as IPX, NETX, and NETBIOS easy. Unfortunately, this doesn't work with Windows.

Netroom on 8088, 8086, and 80286 PCs

Netroom doesn't demand a 386 PC, although it certainly prefers one. It can manage memory on 8088, 8086, and 80286 PCs if they have EMS 4.0 expanded memory hardware, which could be an EMS 4.0 memory board or just a chipset—such as the NEAT chips—that can map memory as EMS 4.0 does.

Netroom and Windows

To work with Windows 3.1, **Netroom** makes these lines in the **SYSTEM.INI** file, in its [386Enh] section:

```
SYSTEMROMBREAKPOINT=False
USERROMFONT=False
DUALDISPLAY=True
```

and if you're not using expanded memory with Windows then use the following line:

```
NOEMMDRIVER=True
```

If you have trouble with Windows, there are tips in the manual to help you. (And you get a screen saver for Windows on the supplemental disk that you get when registering **Netroom**.)

A special **WINMEM** utility that gives each DOS session under Windows its own upper memory area so that each DOS session can have its own memory-residents and drivers. There are memory managers dedicated to 286 and older PCs. The next chapter tells about them.

CHAPTER

9

MEMORY MANAGEMENT

Manage Memory
on 8088/8086/80286 PCs with
the QRAM or MOVE'EM Utilities

The processor in your computer teams up with your operating system software to determine memory management. The 80386 chip added advanced memory management circuits to the PC design. These circuits are also in the 80486 and Pentium chips of the latest PCs. These circuits are vital to using **QEMM-386** and **386MAX** (notice the number is even in their titles) and even DOS's own **EMM386** utility.

But you can manage memory even on PCs without the 386, 486, or Pentium. These are the PCs built with the 8088, 8086, or 80286 chips. In other words, the PC and AT generations. None of these machines can reasonably run Windows 3.0 or 3.1. Nor can they run OS/2, Windows NT, or UNIX. You're stuck with DOS, or a direct DOS competitor (see Chapter 4 for examples of competitors). So all suffer from the DOS 640K barrier. The 8088 and 8086 PCs cannot use extended memory, but the 80286 PCs can.

8088, 8086, and 80286 PCs can have expanded memory. And as you'll see shortly, expanded memory is the key to memory management here. Without it, your memory management choices are far more limited. With expanded memory hardware you have a lot more management power.

On 8088 and 8086 PC compatibles you can at least:

▼   Choose a DOS version that uses little memory.

▼   Choose programs that use little memory.

▼   Limit the use of memory-residents (and choose small ones).

▼   Limit the use of drivers (and choose small ones).

On 286 PC compatibles you can also:

▼   Move some drivers or part of DOS into the HMA (see Chapter 1 for an explanation).

▼   Use extended memory for RAM disks and disk caches.

▼   Use programs with built-in DOS extenders—that use extended memory (see Chapter 1 for an explanation).

And that's about it. However, you can also add expanded memory hardware such as an EMS memory board (version 4.0 is best) or a memory-managing chipset to the 8088, 8086, or 80286 PC compatible. In addition, you can also load memory-residents into upper memory and load drivers into upper memory.

The chips around the microprocessor are called a *chipset*. These link the microprocessor to the memory chips, the bus, and other parts of the PC. A few chipsets—such as the NEAT or LEAP or AT/386 chipsets from the Chips & Technologies company—have built-in circuits that give them some of the abilities of an EMS expanded memory board. Your PC's manual should tell you if it has such hardware.

There are also some specialized processor replacements you can add to an 8088, 8086, or 80286 PC to give it more memory management power. Sometimes these processor replacements are 386 chips in the form of either a tiny board that plugs into the original processor socket or replaces the entire motherboard. Sometimes they are memory management circuits such as the specialized chipsets would have. These chipsets are typically on small boards: You remove the processor from the PC, plug it into the small board, plug that board into the PC's processor socket, and then add memory management software. This much trouble was once worthwhile, when new 386 PCs cost many thousands of dollars. Now that 386s are available for less than $800—including hard drive, wider bus, newer slots for expansion, and so on—it is rarely a good investment. If you have the money for such a specialized upgrade, you're probably better off just moving to the 386 or 486 generation.

If you have the expanded memory hardware in your PC, you'll need memory management software to make it run.

To use the HMA and extended memory, you can use the **HIMEM.SYS**, **VDISK**, and **RAMDRIVE** utilities that come with DOS.

Get the latest version of DOS—DOS 6, 6.1, or 6.2—for better memory management, no matter what generation PC you have.

To free more conventional memory by loading drivers and memory-residents into upper memory, you'll need more than DOS provides. You'll need a program such as **Netroom** (which alone among the

386 programs mentioned before in this book is also good for 8088, 8086, and 80286 PCs), **QRAM** (the 8088/8086/80286 alternative from QEMM maker Quarterdeck), or **MOVE'EM** (the 8088/8086/80286 alternative from 386MAX maker Qualitas).

Netroom

Netroom will let you load drivers and memory-residents into upper memory. For details, see its description in Chapter 8.

MOVE'EM

MOVE'EM is made for 8088, 8086, and 80286 PCs. It used to come free with **386MAX**—packed in the same box and on the same disk. In fact, you could install it with the **386MAX** installation.

MOVE'EM does not come with the latest version of **386MAX 7.0**: you'll need to order **MOVE'EM** separately. You must have LIM EMS 4.0-compatible hardware to use it, such as an EMS 4.0 expanded memory board or an EMS compatible chipset.

To put **MOVE'EM** to work automatically, you can run the **MAXI-MIZE** utility, just as with **386MAX**. This utility will examine your PC, especially its drivers and memory-residents, and see how many will load into UMBs. **MAXIMIZE** options that demand a 386 or later processor will not be available when you have less in your PC.

MOVE'EM's first step is to make sure that the **HIMEM.SYS** extended memory manager is loaded. Then, it checks for the EMM expanded memory manager that came with your expanded memory hardware. Next, it loads its own **MOVE'EM.SYS** memory manager. It creates UMBs and puts the necessary lines into **CONFIG.SYS** and **AUTOEXEC.BAT** to load drivers and memory-residents into upper memory.

If you use **MOVE'EM** on an 8088 or 8086 PC, make sure that the **HIMEM.SYS** line is not in **CONFIG.SYS**. Also remove the **DOS=HIGH** command. Neither works on these PCs.

If you want to fine-tune the memory management, **MOVE'EM** obliges with an editor for the **CONFIG.SYS** and **AUTOEXEC.BAT** files. It also comes with the Qcache disk cache replacement for SMARTDrive and a RAM disk utility called **386DISK**.

QRAM

While **QEMM-386** is for 386, 486, and Pentium PCs, Quarterdeck's **QRAM** (pronounced *cram*) is for the older 8088, 8086, and 80286 PCs. To do much good, it needs expanded memory hardware, as already explained.

QRAM installs to your hard disk just as **QEMM** would (as detailed in Chapter 6). Then you run the **OPTIMIZE** utility, again as with **QEMM**, and follow the on-screen instructions to analyze your PC automatically and put the best memory management commands into your **CONFIG.SYS** and **AUTOEXEC.BAT** files. During this process your PC will reboot several times. The **QEXT.SYS** extended memory manager will load on 286 PCs, although you may want to keep the **HIMEM.SYS** driver instead for best compatibility with DOS. Try **QEXT.SYS** only if you're a **DESQview** user (a multitasking utility). Then, your EMM driver will load, followed by the **QRAM.SYS** expanded memory manager. The resulting configuration will use the **LOADHI** commands to load drivers and memory-residents into UMBs.

If you see a *Nothing to do* comment from **QRAM**, you probably don't have your LIM EMS 4.0 memory or EMS card configured properly.

QRAM supports backfilling—which was discussed in Chapter 1—of conventional memory for better multitasking. If you decide you can improve on the optimized configuration, you're free to work with the loading high commands, using most of the same options as with **QEMM**. **QRAM** comes with the **Manifest** system analysis utility so that you can get a detailed look at what's in memory. **QRAM** also comes with other utilities such as a disk cache and a RAM disk.

Now on to entirely different hardware and software, with equally different memory management: The Apple Macintosh.

CHAPTER
10

MEMORY MANAGEMENT

Macintosh Memory

The Mac has established itself as the next-most-popular fundamental design, after the PC. Well, it is way behind the PC, really, with perhaps only 10-20% as many Macs around as PC compatibles. Until recently, the Mac was more expensive than the PC and could be bought from only one company: Apple. Now they cost about the same as PCs, although perhaps they are still a little more expensive. They aren't yet available from other companies, but that is changing too as IBM and Apple have agreed to cooperate on a new generation of processor chips called the PowerPCs that will be the heart of IBM's new PCs and Apple's new Macs.

The real difference between Macs and PCs is in the operating system. PCs use DOS or a DOS compatible or the Windows operating system. That's what you've seen throughout this book. A few use

OS/2, Windows, NT or Unix operating systems without the DOS restrictions on memory management. The Macintosh has its own operating system, with its own approach to memory. Again, it doesn't have the same restrictions as DOS. In fact, although it uses memory for the same tasks—holding programs and documents—it does not have nearly as many restrictions and complications as DOS. So its memory management is important, but not as desperately important, and it is handled very differently.

The Macintosh operating system, incidentally, introduced personal computers to the menus, mouse, and icons now so well-known from Windows. Figure 10.1 shows a typical Mac interface. The Mac was more expensive for years in part because it had a deserved reputation of being easier to use and easier to learn than the PC. Many people still think it is easier, although fewer people hold this belief now that Windows brings much of the Macs' approach to PCs.

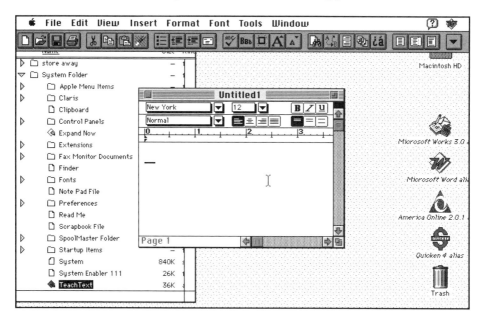

FIGURE 10.1
The menus and icons of the Macintosh interface.

Mac Memory Has No 640K Barrier

The first Macintosh in 1984 was planned to have only 64K of memory. That was more than the typical 48K personal computer of the day. But by the time it shipped, the Mac memory had doubled to 128K. This amount of memory was still barely enough to run a program, and only very short documents would fit. Soon the Fat Mac shipped with 512K RAM, and after that the Mac Plus was available with a full 1M. Today's typical Mac has 4M and many carry 8M.

The Macintosh operating system doesn't have a wall like the 640K barrier in DOS. Nor has the Macintosh design stepped through the large number of chips that the PC design has jumped through, moving from processors that could address only 1M to processors that could address thousands of times that much. There has been a family of processors—the 68000 family—in the Macs. But from the 68000 to 68020 to 68030 to 68040, there hasn't been as sudden a leap to better memory-handling circuits as in the 8088 family of PCs. One step is apparent, though. When the Macs stepped up to the 68020 some had the option of adding a separate Paged Memory Management Unit (PMMU) chip. This chip permitted virtual memory in the Mac, as explained later. The 68030 and later chips had built-in PMMU abilities, and so they didn't need this chip added separately.

The system software itself does take up memory, each program takes memory, and many programs need more memory when working on large documents. But the Mac has no special portion of memory for you to worry about conserving. Instead, you just try to conserve all memory as practical so that you can fit more programs, larger programs, or larger documents into the system.

Different Macintosh designs do limit how much memory you can install and use, sometimes without Apple even knowing that it is doing so. The number of slots for plugging in memory, the capacity of the slots, and most importantly the tinkering with system software controls on memory can set limits. Almost any Mac built within the last several years will fit and use at least 8M. Some can't take any more or won't understand it if you do add it. Some of the most recent Macs can hold and use as much as 256M of memory.

Quick Rules of Thumb

A few quick hints about conserving Macintosh memory are summarized here.

- ▼ Know how much memory is in your Mac.
- ▼ Install more memory—at least 4M, and 8M if possible. (And make sure that your Mac can use it, turning on 32-bit addressing if necessary.)
- ▼ Defragment memory.
- ▼ Eliminate any utilities, *INITs* (initialization programs), extensions, and fonts you don't absolutely need.
- ▼ Decrease the disk cache size.
- ▼ Use virtual memory (if it's available on your Mac).
- ▼ Run only one program at a time.
- ▼ Set programs to use minimum memory.
- ▼ Set the Finder to minimum memory (in System 6).
- ▼ Use System 6 if you can (even though you lose the System 7 features).

System 6 and System 7

As the Macintosh operating system evolved over the years, it was given progressive version numbers. The only two systems you're still likely to find on Macs are System 6 and System 7. Actually, more precisely, the latest (depending a little on which Mac model you're looking at) are System 6.0.7 and System 7.1 and System 7 Pro. But basically it breaks down to Systems 6 and 7.

They don't look much different. Beginners will notice only a few new icons on-screen. But underneath, System 7 contains many improvements over System 6. And some of those improvements are in memory management. Yet, System 6 uses less memory than System 7, while System 7 has some new features that can make it easier to use and more powerful.

If you're looking to use the least possible Mac memory, use System 6, if you can. Some of the latest Macs must use System 7.1. If you want more power and can spare the memory, use System 7.1.

Don't use just System 7; upgrade to System 7.1, which has built-in features, which you can't see, to use memory more efficiently.

But how much memory the system software uses also depends on what you put into it. The most elemental system can have added fonts, extensions, control panels (from INITs—"initializing" utility programs), and options (such as the adjustable-size disk cache or RAM disk). For example:

System 7	needs 1264K	total 1264
but these extras require more memory:		
256K cache	adds 256K	total 1520K
virtual memory	adds 380K	total 1900K
AppleTalk for laser printing	adds 107K	total 2007K
file sharing	adds 264K	total 2271K
popular utilities such as:		
QuicKeys for macros and Adobe Type Manager for fonts	add about 500K	total 2771K

So a System 7 Mac can eat nearly 3M before starting a single application program. And System 7 is popular in part because it can run more than one program at a time. That's why 4M is a minimum for System 7 but 8M is more practical.

System 7 Pro is the latest operating system, with yet more features, power, and memory hunger. Don't bother with it unless you have 5M and are a constant and expert Macintosh user. It isn't yet standard and tested enough for the average user.

Adding Memory

Your Mac can make good use of 4M to 8M of memory. If you have less than 8M and want to run the Mac faster and more smoothly, consider installing more memory. For many Macs this isn't too hard or too expensive—adding 4M to the average Mac takes 20 minutes or so and $160.

 The type, price, and installation of memory differs greatly from one Mac model to another, with some Macs requiring that you not install the memory yourself.

You can follow the same general rules for adding memory to Macs as are explained in Chapter 3 on adding memory to PCs. Make sure that you read the manual for your particular Mac model, because the chips and boards differ greatly from one Mac model to the next.

Most Macs use SIMMs, but many older models use the 36-pin SIMM, while the latest models (since the LCIII and including Centris and Quadra models) use 72-pin SIMMs. See Figure 10.2. You can still find the older SIMMs. The good news on the newer 72-pin SIMMs is that they're the same as PCs use. That means you'll find them in more places and at lower prices.

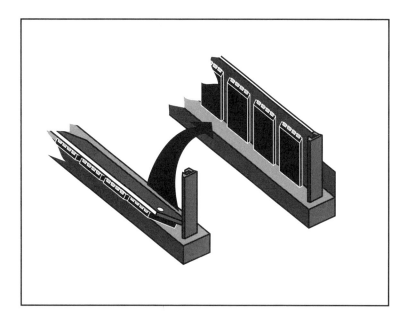

FIGURE 10.2
SIMM memories for Macs.

The move to standard SIMMs also makes installation easier. The older 36-pin SIMMs snapped into slots, and those slots were often organized into *banks* of four slots. Each slot in a bank on such an older Mac needed SIMMs of the same capacity. You couldn't put a 1M SIMM and a 4M SIMM into two slots of the same bank. If you bought new SIMMs with higher capacities, you needed to take out the older, smaller SIMMs. Sometimes you could put them into another bank on the Mac; other times you just lost them, perhaps donating them to a school or other nonprofit organization. 72-pin SIMMs don't worry about slots and banks. You can mix and match them.

Some Special Cases

Mac II and IIx owners need special SIMMs that have nine memory chips per SIMM instead of eight. Also, the Mac II and IIx have two banks. Bank A must have smaller capacity SIMMs than bank B, unless the system has been upgraded to the SuperDrive floppy-disk drive for high-density disks.

The IIci has two banks. Slots in each bank must have the same capacity SIMMs, although the two banks can have different capacities. But if you use the built-in video of the IIci and have different capacities in the two banks, bank B must have higher capacity.

On the Quadra 700 or 800, you must remove some internal components to get at the RAM chips.

PowerBooks use memory all their own, and you must have a dealer install it.

To open an older Mac such as a Plus, SE, or black-and-white Classic, you'll need an $8 toolkit available from most Macintosh memory sources.

When you do buy the chips, remember to use the stated speed or faster (150 ns on slow Macs, 120 ns on IIs, 80 ns on IIci, for example). Buying faster chips than are required won't speed your Mac—it's just a waste of money. (Faster chips cost more.)

Don't count on taking your RAM from one Mac and moving it to another. There are too many differences in Mac models.

If you're not comfortable with installation, buy your chips at a computer store that installs and tests them. This costs about twice as much as buying the chips directly from a chip company and installing them yourself.

You'll know you've installed the memory correctly if you hear the familiar power-on chord when you start your Mac. If you instead hear four notes in sequence, then you may have one or more SIMMs that aren't fully in place or are defective.

Measure Your Macintosh Memory

Some utilities analyze your Mac in detail, but you can learn quite a bit about what memory is in your Mac and what it is doing by just pulling down the Apple menu. (Make sure that you're out of any programs and to the Finder. Then, select the Finder from the menu on the far right, move the mouse cursor to the Apple in the upper left corner, and click the mouse button.) On a System 6 Mac you'll see

> *About the Finder...*

On a System 7 Mac you'll see

> *About this Macintosh...*

as shown in Figure 10.3.

FIGURE 10.3
Pull down the Apple menu to see About this Macintosh.

You'll see a small window that graphically details the memory use in your Mac, as shown in Figure 10.4. There's a lot of information here. At top left you see the Macintosh model that you're using (a PowerBook 180 here). At top right you see the system software that you're using (System 7.1 here). Then, there's a listing of built-in memory (how much RAM chip memory, 4096K or 4M here) total memory (how much RAM and virtual memory added together— read about virtual memory later in this chapter—8192K or 8M here). And beside that is a note that 8192K or 8M of the hard disk is being used as RAM—another reference to virtual memory. Finally, you can check the size of the largest unused block of memory—the largest, continuous, "contiguous" stretch of memory that isn't in use. This is the most important piece of information on the About This Macintosh window because any new programs that start want this block. If it isn't large enough for them, they won't start.

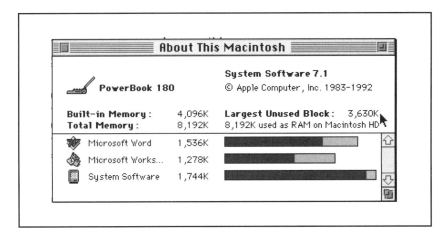

FIGURE 10.4
The About This Macintosh window tells about memory use.

The bottom part of the About This Macintosh window tells you how much memory has been given to each program that's running. The memory allocated for each program to use that is not available to other programs is that program's *partition*. You'll see the program icon, program name, numeric partition size, and graph of partition size. Notice that inside most graphics of partition size is a darker area. Your Mac will tell you what this is if you turn on Balloon Help (under the Question Mark help menu, as shown in Figure 10.5) and then move the mouse cursor to the About This Macintosh window (as shown in Figure 10.6). The partition is the full gray area, but the program is currently using only the black area. You may even see this change, fluctuating up and down, as you watch.

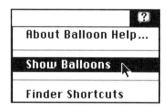

FIGURE 10.5
Turn on Balloon Help to get more details from the About This Macintosh window.

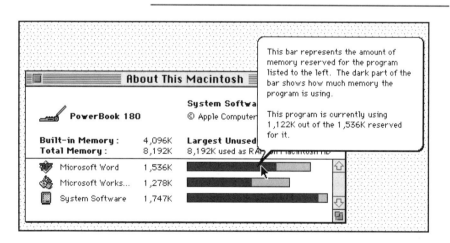

FIGURE 10.6
In the About This Macintosh window you can see both the size of a program's partition in memory and how much of that partition the program is currently using.

Defragment Memory—The Largest Unused Block

When you start a program, that program needs a large unused block of memory. Each program needs a different amount, which you can adjust. When you quit the program, it gives up that memory partition.

Sometimes you'll discover that although your Mac has a lot of unused memory, it doesn't add up to a large unused block. As a result, your program may not be able to start. This is called *memory fragmentation*. Figure 10.7 shows how this can happen.

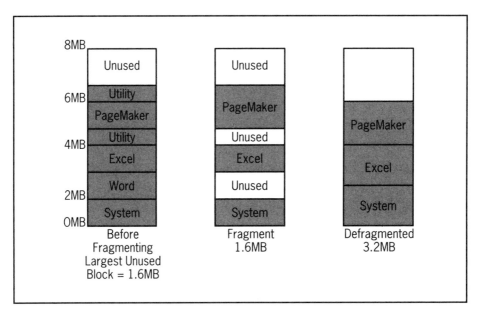

FIGURE 10.7
Fragmentation of Macintosh memory.

Because the Mac doesn't shift partitions to fill areas left open by programs you've quit, large amounts of your memory can be trapped in unused blocks that aren't side by side.

To put this memory together to make a larger block, you need to quit other programs and restart them. This *defragments* memory as also shown in Figure 10.7.

When you start those programs again, they'll take partitions in close order, without the gaps. This should leave the free memory as one large block.

 There's a way to avoid fragmentation. Carefully plan the programs you run, starting first those you'll use all day and later those you may quit.

Allocate the Memory an Application Uses

The Macintosh sets aside a certain amount of memory—in a partition for each application. Each program you start tells the Mac how much memory it wants in its partition. You can adjust that amount if you're using System 6.0.7 or higher or System 7.

 To see if a program really needs its full partition, start the program and then check the About This Macintosh window. The partition is as large as the full gray graphic bar. Only the black bar portion is in use, and the Balloon Help can tell you just how much this is.

You should increase the amount of memory the application asks for if you have large documents, many graphics, large monitors, multiple files, and certainly for any combination of those. You may want to reduce the amount of memory programs ask for if you want to get more of them running simultaneously.

 Don't reduce below the minimum in the suggested size box of System 7.1 unless you remember you're risking program failures and crashes.

To adjust the memory a program asks for:

1. Quit the program (if it is running).
2. Find the application's icon.
3. Click once on the icon to highlight it.
4. Choose **Get Info** from the File menu. You'll see the Info window appear.
5. Change the settings in the Info window.
6. Close the Info window.
7. Start the program.

First, find the main icon for your application. In the Microsoft Works example here, the icon is in a Works folder inside the Applications folder. See Figure 10.8. Then, highlight the icon by clicking on it once and press **Cmd-I**. (The **Cmd** key is the key with the Apple and the four-leaf-clover pattern on it.) You'll see the Info window shown in Figure 10.9 open.

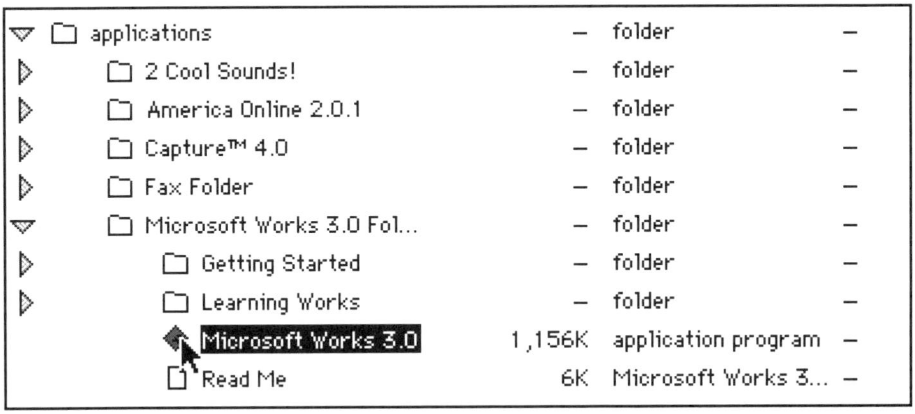

FIGURE 10.8

To allocate memory for a program, first find that program's icon.

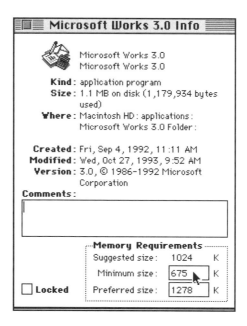

FIGURE 10.9

The Info window is your place for setting a program's memory demands.

At the bottom of the Info window you'll see a Memory Requirements box. In it are several memory sizes. (The precise names depend on the system version you're using.) You may see Application size and Current size or a threesome—Suggested size (which is set permanently by the programmers), Minimum size (which you can change), and Preferred size (which you can change).

The Suggested size is the minimum amount of memory for guaranteed safe operation of the program. The Minimum size is the least amount of memory the program requires to start. If less than this amount is available, the program won't start immediately but will ask you if you want to either quit some other program first or start with less than minimum memory. Figure 10.10 shows an example. Minimum size only appears in System 7.1. The Preferred size is how much the program will take when that much or more memory is available. The program won't take more than this.

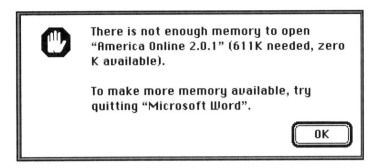

Figure 11.10

The Mac will tell you when there's not enough memory free even for the minimum an application needs.

Set Minimum size to a smaller size for those times when you use the application alongside other applications. Set Preferred to a larger amount for those times when you use the program by itself.

To change Minimum size or Preferred size, double-click in either box and then type the amount you want. Then, click on the **Close Box** at top left of the window. Now you can start the program by double-clicking its icon. It will use the new memory specifications. You don't have to restart the Mac, the way PCs must restart after many memory changes.

Allocating Finder Memory

The Finder—the basic program that works with the system to list programs on-screen and to show you icons that you can double-click to start those programs—is a program itself. It too has a memory allocation. In System 6 you could set this just as with other programs, by working in its Info window. But in System 7 the Finder is supposed to be self-allocating. You can't adjust it. That is, you can't adjust without using a clever trick. Try restarting the Mac with a System 6 floppy disk, getting the Info window for the System 7 Finder, changing its memory allocation, and then restarting with System 7.

Why change Finder allocations? Because the more windows you want to have open on-screen at once, the more icons on-screen, and the more memory the Finder needs. If it doesn't have enough, it will warn you and even keep you from opening more windows. Also, the PrintMonitor program for background printing works better if the Finder has more memory.

Memory Control Panel

Your Macintosh also offers several memory options that aren't adjusted for each program. These include virtual memory, 32-bit addressing, disk caching, and use of a RAM disk. They affect the way memory treats all programs. You'll find them in the Control Panel for memory.

To get at the Control Panel for memory:

1. Go to the Apple menu at the top left of the main display.
2. Pull down that menu with the mouse.
3. Select **Control Panels**, as in Figure 10.11.

You'll see a window full of individual control panels, as shown in Figure 10.12. (If what you see instead is a list of control panel names, use the View menu to see them **By Icon**.) Here you double-click on the **Memory** Control Panel icon, as shown in 10.12 and in close-up in 10.13.

FIGURE 10.11

FIGURE 10.11
Selecting Control Panels.

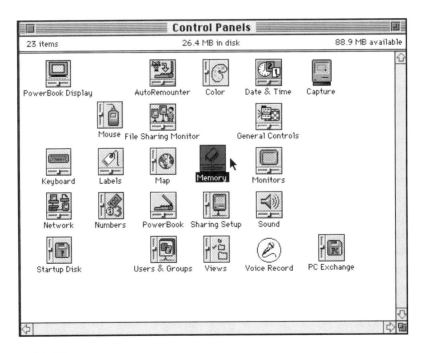

FIGURE 10.12
Choose the Memory Control Panel icon.

FIGURE 10.13
The Memory Control Panel icon.

What do you see? The Memory Control Panel may contain four areas: Disk Cache, Virtual Memory, 32-Bit Addressing, and RAM disk, as shown in Figure 10.14. The following sections explain how to use each of these memory options.

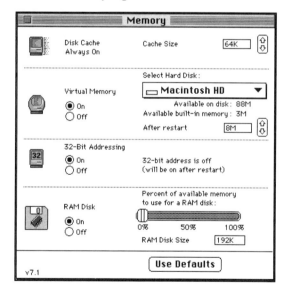

FIGURE 10.14
The Memory Control Panel.

Disk Cache

A disk cache, as explained in Chapter 1, is an area of memory set aside to hold information frequently requested from disk. By looking first to the cache, which is composed of memory chips and is far faster than any disk drive, programs feel as though the disk operates much faster than it did before. This is quite noticeable when you have disk-intensive programs, those that frequently read from and write to the disk. All you need to put in a disk cache is memory to devote to the cache itself, memory to hold the disk cache program, and that program.

The Macintosh comes with a disk cache program. In System 7 it's called *Disk Cache*; in System 6 it's called *RAM Cache*. (That's a misnomer, by the way, because a RAM cache is really an area of very fast memory caching frequently used information from standard, slower memory chips.) You set the size of the cache in the Memory Control Panel. See Figure 10.15.

FIGURE 10.15
Disk Cache in the Memory Control Panel.

Notice that you don't have to turn the cache on. It is always on. You just determine how much memory will be in the cache. Click on the upper arrow to increase; click on the lower arrow to decrease. The minimum is 32K. But 32K won't improve performance as much as 64K or more. More than 256K probably won't add any more speed to your disk operations, and it will spend memory that might be needed for other programs and uses. The best level depends on the size of your hard disk and whether you're using virtual memory too, so for perfect tuning you must experiment. Once you are happy with the size of the cache, you must restart your Mac to put the changed cache into action.

 If you can spare the memory set the cache to about 32K for each megabyte of RAM in your Mac.

Don't set a cache higher than 512K or you could actually slow your Mac.

Most IIci Macs have a special *cache card*, a memory card with fast RAM chips just for caching memory from the rest of RAM memory. This card can increase system performance 10 to 15% but is entirely separate from the System 7 Disk cache.

RAM Disk

A RAM disk sets aside part of memory and treats it like a very fast disk drive. This is not the same as a disk cache, as Chapter 1 explains. Because the information in a cache can be had in a hurry, the average time for getting disk information decreases. A RAM disk puts all of the information from some files and programs into RAM. If a request is made for that information, it all comes much faster. If a request is made for something outside of the RAM disk, it all comes much slower. Most computers with enough memory have both a RAM disk (for important files and programs that need to be as fast as possible) and a disk cache (for speeding retrieval of everything from disk).

To make a RAM disk you need the area in memory to dedicate to the disk, the area in memory for the program that will control the RAM disk (this can be quite small), and the RAM disk program. The Mac comes with a built-in RAM disk program, which you manage from the memory Control Panel.

The default for a RAM disk is off, as shown in Figure 10.16. Decide if you need a RAM disk by asking: Do I have programs that rely on frequent disk access? Do I have 1M or more to devote to a RAM disk (it won't be available for other uses)? Am I protected from power loss?

That last question is vital. A RAM disk is thousands of times faster than a standard disk, so it's great for holding programs (they'll launch faster) and files (they'll load faster). But RAM loses all its information when your computer loses power, and so anything in a RAM disk will disappear when you turn off your computer or accidentally lose power. The only ways to avoid that are to have a RAM disk controlling program smart enough to save all contents to disk both frequently and on shutdown or to have an uninterruptible power supply (UPS) so you don't lose power. The RAM disk built into the Mac is not that smart. (The PowerBook 100 RAM disk is an exception, always keeping its information, even when you shut it down.) It will protect memory when you restart, but not when you shut down, as you are warned in the example shown in Figure 10.17.

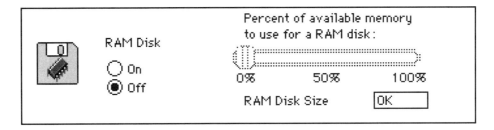

FIGURE 10.16
Turn the RAM disk on and manage it from the Memory Control Panel.

There are some commercial RAM disk managers such as Connectix's Optima, that are smart optima. Automatically stores its contents to the hard drive before allowing shutdown and then automatically sets the RAM disk up again when you start the Mac.

FIGURE 10.17
You will lose everything on a RAM disk when your Mac shuts down.

If you're using the Mac's own RAM disk, then be sure that you remember to copy information back to your hard disk from the RAM disk, have a RAM disk that at least doesn't vanish on restart, or won't be lost entirely if you lose power accidentally (that is, you put files in the RAM disk that are also on the hard disk).

If you copied your main application or even your system to the RAM disk, then power loss would still leave you with the originals on the hard disk.

You can't afford to keep a document you're working on in a RAM disk, unless that RAM disk is a commercial, protected RAM disk.

Get a Reset switch for your Mac, if possible. This programmer's tool let's you get the Mac running again after a crash, without a complete restart. That could save your RAM disk information.

If you decide you can afford a RAM disk, then create it in the Control Panel by turning on the RAM disk option (click **On**) and setting the slider to the size of RAM disk you can afford. (Bigger is better, but you have to balance that against other RAM uses and make it just the size necessary for the files you plan to copy to it.) See Figure 10.18.

Now restart your Mac from the Special menu. When the screen interface reappears, you should see a RAM disk icon, right alongside the other disk icons, as shown in Figure 10.19. You can copy files to this disk and double-click on them to run from this disk just as from any other disk. You can even erase this disk.

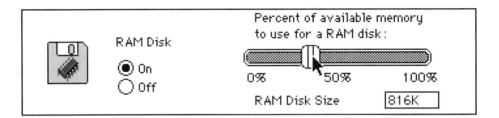

FIGURE 10.18
Turning the RAM disk on and setting its size.

FIGURE 10.19
RAM disk icon for operating RAM disk.

 PowerBooks often have limited memory, but by judiciously creating a RAM disk just large enough to hold a most frequently used application, you can extend battery life tremendously. The RAM disk can be accessed any number of times without ever spinning the hard drive, saving a lot of energy. The RAM disk will keep information through sleep, though not through shutdown.

 On PowerBooks with System 7, the RAM disk manager may be available through the Portable Control Panel instead of the Memory Control Panel.

When you're done with the RAM disk and want that memory back for other uses, you can't just drag the RAM disk icon to the trash (as you would to eject other disks). See Figure 10.20. First, you must clear all files from the RAM disk (copy them to the hard disk if you're worried about lost information) into the trash, empty the trash, and then use the Memory Control Panel to turn the RAM disk off—or at least change its size.

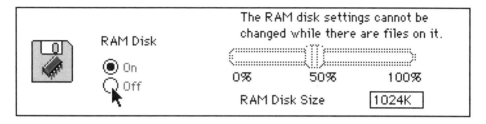

FIGURE 10.20
You cannot eliminate a RAM disk until it is empty.

Virtual Memory

Your Macintosh can use hard disk space to "fake it" as additional memory. This is called *virtual memory* because the memory is virtual, it isn't really there. Instead, when the memory beyond chip memory is needed, something that's in chip memory is copied to disk. That leaves the chips open, ready to pretend to be more memory. When the original items that were in memory are needed, they are copied back into chip memory, swapping with the new stuff there, which is in turn copied to the disk. (This is explained in Chapter 1.)

The disadvantage of virtual memory is that it isn't as fast as chip memory. However, it is cheaper and more plentiful than real memory, and it is sometimes useful so that you can run programs and open files you couldn't run otherwise. Also, virtual uses more power, a big disadvantage on a PowerBook portable.

Most new Macs have a built-in virtual memory utility. It is standard in System 7 on Macs with an 68030 or better processor. You won't find it on the Plus, SE, old Classics, original Mac II, and original LC. The II and LC can get it if you add a 68851 PMMU chip, System 7, and 4M or more memory. To get virtual memory with System 6, get the **Virtual** utility from Connectix Corporation.

You can see if your Mac was set up with the possibility for virtual memory by checking the Memory Control Panel, as shown in Figure 10.21. If the Virtual Memory section shows up, then you can use it.

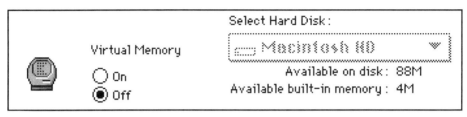

FIGURE 10.21

Virtual Memory is available on your Mac if it shows up in the Memory Control Panel.

The Memory Control Panel lets you determine which disk drive to swap chip information. That's the swap file. Click on the disk drive pop-up menu, as shown in Figure 10.22.

The drives that appear here are your only choices. For any drive you select, you'll be shown, just below the drive listing, how much memory is available on that drive. In this example, only the Macintosh HD (hard drive) can provide virtual memory. And it has 88M of available memory. (A utility called **Virtual Memory Tuner**, which you can find at many user groups or from online services, lets you use a removable cartridge hard drive.) You'll also see here how much real memory, chip memory, is in the Mac.

FIGURE 10.22

Choosing the disk from which to borrow memory for virtual memory.

To keep virtual memory as fast as possible, keep your hard disk fast. Defragment the disk with a disk defragmenting utility.

Then, decide how much memory you want total, adding together the real memory and the virtual memory (disk memory masquerading as RAM). To get 12M total on this system, you need to click on the up arrow until *12M* shows in the Control Panel. You'll notice that it won't happen until you restart the Mac.

After restart, your About This Macintosh window will show the total memory of both RAM and virtual. System 7 will have set aside a swap file on the designated hard disk. That file will be equal to both the built-in RAM and the extra virtual memory you want. For example, although you're only adding 4M of virtual to get the total 8M of memory in this system, the swap file would be 4M plus the 4M of RAM, for a total of a 8M swap file on disk.

The **Virtual** utility from Connectix makes a smaller swap file, only equal to the size of additional virtual memory.

Virtual memory is slower than RAM. But you won't notice much slowdown from turning on virtual memory if the program you're working in runs from real RAM. You'll certainly notice slower work when you run very active software, such as a scanning or OCR program, from virtual memory.

PhotoShop has its own virtual memory scheme, and if you add that to the Mac's virtual memory you could slow everything with both swap files on and off disk.

Don't set total memory to more than twice real memory unless you're ready for major slowdowns.

Virtual memory can keep your disk running more and so cut into battery life on a PowerBook, as you'll be warned by the message shown in Figure 10.23.

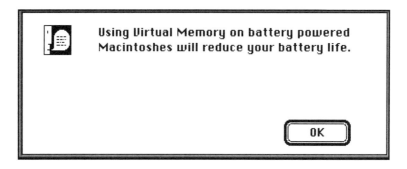

FIGURE 10.23
PowerBook warning that virtual memory carries a battery-life cost.

32-Bit Addressing

No Macintosh can use more than 8M of memory with the Mac's original 24-bit addressing. Even using virtual memory, the maximum possible is 14M. Install 20M of chips, you'll still get to use only 8M. To get at more than 8M you need 32-bit addressing. With that memory option, the Mac can theoretically reach 4096M. No Mac has that much memory, but the latest Quadra 950 can hold 256M. Other Macs could use the extra addresses as large virtual memory.

To get 32-bit addressing working you need three things: more than 8M of chips, System 7, and programs that are 32-bit clean (written to understand 32-bit), and a 32-bit addressing control program.

If your Mac has less than 8M of memory, don't turn on 32-bit addressing. There'll be no benefit, and it could cost you if any of your programs can't handle 32-bit addresses.

Many old programs, or old versions of current programs, weren't written with 32-bit in mind. There's no way for you to tell by looking at the program, no way to know for sure until the program crashes in 32-bit. You can guess there's trouble if you turn on 32-bit addressing and start getting error messages such as *bus errors*. The trouble might even be with system software, such as a hard disk driver or extension. To avoid the problem, get updates of your software—most companies should have new versions that handle 32-bit addressing. If an extension seems to be the problem, restart your Mac, hold down the **Shift** key (disabling extensions), and then remove the extension.

The **Maxima** utility from Connectix lets a Mac get at 14M without turning on 32-bit addressing. And any chip memory beyond 14M can be used as a RAM disk with **Maxima**.

To turn 32-bit addressing on, get into the Memory Control Panel and click on **On**. You'll notice that this won't affect your Mac until you restart, as shown in Figure 10.24.

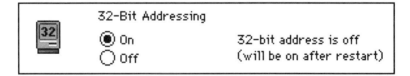

```
┌─────────────────────────────────────────────────────────────┐
│  [32]   32-Bit Addressing                                     │
│         ⦿ On          32-bit address is off                   │
│         ○ Off         (will be on after restart)              │
└─────────────────────────────────────────────────────────────┘
```

FIGURE 10.24
32-bit addressing doesn't take hold until you restart.

The **Mode32** utility from Connectix offered 32-bit addressing to many older Macs and was even part of the system software Apple supplied with some Macs. It is now obsolete in System 7 because of the built-in Control Panel 32-bit addressing utility.

Manage Memory for OS/2, Windows NT, and UNIX

DOS is the root of most PC memory management complications. DOS, as the fundamental operating system software in nearly all PCs, sets memory limits that are far tighter than most PC hardware allows. If you could give up DOS, you wouldn't have to worry or learn as much about memory management. You would still want to install plenty of memory chips, but then you could let your programs use them without bothering about a 640K barrier, conventional addresses, loading high, and so on. So why not jump to another operating system? Why not give up DOS? Because most PC programs were written for DOS, and demand DOS.

As explained in Chapter 5, you can use Windows 3.1 to elude most DOS memory troubles. Windows has its own memory manager and doesn't stick to conventional memory. But Windows 3.1 isn't really a completely new operating system. It still uses DOS to start your PC but shows its DOS roots in many ways. To get away from the DOS memory limits fully you need a fundamentally different operating system. Three prime choices are OS/2, Windows NT, and UNIX. These three operating systems are not only not DOS, and not based on DOS, but they are also fully multitasking operating systems that are able to run any number of programs at once.

OS/2 (pronounced *oh ess two*) was developed by Microsoft and IBM, but it is now solely an IBM product. Its latest version, 2.1, is far different from the earlier versions 1.3 and 2.0. It will run DOS, Windows, and OS/2 programs. This chapter discusses only version 2.1.

Windows NT isn't Windows at all. Developed by Microsoft as its next-generation operating system, the *NT* stands for New Technology. Its Windows name is not only good for marketing, because of the success of Windows, but it also refers to the fact that it will run Windows 3.1 programs. Don't confuse Windows NT with the coming revision of Windows 3.1, to be called Windows 4.0 (and known now by the code name *Chicago*). Windows 4.0 will still show DOS roots, although less so than Windows 3.1.

UNIX has been around a lot longer than OS/2 or Windows NT. It permits much more memory than DOS but does not run DOS or Windows programs—yet. That makes it a larger switch than moving to OS/2 or Windows NT.

OS/2

OS/2 is not just *multitasking*—running more than one program at a time—but it is also *multi-threading*—running separate parts of a single program simultaneously. Basically, it can multitask within a program, if that program is written for it. For example, a word processing program might have a spelling checker thread that could run at the same time as an automatic hyphenation thread.

OS/2 needs at least 4M to start, but you'll want 8M as a practical minimum. 16M is a better amount. And you'll want a 486 or Pentium processor. It also needs lots of disk storage space, 30M for itself, more megabytes for programs, and more megabytes for any disk you'll use as virtual memory.

OS/2 needs memory chips that are solidly reliable and all running at the same speed.

You may want to run lots of DOS and Windows programs under OS/2. After all, there aren't nearly as many OS/2 programs yet, so you may have to use DOS or Windows applications in many circumstances. OS/2 can do it. If you have enough memory you can run up to 89 DOS programs at once, and run Windows programs. IBM even claims OS/2 can run these programs better than DOS and Windows themselves can, for several reasons.

 ▼ OS/2 can run several DOS and Windows programs at once.
 ▼ OS/2 can protect DOS and Windows programs from one another. (If a DOS or Windows program crashes in OS/2, you just close the session it's in; any other programs that are running are not affected. When they crash in DOS or Windows itself, that crash can also ruin any other programs running.)
 ▼ OS/2 can run the DOS and Windows programs faster. (OS/2 has a more efficient filing system on disk, which can give better performance.)
 ▼ OS/2 can give DOS more conventional memory (even using its own virtual memory system). And, it can provide expanded and extended memory.
 ▼ OS/2 automatically manages DOS memory.

When you run a DOS or Windows program under OS/2 that program runs in a *session*—memory and processor time set aside to pretend to be DOS or Windows. (Officially, the DOS session is a VDM or Virtual DOS Machine.) Such programs can run windowed or full-screen, depending on which icon you use to start the session. Full-screen DOS runs faster because programs are in text mode.

 Don't run Windows sessions programs in Enhanced mode; run them in Standard mode.

 OS/2 lets you cut and paste information among DOS, Windows, and OS/2 programs on-screen.

 Don't try to run a DOS program under OS/2 until you have installed DOS support.

 You'll use less memory on Windows programs if you run each Windows application in its own session.

 If you run more than one Windows program in a single Windows session, any of those programs can crash the others.

To get maximum memory for a DOS session, you put special commands in the OS/2 **CONFIG.SYS** file, just as if you weren't using OS/2. These commands include:

DOS=HIGH,UMB to move part of DOS out of conventional memory

DEVICEHIGH to move DOS drivers out of conventional memory

LOADHIGH to move memory-residents out of conventional memory

Other commands include:

DISKCACHE to make the hard disk operate faster, just like a DOS cache

MEMMAN to turn off virtual memory to run a particular program faster

RMSIZE to set the amount of memory a DOS session can use

VDISK to create a RAM disk

VEMM to let a DOS program use expanded memory

All of these commands in **CONFIG.SYS** will apply to any DOS or Windows sessions you start. You can customize other settings for each particular session. Get at them in the Settings notebook, in DOS Settings or Windows Settings (click the right mouse button on a program). These settings include specifications such as whether the program needs EMS, XMS, or DPMI memory. OS/2 will provide whatever kind the program wants, up to a 2M default total. You can increase that total, too.

If you know your DOS program won't use EMS, XMS, or DPMI memory, reduce the defaults to zero to leave more memory for other sessions and uses.

You can increase conventional memory in a DOS session by setting **video_mode_restriction** to CGA.

The **hw_rom_to_ram** setting tells the PC to copy the ROM BIOS to RAM. It runs faster that way but eats up 100K of memory. Fortunately, that memory is not taken from DOS session conventional memory.

Don't run a DOS disk cache under OS/2.

Don't run a DOS memory manager such as QEMM, 386MAX, or even DOS's own EMM386 under OS/2. They need full control of the processor chip, and this requirement conflicts with OS/2. Besides, OS/2 can accomplish the same thing as a DOS memory manager.

Don't use a program that needs VCPI DOS extender memory. Get a newer version that supports DPMI.

The OS/2 disk cache should be about 256K.

The disk cache *lazy write* option is for *write caching*—delaying writing information to disk until a large quantity is ready. By writing less often, performance increases. The disadvantage is that an unexpected power loss could lose that data.

The **VDISK** RAM disk utility with OS/2 is quite useful if your program uses temporary files and if you have about 12M or more memory.

If you see *TRAP* error messages from OS/2, then you may have a bad memory chip. Use a utility to test the memory in your PC.

Windows NT

Windows NT is, like OS/2, a multitasking operating system that owes nothing to DOS and its memory limits. It will run not just on the processors familiar to PC owners but on other processors with higher speeds and quite different designs. It will even be a multi-processor operating system, running on computers with more than one processor. It looks almost identical to Windows 3.1 on-screen. But it has an entirely different foundation.

More than OS/2, Windows NT is a networking operating system. It is built to work on a server in a network, with linked PCs that exchange messages and share disks and printers.

NT can give each application up to 2G of memory—more than 2000M—which requires more chips than any PC has and so, naturally, brings virtual memory to bear. Like OS/2, Windows NT has a file system—for organizing files on disk—that is more efficient than DOS's.

NT can run programs written expressly for it and also Windows 3.1, DOS, and even OS/2 1.3 programs. It will not run OS/2 2.1 programs.

Because Windows NT is a 32-bit operating system, it can theoretically reach 4G of memory. In fact it uses 64-bit addresses when accessing the disk, so it can reach even more memory there.

Unlike the segmented memory in DOS and Windows, Windows NT uses a *flat memory model*, that is, memory addressing without segments. Memory is a clean slate of addresses from 0 to 4G. Using virtual memory, it can reach as much as 2G for each program and a full address space of 16 billion G.

Like OS/2, Windows NT gives memory to programs and then prevents other programs from interfering with that memory. This segmentation helps isolate programs from one another, so that if one program crashes the others won't come down, too.

A minimum practical PC for Windows NT has a 486 processor and 12M of memory.

 If you have DOS programs that need to talk directly to the PC's hardware—typically games do so—you should install DOS alongside and separately from Windows NT.

You can change virtual memory settings—adjust the paging file or swap file NT uses—with the System dialog box's Virtual memory dialog box. This affects the **PAGEFILE.SYS** file on disk. You see a list of disk drives, specify how large the file should be initially on the selected disk, and also set the maximum size it should have there and the minimum, recommended, and currently-allocated size of the page file on all disks.

For Windows 3.1 programs, NT supports virtual memory as 386-Enhanced mode would. You can adjust memory use in **WIN.INI** and **SYSTEM.INI** files as you would with Windows 3.1. There's also a **REG.DAT** file for tracking the settings in NT. If you have programs that need PIF—DOS programs to run under Windows—you can do so under NT as well.

For DOS programs, you can edit **AUTOEXEC.NT** and **CONFIG.NT** files as you normally would **CONFIG.SYS** and **AUTOEXEC.BAT**. Commands for memory include:

DOS	to move part of DOS into upper memory and to create Upper Memory Blocks
INSTALL	to load memory-resident programs into conventional memory
LOADHIGH	to load memory-resident programs high

Windows NT can load DOS memory-resident programs much like using DOS. They run in the window they are started in and work only in that window.

Don't start memory-residents from **AUTOEXEC.NT** or **CONFIG.NT**. That procedure starts a version every time you run a DOS program, wasting memory.

The **DOSONLY** command permits only DOS-based programs to start from the **COMMAND.COM** prompt.

NT can simulate EMS expanded memory for programs that need it. You specify the kilobytes required and the kilobyte limit. NT can also give XMS extended memory for programs, again you specify the kilobytes required and kilobyte limit.

UNIX

UNIX was developed way back in 1969 at Bell Laboratories. It became the most popular operating system with scientists and engineers using minicomputers and *workstations*—super-high-powered desktop computers. In fact, though, because UNIX is so old, it has had time to spread—with many versions from many companies now, each different enough to run only its own programs.

UNIX is famous for being complicated, but recently several graphical user interfaces have appeared for it, making it look and work more like Windows or the Apple Macintosh.

UNIX has a flat address space much like Windows NT. It can reach huge amounts of memory, with no 640K barrier, with the specific amount depending on the version.

The problem with choosing UNIX is that it runs neither DOS nor Windows programs. There are UNIX programs, but far fewer than for DOS or Windows, and you must find one made specifically for the version you're using.

GLOSSARY

MEMORY MANAGEMENT

286

    See *80286*.

386

    See *80386*.

486

    See *80486*.

80286

    Microprocessor chip used in original IBM AT and in many compatibles. Can address 16M of memory, although limited to 1M when using DOS. Faster than 8088 and 8086 but slower than 386, 486, or Pentium. Cannot map memory the way 386 and later processors can, so much less efficient at memory management. Needs an EMS board for many memory management chores or an associated chipset collection of support chips that add memory management circuits.

80386

Microprocessor chip used in fast AT compatibles (now referred to as PC compatibles) and in some PS/2 systems. Can address 4G of memory, although limited to 1M when running DOS. A 386 chip includes circuits for handling expanded (EMS) memory and other memory management circuits for easy remapping of memory. (This chip is sometimes called the 80386DX.) Faster than the 80286, 8086, and 8088.

80386SL

Low-power version of the 80386SX chip, tailored for use in portable computers.

80386SX

Inexpensive version of the 80386 microprocessor chip.

80486

Microprocessor chip in very fast (designed in 1990 through 1992) PC compatibles. Combines 80386 chip and a math coprocessor, so has all memory-addressing abilities of 80386, but is faster, particularly on complicated calculations. Faster than the 80386, 80286, 8086, or 8088, but slower than the Pentium.

80486SX

An 80486 microprocessor without its built-in math coprocessor, and so a cheaper chip for less-expensive systems. Has all the speed and memory abilities of the 80486.

8086

Microprocessor chip used in some PC compatibles. Can address 1M of memory. Slightly faster than 8088. Features a 16 bit internal data path.

8088

Microprocessor chip used in original PC and XT. Also used in many PC compatibles. Can address 1M of memory. The slowest chip in the family, because it only handles 8 bits of data at a time.

A

A-20

The 21st address line (they're counted from A0) is the wire the microprocessor must use to get at memory beyond conventional 1024K.

A-20 handler

A program that handles the A-20 address line and so handles extended memory and the HMA. **HIMEM.SYS** from DOS fills this function as do the many replacements for it in third-party memory managers such as **QEMM** and **386MAX**.

accelerators

New processor chips or boards with processor chips plugged into a PC or compatible to give it more processing speed.

adapter

A piece of hardware or software that helps one element of the computer understand another. Often *adapter* is used for the hardware intermediates and *driver* is used for the software intermediates.

address (noun)

The numeric name of a location in memory. Memory is organized by assigning addresses to all locations where information can be stored. It's the same idea as assigning numbers to houses on a street, to organize and identify them. Memory addresses start at 0 and increase, the end point depending on how much memory is in the computer. Addresses can be in decimal numbers (such as 12 or 63555), in binary (such as 00101 or 11111), or in hexadecimal (such as FF00 or A0).

address (verb)

To reach out and find a certain location in memory.

address line

A wire on the microprocessor's and computer's bus that signals memory addresses. Most computers have at least 16 of these, some have 20, and the latest have 32.

address space

The largest amount of memory a computer can address. A larger address space means the computer can handle larger programs and files.

algorithm

A recipe, a list of instructions, for a computer to reach some goal.

alternate maps

When a PC uses expanded memory, it "remaps" addresses in memory, taking addresses away from some memory chips temporarily and giving those same addresses to other, more immediately useful, memory chips. To get back to the original memory address assignments, the computer, its operating system, and its memory manager software must keep track of those original assignments. This is done in a *map*. The alternate maps—for various sets of address assignments—can be held in software (which is more flexible) or hardware (which is faster). Expanded memory boards with more hardware circuits for alternate maps are therefore better for faster multitasking.

alternate register set

See *alternate maps*.

application

A computer program that handles a specific working task, such as word processing, spreadsheet calculations, or database management. Distinct from computer programs that handle basic system functions—known as operating systems—or communications with peripherals—known as drivers.

ASCII

Acronym for American Standard Code for Information Interchange. Some files of information on disk have lots of special codes that indicate such things as fonts and graphics. Also known as *plain text*, ASCII files have only the basic text characters, symbols, and numerals. Most memory configuration files—such as DOS's **CONFIG.SYS** and **AUTOEXEC.BAT**—must be in ASCII form. Most word processors can save files in ASCII form.

AT-class

A PC compatible with a 286 processor (and sometimes this phrase also refers to PCs with 386 and later processors).

AUTOEXEC.BAT

A file of information on your disk that DOS automatically looks to for its initial instructions when the PC starts. Many memory management techniques require that you put instructions into the **AUTOEXEC.BAT** file. This is a plain text or ASCII file that you can change with any word processor that can save its files in ASCII form. DOS 5 and higher have their own text-editing program called EDITOR that works in ASCII.

B

backfill

To replace conventional memory with expanded memory. Doing so gives faster task switching. See *expanded memory*.

background

A program is said to run in the background when it continues to do some processing, even though that task is not the top or active program on the screen. Few programs running under DOS can actually multitask or run entirely in the background, but some can at least perform calculations or monitor a phone-line connection. The more programs that can run in the background, the more you can get done in the same amount of time. Some other operating systems and some utilities that run on top of DOS—such as DESQview and Microsoft Windows—can handle multitasking and background operation.

bank-switching

One way to let a computer address more memory than its natural address space permits. For example, a stretch of 16K of memory addresses is singled out as a swapping area. Then, the information that is stored in other 16K chunks of memory is moved into and out of that location. If information is needed from one particular chunk, that chunk is given those addresses. If a program then needs information from another chunk, the first chunk is moved out, and the second chunk is moved into the swapping location. Special registers or program instructions are used to keep track of which chunk is needed at which time and to redirect requests to the swapping area so that they actually target the needed information. Expanded memory functions as a bank-switching scheme like this.

batch file

Any file with a .BAT extension on its name that DOS tries to run as a program. You can create your own batch file by typing a sequence of DOS commands into a word processor and then saving them as an ASCII file with a .BAT file extension name. The most famous batch file is **AUTOEXEC.BAT**. See *AUTOEXEC.BAT*.

binary

Consisting of only two possible fundamental values. Known as base two or binary information. Computers deal with all information as strings of 0s and 1s. The computer can build up complex numbers and values by stringing lots of these 1s and 0s together.

BIOS

Acronym for Basic Input/Output System. The most fundamental software in the PC, even more elementary than DOS. It tells the PC processor how to start, where to find the disk, where the display screen is, and so on. The BIOS subroutines and startup code are typically kept in a ROM chip.

BIOS data area

A special area in conventional memory that stores BIOS information concerning how the computer is currently set up. Occupies a small amount of conventional memory.

bit

A single piece of information in a computer. Short for binary digit. See *binary*.

board

A flat panel with circuits on it, such as the main electronics board in the computer (the motherboard) or the various extra expansion boards you can add to the PC.

boot

To start the computer. Cold boots occur when you turn on the power. Warm boots occur when you tell the processor to start from scratch, while keeping the power on. (Most PCs do this when you hold down the **Ctrl**, **Alt**, and **Del** keys simultaneously.)

buffer

An area of memory that holds frequently used information from some larger storage. A disk cache is a kind of buffer.

BUFFERS

A DOS resource that lets you set aside some memory to keep frequently accessed disk information, to speed disk performance. BUFFERS appear as a command in **CONFIG.SYS** and take up some conventional memory.

bus

A team of electrical lines carrying information in a computer. Most processor chips have a data bus that carries any data signals and an address bus that carries any address values the processor sends to locate information in memory. Also, the combination of data, address, and other signals that are brought together at slots where you can plug in extra circuit boards. For a PC to accept and use such a board, that board must be compatible with the type of bus the PC uses.

byte

Eight bits of information taken as a single packet. The smallest practical unit of information in most computers. See *bit*.

C

cache

See *buffer*.

caching

To use a cache.

card

See *board*.

CGA

Acronym for Color Graphics Adapter. The first color video adapter hardware IBM produced for the PC. Many compatible computer makers then made CGA-compatible adapters for their PC compatibles. A low-resolution display that's no longer popular.

CEMM.SYS

Compaq Expanded Memory Manager, the main memory management software used in some Compaq PC compatibles.

CHKDSK

A program that analyzes your disk and as an aside tells you how much conventional memory the PC has.

CMOS

Acronym for Complementary Metal Oxide Semiconductor. A special kind of memory chip that requires very little power to keep its information. A small amount of CMOS memory kept awake by a tiny battery is put into most of today's PCs to hold configuration information that must be saved even when the PC is turned off.

command

> Functions that DOS, application programs, and utilities can perform when you issue the command to do so. Various methods of issuing these commands exist—each program has its own. For example, you can type the name or acronym of the command and then press **Enter** or **Return** or select the command from a menu. Programs that run under environments such as Windows have their commands organized in similar ways and use similar methods of issuing commands. This makes new programs easier to learn.

clone

> A computer that is entirely compatible with an IBM design. Also connotes an inexpensive compatible, from a relatively unknown company.

COMMAND.COM

> The main program that DOS loads when it starts to let the PC understand what you're typing and where the commands you type should be sent inside the computer.

command line

> Codified instructions that users input to control a computer.

command path

> See *PATH*.

compatible

> When one computer or program works in the same way as another. There are many different kinds of compatibilities. A computer that can run the same programs as another computer is compatible with that computer. A program that can use the same operating system, files, commands, or drivers as another program is also considered to be compatible with that program.

compression

To reduce the amount of disk space that a file occupies. A compression program can squeeze redundant information out of the file. Some memory management programs compress the ROM BIOS in a different way, by leaving out unnecessary or rarely used parts of it—such as the BASIC language—when copying it to higher performance shadow RAM.

CONFIG.SYS

A file of information that DOS always looks for, along with **AUTOEXEC.BAT**, when you start your computer. It contains instructions on the system configuration—such as how much memory to set aside for buffers and where the driver is for the mouse. You can create or change your PC's **CONFIG.SYS** file with any word processor that can save a file as plain ASCII text. **CONFIG.SYS** is loaded before **AUTOEXEC.BAT**.

configuration

A computer or program's setting. This includes such things as which options are turned on and how commands will behave. How a configuration is set affects how the computer or program uses memory.

conventional memory

The most basic memory. It is the most important memory for most programs and the memory that is most often exhausted because of so-called RAM-cram. It is the memory from address 0 to address 640K. Note that memory is given different names, depending on how it is organized for the computer to use.

coprocessor

A special processor chip that speeds the computer by aiding the main processor, often by specializing in particular computations such as mathematics.

CPU

Acronym for Central Processor Unit. A generic name for the microprocessor that is the heart of most computers. The type of CPU used is a central factor in determining how much memory a computer can use and how it uses it.

crash

When the PC stops working because a program has failed.

D

dd

See *device driver*.

DDE

Acronym for Dynamic Data Exchange. A feature of the Windows program or environment and of the OS/2 operating system that lets two or more programs or files automatically exchange information. Typically used to keep information up to date when it appears in several places. For example, if a chart that has been pasted into a word processor document is based on a spreadsheet file and the values in that spreadsheet change, a DDE link automatically copies the changes to the chart.

DEBUG

A utility program that comes with DOS. It can inspect and change what's at any address in memory. Also refers to the process that programmers use to detect and fix errors in programs.

default

The original settings.

DESQview

An environment, much like Windows, that helps organize and manage the memory in a PC and allows the PC to run more than one program at a time.

device driver

A small program that tells peripherals such as modems, printers, and special video adapter boards how to communicate with other software in the computer. Most memory management on PCs insists on trying to move drivers from the more precious conventional memory to high memory.

DEVICEHIGH

The DOS command for loading drivers high.

DIP

Acronym for Dual In-line Package. The traditional way of packaging memory chips, putting single chips into small plastic or ceramic packages with two parallel rows of legs.

directory

Any named area on a disk that holds programs and documents as files.

disable

To turn off.

disk cache

A small piece of memory that is set aside to hold frequently accessed information from a disk drive. Using a disk cache increases the apparent speed of the disk drive.

disk-intensive

A program that depends on reading and writing a lot of information from a disk. This is the opposite of compute-intensive. Disk-intensive programs can be given a big performance boost by using a disk cache.

display

What appears on the screen. Sometimes this word is used to mean the screen itself.

document

> The information you're working on in a word processor, spreadsheet, or other program.

DOS

> Acronym for Disk Operating System, from Microsoft, IBM, Novell, or others. The basic software that runs on almost all PCs. Most of this book is about managing memory under DOS. Because Microsoft's operating system is by far the most popular, sometimes people say DOS when they actually mean MS-DOS, Microsoft's DOS. See *operating system*.

DOS environment

> A short set of instructions that DOS keeps in memory as notes to itself on PC configuration.

DOS extender

> A special piece of software that lets DOS reach beyond its normal limit of 1M of memory address space. Extenders don't let just any program reach the extra memory. DOS extenders are typically built into individual programs by the programmer—the user doesn't even know they are there. The VCPI and DPMI specifications help avoid conflicts between programs that use DOS extenders and other programs. Windows has a built-in extender.

DOS resources

> DOS utilities such as **FILES**, **BUFFERS**, **FCBS**, and **LASTDRIV** that occupy some memory.

DPMI

> Acronym for DOS Protected Mode Interface. A specification for programs that want to use DOS Protected mode and extended memory. Programs that support DPMI, such as Windows 3.0 and 3.1, won't conflict with each other. It

is similar to, but more advanced than the older VCPI standard for DOS and extended memory.

DPMS

Acronym for DOS Protected Memory Services, Novell's version of DPMI. It focuses on moving memory-residents and drivers into extended memory instead of into high memory.

DRAM

Acronym for Dynamic Random Access Memory. The most common type of memory chip.

driver

See *device driver*.

DUMP

A complete listing of what's in some part of memory; an option from the DEBUG program.

E

EDC

Acronym for Error Detection and Correction. Circuits that accompany memory and prevent any mistaken bits from creeping into the information. (Damaged chips, static electricity, or cosmic rays—as science fictional as that sounds—can change the bits in memory chips.) Few PCs have EDC, but many do have so-called parity chips, a ninth bit added to each set of eight bits to help detect errors.

EEMS

Acronym for Enhanced Expanded Memory Specification. The improved expanded memory scheme introduced by AST and several other companies to outperform the

Lotus Intel Microsoft (LIM) EMS Version 3.2 specification. The EEMS innovations became part of the LIM EMS 4.0 standard.

EGA

Acronym for Enhanced Graphics Adapter. The video adapter that IBM introduced after CGA. EGA has higher resolution and more colors than CGA, was the standard for several years, and was copied by many PC-compatible makers.

EISA

Acronym for Extended Industry Standard Architecture. Bus that is faster than the older ISA and competes with the MCA bus.

electronic disk

Another name for a RAM disk.

EMM

Acronym for Expanded Memory Manager. Software designed to handle expanded memory.

EMM386.EXE

The EMM that comes with DOS 6 or Windows.

EMM386.SYS

The EMM that came with DOS 5, now obsolete on systems that can get **EMM386.EXE**.

EMS

Acronym for Expanded Memory Specification. The specification for Lotus Intel Microsoft expanded memory. See *expanded memory*.

emulate

To make behave like something, as in "emulating expanded memory from extended memory" where the PC and a memory management program take extended memory and convert it temporarily to expanded memory for programs that need EMS.

Enhanced-386 mode

The most flexible, multitaskable mode of Windows, which works only on 386, 486, or Pentium PCs with enough RAM.

environment

1) The DOS settings that describe how memory is set up.
2) A piece of software that adds to DOS, to manage memory, present menus, and display windows for programs. Windows and DESQview are two of the best-known environments.

ESD

Acronym for ElectroStatic Discharge. A static electricity discharge that can damage memory chips when you install or inspect them. Even small charges on your body, built up without your knowledge, can weaken or ruin chips.

EXCLUDE

Option found on most memory managers that lets you explicitly tell them not to use certain addresses in high memory. Typically you would use this option to avoid a conflict with some other software or hardware that you know will use that memory but that the memory manager may not notice.

expanded memory

A type of memory that lets a PC reach more than its normal 1M of memory through bank-switching. Version 3.2 of the LIM EMS standard for expanded memory restricts the expanded memory to holding data, and so is obsolete. It has been replaced by Version 4.0, which allows programs and memory to be stored in up to 32M of memory outside of the standard 1M.

expanded memory manager
A program to manage expanded memory.

expanded memory specification
The official EMS for how expanded memory works.

expansion slot
Slot on many PCs that you can plug new circuit boards into, to add more memory or a peripheral to the computer.

extended memory
Memory above the 1M address that normally limits DOS programs. It is not bank-switched memory, like expanded memory. It cannot be used by normal DOS applications. It appears only on systems that use the 80286, 80386, 80486, or Pentium chips, not on systems with the 8088 or 8086 microprocessors. Most PCs can use extended memory for RAM disks. Programs with built-in DOS extenders can use 15M of extended memory. Expanded memory simulation programs, or LIMulators, can make extended memory behave like expanded memory, making it useful to many more programs. Some operating systems, such as OS/2, can use extended memory as their own conventional memory.

extended memory specification
See *XMS*.

F

FCBS
Acronym for File Control Blocks. A DOS resource that was useful in DOS version 1 but is now obsolete. It is kept around in some configurations only for old programs that still expect to see it.

file

The smallest element of information that's assigned a name on a disk. Programs, documents, and operating system information are stored in files. When you see a directory of what's on your disk, you're seeing a list of the files on the disk.

file name

The name of a file, which in DOS is up to eight letters long, followed by a period and then a three-letter file name extension, which typically tells the file type.

FILES

A DOS resource that tells how many files may be open simultaneously. It occupies some memory.

foreground

When multitasking, the program that you can see and that is running is in the foreground.

G

G

See *gigabyte*.

gigabyte

A large amount of memory, about a billion bytes, but more exactly 1024M.

GPF

Acronym for General Protection Fault. A conflict in memory that can crash a PC.

graphical user interface (GUI)

Software that displays windows, menus, and icons on the PC screen to make identifying and manipulating files and information easier. Graphical user interfaces demand a lot of memory. The Apple Macintosh had the first popular graphical user interface. Windows is a PC graphical user interface.

GUI

See *graphical user interface*.

H

handle

A name given to a page in expanded memory; a name the memory management software can use to keep track of that page.

hang

See *crash*.

Hercules

A graphics adapter type, one of the few video graphics adapters not created by IBM that has become a standard and has been copied by compatible computer manufacturers. The Hercules adapter standard is now obsolete, superseded by VGA.

hexadecimal

Base-sixteen counting, using the numerals 0,1, 2, 3, 4, 5, 6, 7, 8, 9, A, B, C, D, E, F. Hexadecimal is very convenient for computer scientists counting memory addresses, and so appears in many memory management programs.

high-DOS memory

Memory from 640K to 1024K.

upper memory

See *high-DOS memory*.

high memory

1) The 384K of memory above 640K and below 1024K (1M). This memory cannot be used by most programs and data files, but it can be used for video, BIOS, and other uses and can be borrowed for use of TSRs, device drivers, and other small programs. High memory is also used in expanded memory schemes.

2) The 64K of memory just above 1024K, which can be used by some PCs because of a trick in the microprocessor, which is only supposed to be able to reach 1024K. Sometimes spelled *hi memory*.

high memory area

See *HMA*.

HIMEM.SYS

The extended memory manager, UMB-maker, and HMA manager that comes with DOS or Windows.

HMA

Acronym for High Memory Area. 286, 386, 486, and Pentium computers can treat the first 64K of extended memory, from 1024K to 1088K (minus 16 bytes), as more conventional memory in one way: a single program that would otherwise be in conventional memory from 0K to 640K may be loaded into the HMA instead by a competent memory manager such as **HIMEM.SYS**.

I

icon

A small image used to represent files or commands in a graphical user interface.

INCLUDE

Option found in most memory managers that let you specify that particular addresses in high memory shall be used as UMBs even though the manager's own analysis says they should not, for fear of conflict with some other program.

interleaving

Splitting memory into different areas that can be refreshed an area at a time, so that the entire memory can be made to appear faster.

interrupt

Signal that a program or peripheral sends when it wants the processor's attention. These interrupts are kept in memory so the processor knows what it is doing and has been doing.

I/O

Acronym for Input/Output.

ISA

Acronym for Industry Standard Architecture. Bus that IBM introduced with the IBM AT and that was widely copied in AT compatibles. It isn't as fast as the EISA or MCA buses but is still in much broader use than EISA or MCA.

J

jumper

A tiny wire or fitting used on a board to change the circuit configuration.

K

K

Acronym for kilobyte. 1024 bits of memory. 1024 is used to count many things in computers. The value is 1024 rather than 1000 because 1024 is a multiple of 2 and memory is organized in powers of 2.

kilobyte

1024 bytes is 1K. Don't confuse this with 1Kb, which means 1KiloBit, or 1/8 of 1K (there are 8 bits to a byte).

L

LAN

Acronym for Local Area Network. Electrical hardware and appropriate software to link a group of PCs together so that they can share files, electronic mail, peripherals, and even programs.

LASTDRIV

The DOS resource that specifies the last usable letter of the alphabet that can refer to a disk drive, also known as *LASTDRIVE*. Letters up to Z are possible, the more available, the more memory taken by the resource (though only a few bytes are involved).

leg

One of the small electronic extensions of a memory chip.

LIM EMS

Acronym for Lotus Intel Microsoft Expanded Memory Specification. See *expanded memory*.

LIMULATOR

A program that uses some extended memory and makes it behave like expanded memory.

load high

To move a memory-resident or driver from conventional memory to upper memory, freeing some conventional memory for other uses.

LOADHIGH
The DOS command for loading high.

local area network
See *LAN*.

low-DOS memory
Memory from 0K to 640K.

M

M
See *megabyte*.

mappable
Memory that can have its address changed by memory manager software. Such memory is more flexible and better for multitasking. A PC with 386 or later processor can map any memory. A PC with 8088, 8086, or 80286 processor can map memory only if it has an EMS memory board or a mappable-memory chipset.

MCA
Acronym for MicroChannel Architecture. Bus introduced by IBM with the PS/2 systems. It is a fast, 32-bit bus that competes with EISA.

MDA
Acronym for Monochrome Display Adapter. The original monochrome video adapter standard used by IBM for its PC, and copied by many compatible computer makers. It is obsolete.

megabyte
1024K of memory, the maximum amount a standard PC can address.

MEM

> A DOS utility program that can tell you how much memory is in your PC and what is in that memory.

memory

> Storage area for information in a computer. Disk drives store information too, but most references to memory, including the title of this book, refer to the semiconductor chips in a computer that are the quick memory used for computing.

memory board

> A panel with memory chips.

memory manager

> A program that handles conventional, extended, and expanded memory.

memory map

> A diagram or list that shows what's in memory.

memory-resident

> Programs stay in memory, even though they aren't active, while you use other programs. Some are drivers that the computer user doesn't pay attention to. Some are utilities that can be brought back to activity by pressing a specified combination of keys. Also called *TSRs*. Traditional application programs stay in memory only until you're done using them. When you quit the program, it is dumped from memory.

memory segment

> A 64K area of memory. The 8088, 8086, 286, 386, and 486 processors handle memory with a segment address and an offset. The segment address refers to 64K at a time. There are 16 segments in conventional memory, named 0, 1, 2, 3, 4, 5, 6, 7, 8, 9, A, B, C, D, E, and F.

menu

A list of commands you can choose in a program.

Microchannel

The bus used in some PS/2 computers.

microprocessor

The main chip that handles the calculations and comparisons that are vital to any program. As the engine is to the car (or, more accurately, as the driver is to the car), the microprocessor is to the computer.

millisecond

One-thousandth of a second. Disk drive speeds are measured in milliseconds (ms).

modem

A peripheral device that connects a computer to a telephone line so that it can communicate information to other computers with modems.

modes

The manner in which hardware and software operates offering different features and access to memory. The typical PC processors have Real, Protected, and Virtual-86 modes. Windows has corresponding Real, Standard, and Enhanced-386 modes.

module

A program or device driver in memory.

monitor

The display screen of the computer.

motherboard

The main circuit board in a PC that typically contains the microprocessor and memory. Some people increase the speed of their PCs by swapping motherboards—by taking out the original motherboard and replacing it with a new motherboard that has a faster microprocessor and faster memory chips.

motherboard memory

Memory chips on the motherboard in many PCs run faster than chips on expansion boards.

mouse

A small, hand-held pointing device commonly used with graphical user interfaces, or graphical DOS applications.

MSD

Acronym for Microsoft Diagnostics. The program that you can use to inspect memory and other aspects of your computer.

MS-DOS

Microsoft's disk operating system.

multitasking

Running more than one program at a time or being capable of doing so. Multitasking systems demand more memory than single-tasking systems. DOS is not multitasking system, even though it can perform some multitasking with an environment such as Windows or DESQview.

multithreading

Running more than one part of a single program at a time. Essentially multithreading is multitasking within programs. DOS is not a multithreading operating system; OS/2 is.

N

nanosecond

One-billionth of a second. Memory chip speeds are measured in nanoseconds (ns).

network
> Short for Local Area Network or LAN.

network adapter
> The piece of hardware that connects the PC to a network.

Novell DOS
> A version of DOS from Novell Inc. with some memory management features that are different from MS-DOS and PC-DOS.

ns
> Nanosecond. One billionth of a second.

O

operating system
> The fundamental software that runs a computer. The operating system takes requests from applications and utilities and shuffles information from and for them to and from disk drives, printers, displays, and other parts of the computer.

option
> Choices that you can make to steer the operation of many programs and commands.

OS
> Acronym for Operating System.

OS/2
> Acronym for Operating System/2. A competitor to DOS and Windows, made by IBM.

P

page
> A 16K block of memory used by expanded memory.

page frame

A 64K block of memory addresses used by expanded memory for mapping pages.

parameter

An option.

parity

An added bit that helps keep a byte from having accidental errors.

PATH

A DOS command for telling the operating system where to find files.

PC

The original IBM desktop computer model. Also a generic name for desktop computers or desktop computers that are compatible with IBM's PC and DOS standards.

PC-AT

The IBM PC successor based on the 80286 microprocessor.

PC compatible

A computer that can run the same software as, and connect to the same hardware as, the IBM PC.

PC-DOS

IBM's version of DOS.

PC/XT

The IBM PC successor that added a hard disk and more memory to the original PC structure.

PCMCIA

Acronym for Personal Computer Memory Card Industry Association. A standard for credit-card-sized memory boards and other devices that plug into a PCMCIA connector. Rarely used for memory.

Pentium

Microprocessor chip used in the most recent PC compatibles (designed in 1993). It would have been named the 80586 chip except for copyright troubles with the number names (competing companies were copying them too easily). Pentium is faster than 80486, 80386, 80286, 8086, or 8088 and has all the memory-addressing features of the 80386.

peripheral

A piece of hardware that is connected to the computer but is not vital to computer operation. Printers, modems, even special disk drives can be considered peripherals.

pin

See *leg*.

pixel

Short for *picture element*. The smallest dot of light on a computer display screen. Putting more pixels on the screen gives higher resolution and, therefore, better images. However, managing graphics using more pixels requires more memory.

port

A connection on the computer through which it can hook up peripherals.

POST

The Power-On Self Test that automatically runs when your PC starts.

print spooler

A utility program that routes pages to print to a waiting area in memory, letting the computer return to other work sooner.

processor

See *CPU*.

protected mode

A microprocessor mode available on the 80286, 80386, and 80486 chips that can reach 16M of memory. DOS cannot run in protected mode without the help of special software such as DOS extender. OS/2 is a protected mode operating system.

protection fault

A conflict in memory that crashes a program or the system. See *GPF*.

PS/2

The family of computers that IBM introduced in 1987 to succeed the PC family. They are software compatible with PCs.

R

RAM

Acronym for Random Access Memory. The most common type of memory chip.

RAM-cram

Too many programs, memory-residents, drivers, and DOS resources in conventional memory's 640K of most-useful addresses.

RAM disk

A section of memory set aside to behave like a very fast disk drive.

RAMDRIVE.SYS

A RAM disk utility program that comes with DOS and Windows.

reading

Getting information from memory.

real mode

The operating mode of the 8088 and 8086 microprocessors that is able to address 1M of memory. DOS is designed to work in real mode. See *protected mode*.

reboot

To turn the computer off and then on again, either by turning it off, pressing the **Reset** button, or pressing **Ctrl-Alt-Del**.

register

A memory location for holding specific information during processing. The microprocessor has its own registers that aren't part of conventional, high, expanded, or extended memory. EMS boards also have registers.

reserved memory

The addresses from 640K to 1024K that DOS reserves for BIOS, peripheral adapters, and other such uses. With the right memory manager software, including utilities that come with DOS, this area is not actually completely reserved. Also known as *high memory* or *upper memory*.

remapping

Logically changing the addresses assigned to areas of memory to rearrange what is in conventional, high, expanded, and extended memory. See *address*.

resolution

The number of dots, or pixels, on the display. Higher resolution makes prettier pictures and more legible text but takes up more memory.

ROM

Acronym for Read Only Memory. A type of memory chip that holds information but can't be written to and can't store new information. ROMs are typically used to hold permanent program routines, such as the BIOS and diagnostics in a PC. Some disks, such as CD-ROM or WORM (write-once read-many), can be used like ROM because the data can be read but not altered.

root directory

The fundamental, unnamed directory on your hard disk. Files such as **AUTOEXEC.BAT** and **CONFIG.SYS** must be in this directory to be noticed and used by DOS.

S

shadow RAM

Memory on some computers that is used to hold copies of the ROMs in reserved memory addresses. RAM is faster than ROM, so shadow RAM can speed performance. It can also conflict with the way some memory managers, such as Windows, use memory. Make sure that your computer can disable any shadow RAM it might have.

shell

A user interface put on top of an operating system. A shell is typically simpler than an environment. DOS (since version 4.0) comes with its own shell.

SIMM

Acronym for Single In-line Memory Module. A way of packaging memory chips, placing them in sets of small circuit boards and calling the results modules. A typical module has nine 1Mbit or 4Mbit chips, one chip for parity and eight to make 1M or 4M total. SIMMs take up less space than the older DIP packaging method and, are easier to install and remove.

single-tasking

Running one program at a time; the opposite of multitasking.

SIPP

Acronym for Single-Inline Pin Package. A memory-chip packaging that puts a set of chips on a tiny board with pins extending from just one edge.

slots

The places in a PC where you can plug in expansion boards.

software

Lists of instructions that computer hardware follows.

SRAM

Acronym for Static Random Access Memory. Type of RAM chip that can be faster than DRAMs but is more expensive and takes up more space. SRAMs are commonly used only in caches.

standard mode

The mode in Windows 3.0 made for the 80286—without the full multitasking of Enhanced-386 mode or the single-tasking of real mode.

SVGA

Acronym for Super-Video Graphics Adapter. A video adapter standard that offers more resolution and color, up to 1024x768, than the VGA standard. VGA has become the standard for PC operation today.

switch

A command option. Can also refer to a device on a computer board that can be turned on or off to indicate a selection mode setting.

T

task switching

Having several programs available to switch among, without actually having them all operating at once.

terabyte

1024G or 1024 x 1024M. No PC uses this much memory, so there's no great reason for having this word in the glossary, except that some 386 and 486 chip documents refer to x number of terabytes worth of virtual memory.

thrashing

Spending too much time in a multitasking system switching from one program to another instead of running those programs. Also refers to a hard disk trying to read or write to a full or badly fragmented disk.

top memory

An area of high memory in some Compaq computers.

TSR

Acronym for Terminate-and-Stay-Resident. Shorthand way of saying memory-resident program.

U

UAE

Acronym for Unrecoverable Application Error. An error in Windows 3.1; also know as a GPF.

UMBs

Acronym for Upper Memory Blocks. Memory mapped to high memory addresses that can then be used to hold drivers, memory-residents, and DOS resources, freeing conventional memory.

UNIX

An operating system that can reach more than DOS's 1M of memory and also offers multitasking.

upper memory

Memory addresses from 640K to 1024K.

upper memory blocks

See *UMBs*.

V

V-86

See *Virtual-86 mode*.

VCPI

Acronym for Virtual Control Program Interface. Phar Lap Software and Quarterdeck's Virtual-86 Control Program Interface. This specification is for DOS extenders.

Vdisk

An early RAM disk utility program that came with DOS.

VGA

Acronym for Video Graphics Adapter. The IBM video adapter standard that succeeded EGA. With greater resolution and color possibilities than EGA, VGA has become the business-computing standard and is widely copied on PC compatibles. VGA uses more memory than EGA.

video adapter

The piece of hardware that connects a display to the PC.

video buffer

An area of memory that holds the bits representing the image on the display screen.

video memory

See *video buffer*.

VIDRAM

A utility with the **QEMM** memory manager package that can borrow unused video memory and add it to conventional memory.

Virtual-86 Mode

Mode for the 80386, 80486, or Pentium processor chips that can run any number of V86 modes. Each mode pretends it is an 8086 chip with only 1M of memory. Each V86 operation is protected in the 80386 or 80486 memory from any other operation, which allows the 386 or 486 or Pentium to multitask DOS programs.

virtual disk

Another name for RAM disk.

volatile

Memory that loses what is stored in it when power is turned off. DRAM and SRAM chips are volatile. Some forms of RAM chips, such as SRAMs backed up by batteries, are nonvolatile. Disk drives are also nonvolatile. CMOS is also volatile. When the system battery gets weak, this could result in CMOS errors and difficulty booting the computer.

W

wait state

When the processor runs faster than its memory, a wait state, or pause in the processor's operation allows processor and memory to synchronize.

window

A space on the computer display screen that's reserved for a particular task. By placing tasks or programs in their own windows and letting those windows overlap on the screen, the computer tries to replicate the familiar image of multiple sheets of paper arranged on a desktop.

Windows

The memory management and graphical user interface environment program from Microsoft. Accurately known as Microsoft Windows.

writing

Storing something in memory.

X

XGA

The IBM video graphics adapter standard that may succeed VGA, with more resolution and color, and higher memory demands.

XMS

Acronym for eXtended Memory Specification. The standard for using extended memory in PCs.

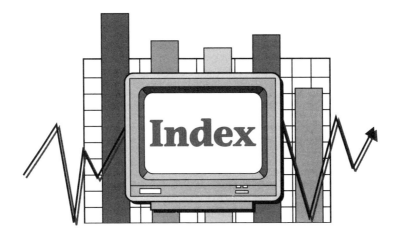

Index

Numerical Index

memory management techniques, 155
minimum/optimum amounts of memory for, 92
Netroom utility on, 247
where to add memory, 94, 97
80286 microprocessor chips, 29, 30, 165, 166, 295-296
80286 PCs
    managing memory with QRAM or MOVE'EM utilities, 249-254
    memory management techniques, 155-156
    minimum/optimum amounts of memory for, 92
    Netroom utility on, 247
    resetting for added memory, 108
    upgrade considerations, 166
    where to add memory, 94, 97
80386 microprocessor chips, 30-31, 165, 296
80386 PCs
    memory management techniques, 156
    minimum/optimum amounts of memory for, 92
    resetting for added memory, 108
    where to add memory, 94, 97, 100
80486 microprocessor chips, 165, 296
80486 PCs
    memory management techniques, 156
    minimum needed for Microsoft Windows, 163
    minimum/optimum amounts of memory for, 93

resetting for added memory, 108
where to add memory, 94, 97, 100

Alphabetical Index

A

A-20 address line, 297
A-20CONTROL:ON|OFF parameter, 127
A-20 handler, 297
A=ALTREGS parameter, 132
About Program Manager option, 161-162
About This Macintosh window, 263-264
accelerators, 297
access time, 12
adapters
    checking memory usage of, 69, 70, 74
    described, 297
    use of video memory by, 58-60
adding memory
    deciding when to, 92-93
    deciding where to, 93-100
    for Microsoft Windows, 164
    on Macintoshes, 260-263
    testing and reconfiguring, 108
address bus, 23, 29
addresses
    for checking contents in memory, 68
    described, 21, 297-298
    unused, 52
addressing, 298
address space, 22, 298

remapping, 27, 40, 41, 326
REM command, 121
reserved memory, 33, 326
resolution, 326
resources, 191-192
ROM chips, 18
ROM (Read-Only Memory), 12, 326-327
root directories, 327

S

sector parameter, 152
segments of memory, 25, 27
self-tests for PCs, POST (Power-On Self Test), 64, 324
SHADOWRAM:ON|OFF parameter, 129
shadow RAM, 55, 64, 327
sharing information in Microsoft Windows, 170
SHELL command, 125-126
shells
 from 386MAX, 223-226
 described, 112, 327
SIMM (Single In-line Memory Module)
 described, 19, 94, 96, 97, 100, 327
 on Macs, 260-262
 replacing, 105-107
single-tasking
 described, 328
 See also multitasking
SIPP (Single In-line Pin Package), 328
640 wall, 33, 109
size parameter, 152
SIZER.EXE, 142
slots, 328
SMARTDrive disk cache

with DOS, 48, 112, 121, 138, 145-150
with Microsoft Windows, 186-188
SoftLogic Solutions' WinSense, 162
software
 described, 328
 for housekeeping chores, 33
 for memory management, 28
 See also DOS (Disk Operating System)
speed considerations
 for caching, 35
 for chips, 102
 for chips for Mac upgrades, 262
 for memory, 12-13
 for Microsoft Windows, 161, 163, 164, 165, 166, 168
 for processors, 28
 of RAM disks, 151
Squeeze from QEMM, 204
SRAM (Static Random Access Memory), 18, 21, 35, 328
Stac compression utility, 166
"Stack overflow" message, 126
stacks, 126
STACKS command, 126
standard mode, 160, 161, 171, 328
startup disks, 119-120
static electricity, 103, 104, 105
Stealth from QEMM, 198, 204-205
Super Video Graphics Array (SGVA), 168
surge protection, 103
SVGA (Super-Video Graphics Adapter), 328
swap files, 182, 184-185
swap option of MemMaker, 142
swapping areas, 300
switches, 328